Praise for Twisted Head

"Capotorto's humorous prose comes to life when he describes his disco-era lifestyle, whether it be dancing the hustle or, as he's primping for the Saturday night disco, overhearing his mom gossiping about Rock Hudson having an affair with Jim Nabors . . . In the end, [he] skillfully weaves stories that are both comic and tragic to capture a family caught between the Old and New Worlds."   —*Publishers Weekly*

"You have read this memoir before: an actor and playwright author tells the story of his tyrannical father, visiting his own demons on his wife and children and especially on the terrified, closeted gay son, who is trying to find how to live. What you do not know, however, is the sweetness, the fluid grace, of Capotorto's writing, which never makes us feel like voyeurs . . . Italian Americans in particular will smile at the taste of food, the shape of hairdos, and the look of interior design they will remember with affection." —*Booklist*

"Carl Capotorto's first book was for me a wonderful reading experience—in part because my own upbringing was strikingly similar to Carl's. On the other hand, you don't have to be Italian to be moved by Carl's powerfully touching epilogue."   —Mario Cuomo

TWISTED HEAD

Carl Capotorto

TWISTED
HEAD

AN ITALIAN-AMERICAN MEMOIR

Broadway Books
New York

Originally published in hardcover by Broadway Books,
New York, in 2008.

All photographs courtesy of the author.

Frontispiece: Eva, the author, and Rosette, dressed in
Sunday finery for a trip "down the city"

Library of Congress Cataloging-in-Publication Data

Capotorto, Carl, 1959–
    Twisted head: an Italian-American memoir / by Carl
Capotorto.
        1. Capotorto, Carl, 1959– 2. Actors—United States—
Biography. I. Title.

PN2287.C263A3 2008
792.02'8092—dc22
[B]

                                                2008016133

ISBN 978-0-7679-2862-5

PRINTED IN THE UNITED STATES OF AMERICA

10 9 8 7 6 5 4 3 2 1

First Paperback Edition

Author's Note

The characters and events in this book come directly from life, and have been recounted here with the greatest accuracy that memory allows. Names and other details have been changed in some cases to protect the privacy of certain individuals.

The story, of course, is told from my own point of view. Some who lived parts of it alongside me might possibly discover that their recollections differ somewhat from my own. Such is the nature of personal perspective.

There is not one single fabrication in these pages. I lived each beat of this story exactly as described . . . and have the scars (and plenty else) to prove it.

For my father—and all the ancestors—
upon whose backs I stand

And for my mother, whose unconditional love
has always meant safe harbor

I guai della pignatta sa sol'o cucchiaio.

(The troubles deep in the pot are known only by the spoon.)

OLD ITALIAN PROVERB

Foreword

The literal translation from Italian to English of *Capotorto,* my family name, is "twisted head." This is no accident. The name was not assigned randomly. Names never are. Our ancestors were frequently branded for a physical characteristic or personality type, trade or special skill, hometown, background, or other prominent feature. Most of the people I grew up with in the Bronx in the 1960s and '70s are good examples: the Mangialardi family (Eat Fat), Mrs. Occhiogrosso (Big Eye), or Marie Sabella (So Beautiful). They were incessant fryers, a bug-eyed doomsday type, and a dolled-up glamour queen, respectively. What else could they be? They were bound by ancestral imperative, these people, unconsciously acting upon orders issued down through the blood from generation to generation. There is a lot in a name. A name is an inheritance. Names are legacies.

What does it say about my people, and therefore myself, that they were called Twisted Head? What traits or skills or qualities must they have exhibited to their fellow townspeople to earn this moniker? We may never know. But we can guess. *Capo* refers not to an actual head (the Italian word for that is *testa*) but rather to a boss or leader—as in *capo di stato* (head of state). *Capo torto,* therefore, denotes a twisted or demented chieftain.

This is where it all starts to make sense.

The very first twisted head, that lumpen little Barese ancestor marching up and down the hills of Gioia del Colle, barking out orders and bossing the villagers around wildly, must have been exactly like my father, a definitive specimen of the bloodline: tyrannical, obsessive-compulsive, imperious. ("I'm not your friend, I'm the *father!*" was a common refrain.)

As for the ancestor's son all those years ago in Italy's deep south, he must have been exactly like me: timid, anxious, fearful. These are the twin prongs of the Twisted Head pitchfork, mirror images of the same dysfunction. For years, I've thought of myself as cursed by the Capotorto legacy, destined to wriggle painfully on the tines of fate for a lifetime. I'd learned to accept it. But I find myself rejecting this contract in middle age, suddenly eager to break free from it all.

This book is an exorcism. With laughs.

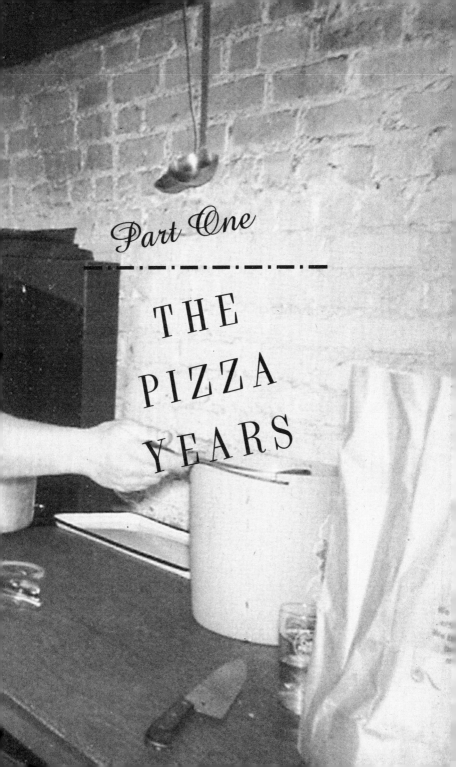

Part One

THE
PIZZA
YEARS

CAPPI AT WORK IN THE KITCHEN

1.

I begin, as I must, with my father. His story starts much earlier (he was born Philip Vito Capotorto in East Harlem in 1922), but I am compelled to introduce him through Cappi's Pizza and Sangweech Shoppe, his fateful venture into the restaurant trade. Built with his own hands out of a pair of burnt-out storefronts during the fall and winter of 1964, Cappi's occupied an awkward stretch of White Plains Road near Pelham Parkway in our native Bronx, directly under the elevated tracks of the Number 2 train but nowhere near the actual station. You really had to go out of your way to get to Cappi's. Once there, you had to endure the terrifying racket of trains thundering overhead every few minutes, sparks raining down from the tracks, crashing onto the pavement, and bouncing off the white metal placard bearing our store motto: "We Don't Spel Good, Just Cook Nice." Adding to the general tension and discomfort were the rules of the house, fancifully printed by hand on a sign the size of a man and posted aggressively at the door: NO RUNNING, NO JUMPING, NO PUSHING, NO SHOVING, NO YELLING, NO FIGHTING, NO CURSING, NO GRABBING.

NO STROLLERS, NO BICYCLES, NO ROLLER SKATES, NO SPECIAL ORDERS, <u>THIS IS NOT A BASKETBALL COURT,</u> NO SHARING, NO EXTRA CHEESE, NO SLICES AT THE TABLE!

The shop was divided into two sections, a vestige of its earlier life as separate storefronts: one half was a typical pizza counter, the other, a simple dining room with little Formica tables and travel posters of Italy on the wall where you could order obscure Italian delicacies, like *capozelle,* the stuffed baked head of a lamb (an example, incidentally, of the word *capo* used in a physical sense); *sanguinaccio,* buckets of animal blood that are boiled and sweetened and churned into a nauseating mock chocolate pudding; *zuppa di trippa,* the lining of a cow's stomach stewed in tomato sauce, and other such delights. My mother, Mary, poor Mary, was in charge of the kitchen, while my father manned the front counter and dining room. She begged him to simplify the menu (though she could prepare world-class versions of everything on it) and lived in mortal fear of orders like shrimp oreganata or broiled cod. Perishable, rarely ordered items such as fish and seafood were kept frozen. Would the customer mind waiting four or five hours while it thawed? It was not unusual to find my mother bent over a steamer pot, weeping, pleading with one frozen lump or another to become soft enough to cook.

The pizza and restaurant sides were distinct entities in my father's mind, and ne'er the twain could meet. The staff, otherwise known as our family of six—my parents; my oldest sister, Rosette; the next oldest, Eva; me; and my baby sister, Maria (less than a year old when we opened Cappi's)—could move between the two areas through a swinging door near the kitchen. But customers had to decide out on the street which entrance to use, and that was that. Their fates were sealed. So if a family of three came in for dinner, say, and Mom ordered eggplant parmigiana and Dad ordered veal cutlet and little Junior just wanted a slice of pizza, guess what? NO SLICES AT THE TABLE. Junior would have to be forcibly removed from his family, sent outside to enter the pizza area through a separate door, and made to stand at the counter to eat his slice alone. The only thing missing was a dunce cap. The parents, of course, would object. My father, the people pleaser, would argue reasonably for a minute and then just throw them out, busting into a full-throttle Ralph Kramden: "Owwwt! Get owwwwt!"

Word spread. Business was slow.

In an effort to boost sales, Cappi had the brilliant idea of offering to throw pizza parties for children. He'd lure a poor, hapless parent into booking the place for a Saturday afternoon and loading in, say, twenty overstimulated eight-year-olds, shrieking, shouting, jumping, and breaking all the Rules. Long before the first pizza was ever served (full pies at the tables were acceptable, just *no slices*), my father would be throwing the entire party out into the street.

"All right, that's it, enough. Get out. Out!"

My own tenth birthday party ended this way, when Steven Morgenthal starting popping balloons with a plastic fork. Cappi exploded. "No more! Party's over! Everybody out! OUT! GET OWWWT!"

I was mortified. I didn't have many friends to begin with, so this was an important social event. A black-and-white photograph taken early in the party shows my guests and me dressed in white shirts and clip-on ties, like for Assembly Day. I was a big shot. This was *my* place, *my* party. Until it wasn't.

As my friends reached for their coats in fear and confusion, my father bellowing at them in his tomato-stained white apron, I ran from the dining room into the kitchen. My mother was turning away from a busy stove when I appeared in the doorway, wiping her hands on a dish towel and preparing to stick ten birthday candles (and one for good luck) into a big, fluffy cake. I wailed up at her like a wounded animal. She dropped everything and bent down to me. That moment is etched into my brain—my mother's instant downshift from a whirl of activity into a tight nest of concern. The seamless, lightning-quick transition moved me. It said that I was more important to her than any task could ever be. (I ended up writing about this moment in a fourth-grade composition assignment entitled "My Red Letter Day," which the teacher had explained was a day we'd never forget.) I choked out my sad little story:

"He threw the whole party out!"

"What?"

"He threw out the whole party!!"

Indignant, my mother marched away to confront my father. Nothing came of it. She was no match for him. She acquiesced almost

MY TENTH BIRTHDAY
PARTY AT CAPPI'S, JUST BEFORE IT GOT SHUT
DOWN. (THAT'S STEVEN MORGENTHAL AT CENTER.)

always, banking on the logic that this would foster peace—the more she swallowed, the less he'd have to dish out. But really it worked the other way around: the more she choked back, the more he shoveled in. I don't remember what happened to the cake. Maybe we ate it. I know I moped around for hours afterward, sighing and anxious. How would I face my friends the next day? Eventually, my father sidled over to me with his tail between his legs.

"You can call them all back if you want to."

"No I can't. It's too late."

It was painfully obvious to all that Cappi wasn't cut out for retail. He must have been grateful for our regular customers, such as they were. My mother still refers to people based on their standing orders of forty years ago.

"You know who I ran into today at Met Foods? Gertrude Fierman. Remember her? She used to come to the restaurant with her mother, they'd order an eggplant parmigian' and a chicken parmigian' and split them—and they always wanted the cheese very burnt. Remember them, with the burnt cheese?"

And I do. Gertrude and her mother were two of our better-adjusted regulars. Some of the others were another story.

Like the Silent Drunk, whose name we never learned—a tiny slip of a man in his mid-fifties or so who'd toddle into the restaurant late on weeknights, inebriated, and just point to items on the menu, mouthing his order, never sounding a peep. (*Zuppa d'escarol'* and spaghetti with garlic and butter were his usual picks.) He traveled with an imaginary, or at least unseen, companion, with whom he'd engage in silent conversation throughout the meal. My mother looked on the bright side. "At least he thinks he's not alone."

But these mimed dates always ended badly, with the little man eventually jumping to his feet, gesticulating and shouting in a soundless rage, tossing a few crumpled bills and some change onto the table, turning his pockets inside out, and making a big show of being empty of further cash. The fights were always about money. I'd park myself in a quiet corner during his visits, pretending to wipe down tables or fill condiment jars or something. Then I'd run on back into the kitchen and report what I was seeing.

"He's a *freak!*" Eva would concur. (She and I, the two middle children, were constant collaborators.)

The Silent Drunk reminded us of the sad-sack hero of "One Meat Ball" by the Andrews Sisters, who, hard up and hungry, wanders into a Depression-era diner "to see what fifteen cents could do."

> *One meat ball*
> *One meat ball*
> *He could afford but one meat ball . . .*

My mother had the original Decca recording. We'd drag it out once in a while and she'd break into a quiet little Lindy Hop. I loved watching her in those moments, imagining what she must have been like as a young bobby-soxer in flare skirt and snood. She had been an early Sinatra groupie, and photos from her youth show a beaming, dark-haired beauty in stylish 1940s fashions, usually surrounded by a gaggle of girlfriends.

"Want to learn the Big Apple?" she'd ask in her lightest moments, demonstrating various foot shuffles and hip rotations. "Shine the apple!" she'd call, dancing an appropriate step. "Now slice it!"

Sometimes my father would take her hand and they'd give it a whirl across the scuffed linoleum tiles, a rare display of affection between them. The whole family knew the lyrics to "One Meat Ball" by heart.

The Circus Act, another pair of regulars known only by the nicknames we secretly gave them, were at their usual table on most Friday nights. Again, I'd watch from a "hidden" perch: he was about seven feet tall, gangly and unkempt, with great shocks of brown, bristly hair pushing out at odd angles; she was maybe four-foot-one, Thumbelina-like and neat as a pin, her head rising not much higher than his hip. They seemed old to me but were probably only in their thirties.

"There's a lid for every pot," my mother would say.

He was a toilet seat salesman. We could tell because he always had samples on hand, falling out of their dirty, bashed-up cardboard boxes. He carried a beaten leather binder stuffed with hundreds of unbound documents, all crumpled and ready to spill. He moved in uneven lurches. He was *spastic* in kid speak, and utterly fascinating. The miniature woman didn't say much. When she spoke, her voice was so soft as to be inaudible. At some point at the end of every meal, the toilet seat salesman would rise spasmodically from the table, nearly knocking it across the room, and lumber off to the bathroom, where he'd remain for a good twenty minutes or more, while his date, alone at the table, shifted awkwardly in her seat, applied and reapplied lipstick, eyed the check anxiously. Eventually the giant reemerged, thundering back to his table in a stink. On at least one occasion he stopped off at the kitchen door to shout the helpful news that "ya toilet's clogged." For some reason, he never tried to sell my father his wares. I guess he didn't like mixing business with pleasure.

Pizza was fifteen cents a slice. Heroes were something like eighty-five cents. You could have a homemade soup-to-nuts meal for about five bucks. Cappi had to move a lot of food to make it work. All regular customers were valuable. Their eccentricities were tolerated, as long as they obeyed The Rules. Some were more fun than others, and a few became family friends. John and Jen were a jolly pair, an unlikely sight in their authentic western gear, right down to the boots and spurs. They were obese, weighing more than six hundred pounds between them, and spoke with thick southern accents . . . though we were pretty sure they hailed from well north of the Mason-Dixon Line. Horse enthusiasts and avid riders both (my mother pitied the poor animals), they hoped one day to own a stud of their own. At some point they moved away, but continued to exchange Christmas cards with my family for several years, always signed "John & Jen." Eventually, a third name appeared: Sandy. My mother wondered aloud every holiday season whether Sandy was a boy, a girl . . . or a horse.

Merle and Barry, a pair of fresh-faced comics in their late teens or so, used to perform their routines in front of the counter as we gathered on the other side to watch. I'd howl with laughter at their bits, clutching my sides and doubling over. I thought they were the funniest things on Earth. One skit that always killed me opened with Merle laughing hysterically; Barry walks up and officiously informs her that she is in a "no laughing zone" and will have to "stop laughing immediately, Madam," which only makes her laugh harder; he insists she stop; she laughs harder still; and round it goes. Eventually Barry starts laughing too, and they walk off together in a gale of guffaws. Curtain. Encore! I couldn't get enough! Merle noticed.

"He is *really laughing*," she once commented, beaming.

It pleased her, which pleased me. I had a crush on Merle. She was going places. She'd landed a bit part in Alan Pakula's *Up the Down Staircase,* playing a high school student named . . . Merle. She even had a few lines with Sandy Dennis. I was too young to see the movie but got the point: Merle was a star.

She and Barry inadvertently provided my stage debut at the tender age of nine. The Bronx's own Lunt and Fontanne, they were starring in a comedy production they'd mounted at a local community theater. I don't remember the details; I have purposely forgotten. At some point during the show, I had to pee. My mother pointed toward the bathroom but must have known it was useless. I had no sense of direction. (At Tung Hoy, the old-school Chinese restaurant my father brought us to on very special occasions, a grand room with a maze of tables and a colorful mosaic dragon snaking along two walls, my mother would have to flag me down after my bathroom trips or I'd wander around in total confusion, hopelessly lost and becoming frightened.) I was able to find the theater's bathroom with relative ease, as I recall, but got tangled up on my way back and ended up walking through a series of doors that led backstage. Lost and disoriented, I asked a teenager who was loafing on a metal folding chair, a slacker stage manager I guess, how to get back to my seat. He smirked and pointed to a big pair of double doors.

"Right through there," he said.

"Here?" I asked hopefully. "This door?"

"Yep," he said with a glint. It didn't feel right, but I pushed through anyway.

A sudden flood of light engulfed me as I stepped into a very bright room filled with heavily made-up people who froze the moment I entered and were now staring at me with openmouthed horror. When I realized I was onstage, I snapped the door shut and sped away. His little metal folding chair had collapsed under the prankster's wild laughter, and now I could hear great peals of it rising from the audience as they realized what had just happened. My mother slumped down in her seat, hoping I wouldn't find her. I waited at the back of the house until the end of the performance. I don't know what Merle and Barry made of my hideous gaffe. I don't remember seeing them much after that. At some point we heard that they'd moved to Hollywood.

There were other regulars too, some who brought cheer into the place and whose visits we anticipated with pleasure, others whose oddness provided welcome distraction. But the stalwart Saturday night crew formed a pillar of Cappi's business: Ann Lazerta and her husband, Little; Ann's sister Flo and her husband, Big; a woman named Rosie and some guy known only as Lenny X (they were married, but not to each other); a short, morbidly obese guy, I forget his name, maybe Vin or Vic, who had an open hole where his ear should have been but would plug in a Mr. Potato Head–like plastic replacement on formal occasions; and a few others. They were to me the height of glamour, feasting and partying at Cappi's every Saturday night until maybe midnight or so, racking up a hefty tab. The women all wore sequins and diamonds and smoked long, skinny cigarettes; they had raspy voices, husky laughs, and flawless manicures. The men wore shiny suits, their fat fingers adorned with chunky rings; they reeked of pomade and cologne and fresh tobacco, all mixed in with traces of women's perfume. (Flo to Ann: "You like this fragrance? Joy. Hundred dollars an ounce.")

When Cappi's closed for the night, the whole crew would amble down the avenue to settle in for more serious drinking and carousing at the Villa Reda, our neighborhood nightclub. A French singer named Jacques Kayal performed there on weekends, determined to have a hit with his Ventures-inflected pop rock novelty number, "I Want a Short Fat Girl with a Brain the Size of a Bird." My mother still has the demo pressing, and Jacques's eight-by-ten glossy sits to this day in a gilded frame in her living room. She had a crush on him. All the women did. He was pretty. He was French. He was a crooner. And, while it was never discussed, I suspect he may also have been a "friend of Dorothy." I thought I noticed something pass between us whenever he looked at me, a flash of recognition. (I remember being aware of my own homosexuality and being able to recognize the same in others from a ridiculously early age, which I think is true for most gay people.)

I developed a crush on Jacques but was really more starstruck than anything else. He had the gleam of celebrity, an air of French ele-

gance not found elsewhere in the neighborhood. His solo concert at Alice Tully Hall, which our entire family attended, sealed the verdict: Jacques was legendary. He didn't visit Cappi's often, but when he did my mother really put on the dog for him, breaking out special desserts and cordials, fussing over him and giggling coyly. She fluttered so when waiting on Jacques that she once spilled a glass of red wine down his shirt, a faux pas that can still make her blush, decades later. I used a ballpoint pen to carve his first name in huge letters into the seat of a chair he'd occupied. My father laughed when he saw it. He thought it was cute. (He could be unpredictable that way.)

"*Don't!*" I screeched a few days later, when he showed it to Jacques. The singer seemed somewhat alarmed by my desperate scratchitti but smiled gamely and said he was flattered.

Big and Little and Lenny and the rest of the guys, most of them, were "connected." Fur coats, jewelry, and electronics would "fall off the truck" into their lucky hands. Many times they offered my father "in." ("You want *in*?") All he had to do was say yes. But my father wanted no part of their thing. He'd entertain them at the restaurant and sometimes even join them for drinks at the Villa after hours, but that was where it ended. I understood his choice even then, and was proud of it. Still, I liked what these slick, Runyonesque characters brought out in him. He'd become a regular Red Buttons around them, telling jokes and singing little novelty numbers in their obscure southern Italian dialects. (He was an expert in this area and remained for the rest of his life the go-to guy for folks longing to hear the spoken music of their ancestors.) At the Villa Reda, between sets of Jacques Kayal, my father used to do an entire act on the tiny, tinsel-curtained stage, performing original patter songs and stand-up routines. Sometimes the crew would command a performance of some snippet or other right there in the restaurant, and I'd get to see a part of the man he rarely showed his family. I remember his bit about the human heart.

"What is it, really? Just a pump. So why don't we call it that? Because it would ruin popular music, that's why."

And then he'd do a medley of tunes, replacing the word *heart* with the word *pump:*

"I left my pump in San Francisco."

"Pump and soul, I fell in love with you."

"Zing went the strings of my pump."

I saw him do this routine only once, performing in his pizza whites and apron in the fluorescent-lit dining room, a poor man's Lou Monte. My family, Eva and I especially, noted with some bitterness that he could be the life of the party when he wanted to be, funny and charming and expansively warmhearted.

"Oh, he's a riot," people would say. "You kids must have so much fun at home!"

Comments like these made our blood run cold. They rubbed salt in the wound.

My father never sang for his family.

2.

The pizza shop was effectively our home. It was where we'd go after school and stay until bedtime. Cappi set up a makeshift "family area" directly behind the double pizza oven (where else?), consisting of a couple of small Formica-topped tables pushed together with six chairs around them, and a secondhand black-and-white TV propped atop a pile of soda boxes. "The table" was where we'd eat our family meals (grace included), do homework, fold pizza boxes (my job), take naps. It was from this hot little corner that we watched the Apollo moon landing and learned of the assassinations of Robert F. Kennedy and Martin Luther King, Jr. Our real home—rarely occupied, since the pizza shop was open twelve hours a day, six days a week—was a fourth-floor walk-up, one-bedroom apartment in a prewar mock Tudor building just a few yards behind the shop. (Spacious for a one-bedroom but still tight for a family of six.)

The earsplitting, eyeball-rattling pattern of train noise was actually worse up there, since the added height put us just about at track level. Trains thundered by on their ruthless schedule right outside our living room window, at a distance of maybe twenty yards. I nearly developed lumbago from leaping up and down to smash my ear against our old black-and-white television set in a desperate effort to miss fewer punch lines on *Laugh-In* and *The Carol Burnett Show.*

My two older sisters and I shared the single bedroom—they in bunk beds, I on a trundle bed along the opposite wall. My parents slept in the living room, Maria in a crib at their side. When Maria outgrew her baby quarters, she took my place in the bedroom and my "room" became a sectioned-off length of hallway into which a narrow bed had been slipped, blocked off by a bookcase. It was a makeshift sleep-in *closet,* really, more of a tall *drawer* than a room. But I loved it. It was mine. The walls protected me. I had a habit of rocking violently in the night, so much so that during the years I shared the bedroom with my sisters, I'd wake up most mornings to find myself in the middle of the room, having rocked myself there, bed and all, overnight. I also rocked rhythmically during car trips, a habit my older sisters teased me about mercilessly. My methodical back-and-forth movements were usually accompanied by chanting. (Maybe I was meditating. Or slightly autistic.)

"Mother-father-sister-brother," I am told, was one of my mantras.

Another was "Rock-a-fell-a-fino," repeated endlessly in staccato fashion, which my family ribs me about to this day. (I must have plucked the pleasingly percussive pair of names right out of the news: Nelson Rockefeller was battling Barry Goldwater at the time for the 1964 Republican presidential nomination . . . with Paul Fino as his running mate.)

The walls anchored me as I rocked and rolled in my sleep. I spent hours gazing up at them, planning to decorate but never actually doing it. The furthest I got was to tear an advertisement from the pages of *TV Guide* and tape it above my head. It was a full-page black-and-white photograph of a teenager with arrows pointing to different parts of his body, leading to little passages of text. The headline read, "How to Tell if Your Child Is a Junkie." An arrow stemming from the teen's arm advised parents to look for track marks; an arrow from his eyes warned against finding them bloodshot and droopy; from his hair, an arrow directed parents to beware of failing hygiene; and so on. I don't know if I fully understood the meaning of the ad. I just liked the picture, so somber and vérité. Its sudden appearance in my "room" alarmed my parents. I remember hearing them wonder quietly why I'd hung it there and whether they should take it down. (They said nothing to me directly, so the picture stayed.)

ME, SLUMPING AROUND THE APARTMENT—ONE OF
MANY DIANE ARBUS—LIKE PHOTOS FROM THE PERIOD

It must have been especially noticeable, since it was just about the only decorative element in the apartment. My mother was (and still is) fastidiously clean, so the place was always spotless ("immaculate" in her parlance), but not a single photograph or painting was displayed, no rugs or knickknacks or coffee tables. Black-and-white family photographs from the period look like they're by Diane Arbus: we are slouched and cheerless (exhausted, I guess, from the grind of the pizza shop), gazing vacantly into the camera, surrounded by blank white walls and strictly utilitarian secondhand furniture. The barrenness of that apartment was partly a function of the fact that it was supposed to be temporary. My parents had moved there from a tiny basement studio on Grace Avenue when they still had only two kids (after having lived with my mother's mother for a while as newlyweds). Their plan was not to stay; they stayed for fifteen years. The eat-in kitchen was the most cheerful room, with faded wallpaper in a classic cups-and-saucers design, and a 1950s red Formica-topped wooden table with matching chairs, all nicely faded with age. There was a broom closet and a dumbwaiter and a vegetable cabinet built into the wall under the window, each of which held its own particular fascination—especially the dumbwaiter, in frequent use not only for carrying up parcels and carrying down garbage but also as a kind of crude telecommunications device: "Yoo-hoo . . . Mary . . . open up, I wanna *aks* you something."

Our ornery downstairs neighbor was in the habit of sticking her head out into the hoistway and raging up at my mother whenever she heard her near:

"You people are animals! Your kids run around like Indians! You're savages! You make noise day and night!"

"What the hell is she talking about, we're never even here," my mother would say. "She's a witch."

She referred to Mrs. Chumsky as a witch so often that I began to take it literally. One day when we happened upon our neighbor on the street, with her hard scowl and wild mane of fried white hair, I asked my mother at full volume, "Mommy, is that the witch?" Mrs. C did the ladylike thing and spat at us. It got so bad that my mother once turned away from the dumbwaiter while Mrs. C was screeching up at her, moved calmly to the sink, poured a cup of cold water, returned to the dumbwaiter, and dumped the water down onto Mrs. C's face. If she wasn't a real witch, she sure squealed liked one. This was a rare act of aggression on my mother's part . . . and I liked it. I asked her over and over again to tell the story.

"Did you really do it? Did you really dump the water in her face?"

She'd casually recount the tale like it was nothing, the sort of thing she did every day. But I could see that she was as proud of it as I was, and for the same reason.

The kitchen window, dressed in kitschy curtains purchased at Harry's Hardware or John's Bargain Store, faced the front of the building and looked down into the courtyard, a small paved area connecting three wings in a squared off U-shape. The window was in the center wing, on the horizontal, but still you could catch glimpses into other people's apartments. I became a bit of a Peeping Tom, though all I ever saw were flashes of fully clad bodies moving through ordinary rooms. In the morning, the courtyard filled with the sounds of alarm clocks, kitchen radios, children crying, couples arguing . . . and became thick with the smells of fresh-perked coffee and frying bacon. A few windows away lived a dark and disturbed young man named Neil, known to physically abuse his mother, Lily, a short, wobbly little woman with extremely bowed legs, always pushing a shopping cart lined in blue plaid plastic. Lily was sweet and gentle and kind, which added greatly to the heartbreak of knowing how she suffered at the hands of her son, a frightful sight in filthy paramilitary clothes, with matted hair and wild eyes. Neil would fixate on a particular record and blast it over and over again at top volume for days. Most haunting was his obsession with "Rag Doll" by the Four Seasons:

> *I'd change her sad rags into glad rags if I could (if I could)*
> *My folks won't let me 'cause they say that she's no good . . .*

By the fiftieth spin or so, the song began to sound like nails on a blackboard. Still, no one was willing to confront the source. Eventually, the record started skipping.

Sometimes Neil would "fix" it, and the needle would lurch forward with a hard scratch; other times he'd just let it skip endlessly.

> *If I could—if I could—if I could—if I could—if I could . . .*

Through the living room wall: the sounds of a man beating his wife. I hear him grunting in short barks; I hear her pleading with him; I hear him strike her; suddenly, chaos—furniture crashing, glass breaking, bodies thumping hard, strangulated screaming. I don't remember the man's name. I remember finding him foul as he hurried by on the street or in the hallway, head bent, unsmiling, avoiding eye contact, balding awkwardly and dressed in a cheap suit. He and his wife, Corrina, were recent immigrants from Italy. She was a big woman who could easily have crushed him if she wanted to. Corrina was shy and quiet, spoke very little English, and flashed a couple of Old Country gold teeth whenever she smiled, which was often. The couple had one child, Nina, younger than I, shy and skittish with good reason. I anguished over the suffering of my neighbors. I'd watch them in the courtyard or on the sidewalk, chatting and shopping and going about their business, knowing what awaited them at home. I could *hear* it when it happened, *feel* its terrifying vibration against the wall. My awareness of their secret suffering was a burden I carried in silence.

I included these people in my nightly prayers, along with other pitiable creatures I happened upon in the neighborhood: the withered, ancient man who sat at the window of his ground-floor apartment a few blocks away, staring blankly at nothing all day long from inside an empty shell; the mentally retarded adult woman I once saw trip and fall while carrying a small child, not injuring the baby but crying like one herself, begging her mother for "one more chance" as the kid was snatched away from her, repeating over and over that she was "sorry, Mommy, so sorry, so sorry"; the mournful old Polish lady who walked around with tears in her eyes but would smile at me through her watery gaze, once stopping me and pressing into my hands a dog-eared hymnal (which I still have), saying, "Take, take, good boy"; the child I watched get beaten by his father right on the floor of Alexander's department store, mercilessly and without cause.

I prayed for all of them.

I prayed for Giulia, the old Italian lady on the second floor, whose obese, alcoholic son would yell and thrash wildly about the apartment when he was drunk, sometimes striking her and spilling his madness into the building hallway, where he'd pass out on the cold marble steps, his weeping mother trying in vain to drag him back inside. I experienced the sadness of these strangers as my own. Sometimes I couldn't shake it.

Not all of our neighbors (Jewish, Italian, Polish, German, Irish mostly) were quite so beleaguered. Miss Sabella, who occupied the apartment above us, and Mrs. Mueller, right next door, both widowed and childless, spent hours talking and gossiping in the hallway. I'd often join them, enjoying the contrast between the two—they couldn't have been more different—and comforted by their homespun routines. Miss Sabella, a tall redhead in her sixties bearing a passing resemblance to Joan Blondell, was always done up to the nines in coordinated fashions of vibrant color, seamed silk stockings, netted hats, ensemble jewelry, high heels, and fancy leather purses. Her lips and nails were painted ruby red, and she spoke in a hurried whisper, as if just squeezing in a few urgent words before being whisked away to some impossibly glamorous event. She liked our family and always had a kind word for me.

"What a sweet boy you are," she'd say, "and so handsome!"

Our stylish neighbor, having lived in her fifth-floor walk-up apartment for more than thirty years, complained bitterly about the building's fall from grace.

"This used to be a white-glove residence. We had a doorman and beautiful carpets in the lobby. Not like now. It's become a tenement. Terrible. . . . Have I mentioned that I was once Miss Bronx for three years in a row?"

Mrs. Mueller, a plain Jane who'd lived in the building for nearly as long, would nod and offer agreement. "Yes indeed, mm-hm, it has, it was, it is, you don't say."

Her gray hair was combed simply. She wore dark cotton dresses, black orthopedic shoes, and cat's-eye spectacles of black and silver. Brigid, her ancient dachshund, had to be coaxed up each and every step of the four flights to their apartment with a dog biscuit. (Skinny Mrs. Mueller wasn't strong enough to carry the poor old beast.)

I never saw Miss Sabella's place, which I imagined looked something like a 1930s Hollywood set, but I once knocked on Mrs. Mueller's door to seek advice about a wounded squirrel I rescued from the lots, the apparent victim of a BB gun attack. I'd loaded the creature into a cardboard box and carried it upstairs. Mrs. M was an animal lover; I was sure she could save it. She invited me inside and led me down a long, dark entrance corridor, which opened onto a cramped living room stuffed with doily-strewn, Depression-era furniture. She sat me down on a dusty old sofa next to an oversize pillow in the shape of a dachsie—the spitting image of Brigid, who snored heavily as she snoozed nearby, a dog at the end of her life. Mrs. M looked down at the wounded rodent, which by now was bloody and panting hard.

"I think the best thing you can do for this animal is to let it die," she said.

Minutes later, the squirrel fell still. I was stunned that Mrs. Mueller couldn't save it and wondered in some part of my mind if she hadn't willed its death.

"Why don't you take it on downstairs and put it back in the lot where you found it?" she offered patiently as the diseased thing stiffened in its box at her feet. I took her advice but never again felt as warmly toward my neighbor.

I named the squirrel Scruffy posthumously and gave it a proper burial, a technique I'd picked up from my sister Eva. She and her friend Darlene from around the corner regularly scoured the neighborhood for wounded cats, birds, squirrels, and other needy critters. They'd nurse them back to health, if possible. If the animal was dead when they found it, or died in their care, they'd build a coffin out of a milk crate, form a funeral procession through the streets—picking up kids as they went along until they had a proper entourage—and bury it in the lots with tears, prayers, and a humble marker.

Eva once rescued a wounded baby sparrow, naming it Windy after the 1967 pop hit by the Association (*"And Windy has wings to fly / Above the clouds / Above the clouds"*). She built a little habitat for the baby bird, fed her with a dropper, and taught her to fly by gently throwing her for short distances, low to the ground, encouraging her wings to grow stronger. During one such flying lesson, which appeared after several days to be working quite successfully, little Windy landed in a patch of tall weeds and was momentarily lost. Eva and I searched the area.

"Here, little Windy. Here, Windy, Windy, Windy."

Suddenly, a high-pitched squeak came from underfoot: I had stepped on the tiny thing and squashed it squarely with my big shoe. Poor, recovering little Windy was now quite dead. Eva sobbed and wailed as she hammered together a fresh coffin, cursing me and driving me away from her. I wrote a five-page apology letter, something I found myself doing often. Eva forgave me. She always did. We needed each other.

Not long after the Windy incident, I earned some brownie points with my big sister by leading her to a kitten I'd found in the A&P parking lot a few blocks away, trying to nurse from a dead mother. Eva carried the sickly thing carefully back to Cappi's, cooing at it the whole way, quickly naming it Nefertiti (Niffi for short). Using nails and wood culled from vegetable crates, she built a two-room kitty condo behind the pizza shop and nursed the feline faithfully for weeks until her health improved. My father tolerated Niffi's presence grudgingly but put his foot down as cold weather approached and we begged for permission to take her into our apartment. No way. We worked on him. He relented. Niffi had grown quite strong by then. And, we were soon to discover, quite *evil*. She started launching sustained, spontaneous attacks, completely unprovoked, choosing a target (usually me), stalking it, and then mauling it viciously, not just once but repeatedly, galloping after her prey like a tiger in the wild, pouncing, clawing, biting, drawing blood, opening gashes.

I spent more times than I care to remember being chased around the apartment this way, howling in fear with Niffi hot on my tail, my mother screaming and yelling but unable to control the vicious animal. When all else failed, Mom would open a closet door so I could hop in and take cover until Niffi calmed down. I remember hovering in the darkness and asking quietly through a tiny crack in the door whether it was safe to come out.

"Not yet," my mother would say, trying to lure Niffi into the bathroom or bedroom—the only rooms with doors.

How that cat was allowed to stay remains a mystery. She turned on my mother more than once (scars remain) and attacked visitors with some regularity. But she really had it in for *me,* perhaps because I was the one who'd discovered her. Maybe she'd have preferred to die in that parking lot along with her mother and siblings, their bodies splayed stiff as boards around her when I'd stumbled upon her pitiful form.

Only in heat would she seek my affection, and then very bossily. She'd wail and moan in that strangely human-sounding voice female cats use during mating season, and push her swollen, pulsating cat vagina into my face. The first few times she exhibited this behavior, I mistook it for affection and tried to stroke her. She turned and attacked, hissing and clawing viciously.

"Don't touch me! Just fuck me!" she screamed.

No wonder I turned out gay. That cat had me terrified. And she knew it. Once when I was alone in the apartment, she began stalking me, and I could see that an attack was imminent. I panicked and dialed the ASPCA.

"Yes, hello, I'm about to be attacked by my cat! *What do I do?*"

"You say you're about to be attacked by your cat?"

"Yes! She attacks me! She's gonna pounce any minute! What do I do?"

"Sir, can you just go into another room?"

"I can't! She's blocking my way!"

And she was. But the operator must have thought it was a prank call and just hung up. Thinking fast, I hurled myself backward across the entrance foyer, fumbled with the front door desperately, and threw myself out into the hallway. A narrow escape.

I hated to be left alone in that apartment. Even long before Niffi, I found the prospect terrifying. My mother still recounts the time from my early childhood when, as she was coming back from hanging laundry on the roof, she heard me sobbing inside.

"I'm all alone! Oh my dear God! I'm all alone!"

I couldn't have been more than four years old, but I remember the episode quite distinctly: It was late afternoon. I was napping on the couch (really an old army cot with a throw blanket and bolsters), having fallen asleep to the reassuring sounds of my mother puttering about in the kitchen. When I awoke, all was silent.

"Ma?" I remember calling. "Mommy?"

Nothing. I got up and walked into the kitchen. "Ma?"

Still no answer. I stumbled through the back hallway leading to the bathroom and bedroom, searched the bathroom, searched the bedroom—all empty. I remember a tidal wave of panic sweeping up my spine and exploding inside my head. I remember feeling *alone* in a way I never had before, alone in a *primal* way. By the time my mother came rushing through the front door, casting her laundry basket aside and scooping me into her arms to comfort the little body racked with sobs, it was too late. I had glimpsed the abyss. I *was* alone. She couldn't protect me from that. No mother could.

I guess that's what the recurring nightmare I had for years in that apartment was all about: I am asleep in the bedroom; I hear the buzzer, announcing a visitor; I rise from the bed, go to the intercom, buzz the visitor in. I crack open the apartment door and listen down the windy hallways; I hear the whiny breath and threatening cackle of a witch—the fairy-tale kind, replete with hat and broom. I rush into the kitchen, where my mother is cooking at the stove.

"It's the witch," I say. "She's coming to get me."

My mother turns to the broom closet, opens the door, and shoos me in. "Quickly," she urges. "Hide in here."

I scramble inside and press my ear to the door. I can hear the witch entering our apartment; I can hear her creeping over to my hiding place; I can feel the hairs on the back of my neck go electric as she opens the broom closet door and finds me.

"Aha!" she shrieks. "You can't hide from me!"

And then she bops me on the head with her broom.

End of dream. Not so bad, really. But terrifying nonetheless.

Home alone one late afternoon around Christmastime, I hear a strange noise in the hallway. I creep over to the peephole, slide the round disk aside on the old-fashioned viewing device, and look through the thick lens: a human eye, clear as day, is staring back at me! I fall backward, gasping. Maybe it's my imagination. I check again. Again—an unblinking eye staring straight into mine! Trembling, I creep over to the black rotary wall phone and dial our neighbor Josie. She lives just up the block.

"Josie, it's Carl. I'm alone in the apartment and someone is outside the door staring through the peephole!"

"What? Are you sure?"

"I'm sure! I checked twice! What do I do?"

"You're probably just imagining it, honey. But I'll call your mother. Just keep the door locked and someone'll come up to get you."

Oddly, I hadn't thought of simply calling down to the pizza shop myself. Things were hectic down there just then, and I had been sent upstairs to do my homework (i.e., get out of the way). Within minutes I hear someone on the stairs. Then I hear my mother chuckling, keys in the door, the door opening.

"Mom?"

"Yeah, it's me." She appears in the doorway with a winter coat slung hurriedly over her apron.

"There was someone there, Ma! I swear! An eye was staring at me through the peephole!"

"Still is," she said. "Take a look."

It was Santa Claus. Days before, she'd hung a molded plastic likeness of Santa's face on the apartment door, and one of its eyes happened to be lined up exactly with the peephole: I'd been staring into the printed graphic of a cheap holiday decoration. Still, taking no chances, I donned my coat and shoes and followed my mother down to the relative safety of the pizza shop, hurrying to keep apace. Walking alone through the hallways had always given me the willies. Whenever I had to go up or down the four flights of stairs alone, I'd ask my mother or Eva to talk to me the whole way, calling up or down in an ever-louder voice until I had arrived safely at my destination. Eva was fond of falling silent at around the midway point, just to torture me.

"Eva? Eva! Eva, are you still there?" Silence. *"Eva?"*

A wild guffaw. "I'm right here, you big baby. Keep walking."

It wasn't just me. Our downstairs neighbor Rosanna Corso also found the cool, dark hallways intimidating. She navigated them with keys splayed through the clenched fingers of her gnarly fist, make-shift brass knuckles.

"See what I do, Mary? Anybody attacks me, I'll gouge their eyes out!"

She demonstrated with a weak and bony key-studded left hook. Rosanna had a tight, nervous way of walking and talking, which was great fun to mimic—something Eva and I did constantly, without cruelty.

"Ya little rare-scals!" she'd peep. "Want some candy?" And she'd open her black patent leather pocketbook to retrieve little bundles of ancient suckers (usually the Christmas variety, striped in red and green), packed by hand into squares of plastic wrap. We never ate them. Though childless and widowed, Rosanna struck me as an older, ethnic version of Jane Wyatt as Margaret Anderson on *Father Knows Best*: crisp, belted flare skirts hugging a slim waist, white tailored blouses, neat shrug jackets in cotton or velvet, sensible heels, tight coif, pronounced but modest makeup, strands of pearls.

"Ya little rare-scals!"

Eva and I noted well our neighbor's obsession with cleanliness and her overfondness for plastic wrap, neatly cut strips of which she used to cover her rings and bracelets, the straps of her handbags, the tops of her shoes. Even the steering wheel of her impeccably maintained 1940s black Chevy was sheathed in protective wrap. She and her husband, before he died, had kept an eye on their pride and joy from their bedroom window, sounding an urgent alarm whenever anybody got too close.

"Away from the car, please!"

On Sundays, they'd get all dressed up, perambulate in a leisurely fashion over to their vehicle, climb carefully into the front seats . . . and then sit for an hour or two, waving politely at neighbors who happened to pass by. They didn't even bother firing up the engine. Only once in a while would the car would actually get *driven*—never at a speed over twenty miles an hour, and always on the same exact route around the neighborhood.

After Mr. Corso died, Rosanna insisted that she wasn't alone. "My sick aunt lives with me now. She never leaves the apartment." We knew it wasn't true. "Hello, Auntie," she'd call as she pushed into her empty place.

Rosette and her friend Peggy once got into big trouble for slipping a note under Rosanna's door that read: "OPEN UP OR WE WILL KILL YOU." Rosanna had asked them to pick her up a quart of milk from Ruby's, the corner store, but then would not open the door to allow its delivery. They could hear her fumbling quietly with the peephole, pretending she wasn't home. I guess she hoped they'd just leave it there, but they pressed the issue. Alarmed and disturbed by their note, she showed it to my father. Rosette caught hell for that.

Rosanna later apologized to my mother for making trouble. "But you can't be too careful these days, Mary."

Outside in the courtyard, kids gathered to play handball or stoop ball with pink rubber Spaldings ("Spaldeens" we called them), or to choose up sides for Ringolevio, an age-old borough game, basically a team version of hide-and-seek. The rules of Ringolevio were such that when a player from one team was found and tagged, he or she became a member of the opposing team, so you could never be sure who was still on your side and who had been tagged and was therefore now your enemy—good training for life. The game could stretch on for hours, and could be played with a nearly limitless number of kids across a great swath of the neighborhood (with the courtyard as home base). You often found yourself playing with kids you'd never seen before and might never see again, so the social pressure was off.

There was no history, no reputation to live up to or disprove. It was liberating.

Our supers, Jo and Joe Galotti, who lived in a basement apartment off the side alley where the garbage cans were kept and seemed pretty depressed, specifically forbade such courtyard antics. Joe would sometimes let us slide, but Jo would come hulking up from her underground lair, all grizzled and wheezing in her well-worn housecoat, gray hair flying, bony knees crackling, smoking four cigarettes in one hand and six in the other (or so it seemed).

"Get outta the court!" she'd bark in a voice that sounded like tires grinding over gravel. She didn't have to tell us twice.

Mitchell Kirschenbaum's mother chased us out of the courtyard too—but only to stop us from torturing her son, a lumpy, doughy ball of a kid with oily skin and eyeglasses that were always sliding down his nose, a quintessential nerd, right down to the speech impediment. He and his family were planning to move out of state.

"We're moving to *Mathathuseths,*" he'd announce haughtily.

We seized upon this like vultures:

"Where did you say you were moving to, Mitchell?"

"*Mathathuseths.* We're moving to *Mathathuseths.*"

"*Mathathuseths?* Ya moving to *Mathathuseths?*"

And we'd collapse onto the pavement, rolling theatrically and howling with cruel and pointless laughter.

"We're moving to *Mathathuseths,* we're moving to *Mathathuseths,*" we'd chant.

Poor fool Mitchell would turn beet red and start bawling. His mother, a short, fat brunette usually wearing stretch pants and tunic tops, took to hiding behind the large cement planters in the courtyard and running out like a banshee screaming, "You leave him *alooone!* Leave him *alooone!!*"

We'd scatter in every direction and seek adventure elsewhere in the neighborhood. There was plenty to be found.

The back alleys of nearby buildings, with their winding cement pathways and darkened storage rooms, were akin to uncharted land, ripe for conquest. "Whoa! Look at this!" We'd call out to one another when one of us had stumbled upon an unseen doorway or a discarded refrigerator or washing machine, boldly venturing to sites farther and farther away from home. These exploratory expeditions were usually embarked upon in small groups that would form spontaneously on any given day just for that purpose—similar to the way Ringolevio games got started.

"Wanna go explorin'?" one boy might say to another.

"Yeah," the other might reply. "Let's find some other kids."

This was decidedly a *boys'* game, which was a big part of its appeal. I was labeled "faggot" at an early age, so my social status was shaky, at best. There was freedom in anonymity.

Bronx Park, two blocks away, was a wilderness, especially the great expanses beyond the playgrounds and bench areas. We'd enter at Waring Avenue, head up a paved path tacking a steep incline, walk across the footbridge over the Bronx River Parkway—taking a moment, perhaps, to spit down at passing cars, or maybe just to wave— pass through the gate (now modern and locked, but once a simple old turnstile), and canter down a sloping trail leading deep into the heart of the park. We spent hours lost in our local forest, the far reaches of which meld eventually into the Bronx Botanical Garden and the Bronx Zoo, certain that we were spying lands never before seen by man. Johnny Sczepanski and I once found what we took to be a fresh stream gushing out of the ground and winding down a rocky path. We drank from it greedily. (Only years later did it occur to me that it was probably a drainage pipe.) We scaled "mountains" here—and along the rocky stretch of White Plains Road just north of Cappi's—crawling across giant boulders to mine mica with our fingernails, collecting samples in Band-Aid cans or the little muslin sacks that Gold Rush gum came in, certain that we were farming a substance of incalculable value, coming to know those rocks so well that we could scamper across them blindfolded.

In the shops and stores crowding "the Avenue" (White Plains Road, west of Pelham Parkway), and nearby Allerton and Lydig avenues, we'd buy (or steal) comic books, baseball cards, water guns. We'd stop at our favorite shops to buy penny candies (Bazooka bubble gum, Tar Babies, Mary Janes, Red Hots) or to slurp down chocolate or vanilla egg creams served in conical paper cups slipped into aluminum goblet-shaped bases. Al's Candy Shop on the corner of Allerton and Olinville made the best in town, frothy, sweet, and bubbly. Behind the counter, Al pumped syrups, milk, and soda from spit-shined stainless steel fixtures into a tall mixing glass, briskly stirring the elixir with a long, slender spoon as he went along . . . a grumpy chemist in a sparkling candy lab. All hopped up on sugar, we'd sneak in through the side doors of our local movie house, the Globe Theater, to catch a few minutes of whatever was showing—a simple pleasure that was about to be snatched from us, *hard.*

3.

In 1967, less than two years after Cappi's opened for business, the Globe made the bold move of going porno. It had been nudging the envelope for months with M- and R-rated movies but pushed it all the way to the wall with its first X-rated feature: *I Am Curious (Yellow)*. My father, enraged, began a campaign to shut the theater down, organizing local priests, rabbis, and concerned citizens to picket the place with handmade signs, bang pots and pans under the marquee, and otherwise discourage potential perverts. This very quickly grew into a broader crusade against pornography, and before long my father had established the Committee to Control Obscenity by Constitutional Means. I still have the letterhead. The address? Cappi's. Yes, Cappi's Pizza and Sangweech Shoppe was the national headquarters of the Committee to Control Obscenity by Constitutional Means.

My father subscribed to the *Congressional Record,* piling copies in great stacks all around our bare-bones apartment, poring through them for relevant references, racing up to Albany in his broken-down lime green Cadillac (sold to him by Squeegee the bread man for under

a hundred bucks) to lobby support among members of the state legis-
lature for an antiobscenity amendment to the U.S. Constitution. Either that, or he was proselytizing from behind the pizza counter.

"How do you feel about pornography?" he'd ask every adult male
customer.

Most people felt it was a matter of free speech, which really got
his goat.

"Oh yeah? Is *this* free speech?"

And he'd flash a picture of, say, a nun in a barnyard with her habit
hiked up over her head, being mounted from behind by a farm animal. He kept a collection of particularly egregious porn samples
handy for just this purpose.

"Or *this*?!"

And it would be a close-up of a way-dilated bodily orifice being
violated by an oversize household object, like a vacuum cleaner hose
or a decorative vase. The customers, of course, would be horrified.
They'd politely explain that while these images were not their cup of
tea, they didn't have to see them if they didn't want to (unless of
course they happened to be ordering a slice of pizza at Cappi's) and
therefore they had a right to exist.

"Oh really? Well guess what? I don't serve perverts here! Now get
out! *Owwwt!*" Another potential customer tossed out on his ass. I'd
say one out of three met this fate.

The porn collection was stored in a tan leatherette case that had
once housed a portable record player (which we referred to as a "Victrola"). I can still see the rectangular patch of darker tan and gold
mesh material on one side of the case, originally intended to mask a
set of speakers but now suggesting a kind of pubic area, and the
brown vinyl piping, frayed slightly, folded around the edges. I felt a
special bond with this hollowed-out object from the moment I dis-

covered it in a small utility closet at the back of the shop. Heart pounding, hands sweating, eyes burning, I'd sneak into the closet at opportune moments, swiftly open the box, and swipe some random samples. Then I'd disappear into the bathroom or into the lots behind the shop to investigate. I was prepubescent at the time, so it wasn't really about masturbating. I was just compelled by the material, repulsed and titillated in equal measure—also terrified, which must have been part of the thrill. Getting caught would be the end of me. The very idea of it gave me the shakes. And then it happened.

I had made the mistake of sharing the contraband with my good friend Eddie. He and his mother, Josie, were regulars of the restaurant (though they often couldn't afford to pay), and had become more like friends than customers. Josie had taken my mother into her confidence, telling hair-raising tales of prolonged physical altercations with her drunken husband, whom she referred to as "it." A cute, skinny thing with bleached blond hair and sunken cheeks, Josie had had spinal meningitis as a child and was very self-conscious about the hard curve it had left in her back. It was not uncommon to find her entering the shop in tears.

"Oh Mary, I just ran into my neighbor Gladys. She touched my back when she said hello, and I know why—it's good luck to touch a hump! I'm a humpback!"

My mother would comfort her, insisting that the hump wasn't visible (it was).

Poor Josie had a weak stomach and could eat almost nothing. "Just a boiled potato, if you don't mind."

My mother prepared special orders for her, bland but healthful, and loaded Eddie up with her best home cooking, never even bothering to hand them a check.

"Don't worry about it," she'd say. "My treat."

My father grumbled and moaned about Josie's lurid storytelling and lack of cash, but he never interfered with my mother's charity.

Eddie was a year older than I, a professional actor. He had appeared in a couple of TV commercials, which was impressive, and was constantly being carted around to lessons of every sort—acting, singing, dancing, guitar, drums, piano, speech, diction, movement, audition technique. (Whatever money he made from his professional work, Josie spent on these lessons and on extravagant Christmas gifts for my sisters and me, and for her nieces and nephews.) Eddie introduced me to his friend Gene, a fellow professional who lived in the neighborhood but went to private school "down the city."

Gene and I hit it off immediately and soon found ourselves sneaking away to play quasi-sexual games of his invention, like Pass-out, which involved inducing brief fainting spells in each other so we could grope without guilt. We'd take turns: one of us would hyperventilate while the other reached around from behind and squeezed all the air out of his partner's chest, causing him to pass out. The conscious player would quickly "feel up" the unconscious one before reviving him. Then we'd switch. Fun. Another game invented by Gene was called Channel 37 Wrestling, seminaked horseplay of a type he claimed to have witnessed on UHF-TV, the utterly useless ancestor of cable, all snow and static. Gene added a bonus round, in which the winner (whom he was in charge of declaring) could command the loser to do anything he wanted for a full thirty seconds. He always seemed to win. And he always wanted my dick in his mouth, or vice versa. This was not exactly mutual fellatio; we did nothing more than hold each other's member between our lips for the allotted time. No movement, no talking, no nothing. I know we were both highly aroused by the game, but it was oddly sexless. I assumed that Eddie knew all about my forbidden "affair" with Gene—and that the two shared a similar intimacy—and therefore felt certain I could trust him. (For some reason, it never occurred to me to share the porn collection with Gene, perhaps because I hadn't known him for very long.) But then we had a fight. Eddie played his trump card.

My mother careened over to me out of nowhere one day, agitated and wearing an expression I didn't remember having seen before— hurt, angry, betrayed, vengeful.

"You showed Eddie pornography?" she hissed into my face. "You said, 'Hey, you wanna see somethin' good?' and then you showed him *pornography*? You think that's 'somethin' good'?"

Son of a bitch had *quoted* me!

"I'm telling your father."

I don't remember what happened after that. Everything must have gone black. I guess I pleaded, begged for mercy, and prostrated myself before my mother; I was good at that. She tortured me with the threat awhile longer, but never carried it out. Mom was good that way. She had our backs.

Eddie and I eventually made up, but I trusted him with no more secrets. Instead, I turned to my friend Marco, who'd arrived from Italy just a few years earlier and saw me as an expert in the ways of Bronx life. I convinced him to help me assemble our own soft-core porn collection by shoplifting adult material from local newsstands. Our favorites were these cheesy chapbooks about the size of a Playbill (easy to lift) with names like *Bold* and *Gent*. The covers were printed on glossy paper in full color; between them were black-and-white newsprint pages containing smudgy photos of retro-looking topless models. It was all very innocent compared with the hard-core action nesting in the old Victrola. Perhaps that was its appeal; maybe I had overdosed on porn before I was ready, and this was my way of turning back the clock. Marco and I commandeered quite a few of these rags, which we carefully packaged in plastic and paper bags and stashed in a shallow grave covered by rocks in a far corner of the lot behind Cappi's.

Then, the inevitable fight.

I remember the phone ringing one night, and my father picking it up. "Cappi's Pizza and Sangweech Shoppe. Cappi speaking."

There was a period of silence; an instant tightening; a couple of urgent questions; and then a massive explosion. Suddenly my father was screaming into my head, pulling me across the shop and out the back door. He stormed up into the lot, dragging me behind, shouting things I don't remember. I thought I was about to be executed. What were we doing out here? My heart twisted into a garlic knot when I realized we were headed straight for the buried porn. Marco must have provided excellent directions, for my father seemed to go right to it, kicking away the rocks and clawing at the dirt, pulling our porn stash out of the ground like some vile harvest.

He unleashed a world-class verbal assault, clutching the books like murder weapons, shaking them crazily into my face. He cried, I think. Here he was, founder and president of the Committee to Control Obscenity by Constitutional Means, a crusader against filth in all its forms, on his knees in an empty lot under the El, learning in the dirt that his son was a porn freak. He began to panic. Suddenly he was demanding to know about "Brian and Neal." Who were they? Where did they live? We were going there *now*!

Marco had sung like a canary. The kids whose apartment my father was now dragging me across the neighborhood to storm were a pair of Irish brothers familiar with our collection. I was confused and mortified. I had never been to Brian and Neal Linnehan's apartment, didn't even know them that well. But they were cool kids and I hoped we could become friends. (Plus, I secretly had a crush on both boys.)

Brian and Neal's father, a recent arrival from Ireland, was the super-intendent of a big old building on a tree-lined street off Astor Avenue. My father pulled me into the lobby, down into the basement, and knocked on the super's door like the law. The door swung open, and there stood Mr. Linnehan in a T-shirt, towel draped over a shoulder, shaving cream on one side of his face, razor in hand.

"Evenin'. Help you there?" he chirped in the most cheerful brogue.

My father, trembling, intoned: "Your sons and my son have been meeting in secret to look at disgusting filth—like *this*!"

He shoved the magazines into Mr. Linnehan's chest. Mr. Linnehan flipped through the magazines, gave a little laugh. "Well, didn't you look at this stuff when you were a boy?"

My father seemed stunned.

"Come in and have a drink with me," cooed the Irishman as he guided my father into the kitchen, calling out to his sons that their friend was here, pointing me toward the living room. (I don't think there was a Mrs. Linnehan.) Brian and Neal were lounging in front of the TV. They greeted me in the most natural manner.

"Hey. How ya doin'?"

"Hey," I say. "Whatcha watchin'?"

"*Batman*. Wanna watch?"

"Sure."

And suddenly everything is normal. The world is not splitting apart. I have not committed some unredeemable sin. I'm just a regular kid, watching *Batman* with my friends on an average weeknight. My father is in the kitchen, visiting with their father. It was possible for it to be like this, regular like this, A-OK—I remember having that thought quite clearly. After a while my father came to collect me. I don't know what spell Mr. Linnehan wove in that kitchen, but Cappi was calm now, even cheerful. I think he might have whistled a little tune on the way home. Maybe he was drunk. I asked no questions.

The incident was never mentioned again, but my father's anti-porn crusade continued. And intensified. There was a hot political debate raging about pornography in those years, with the Supreme Court hearing a string of pertinent cases. In 1964 it had adopted the Brennan Doctrine (based on a majority opinion written by Justice William J. Brennan, Jr., in *Jacobellis v. Ohio,* a landmark case involving Louis Malle's *Les Amants* and Henry Miller's *Tropic of Cancer*), which held that speech could be considered obscene—and therefore exempt from First Amendment protection—only if it was found to be "utterly without redeeming social value." My father seized upon this phrase, spying a crack in the door: surely the sort of material he collected in the old Victrola could easily be deemed valueless, and could therefore be outlawed. I heard him repeat the phrase so often that I eventually started using it myself—in the street, sometimes, as in "This game is *utterly without redeeming social value,*" but most notably when I wrote a letter of complaint to our local assemblyman about the garbage and debris littering our beloved lots. "This garbage is *utterly without redeeming social value,*" I argued, and therefore ought to be removed.

"The apple never falls far from the tree," sighed my mother as she helped me address and stamp the letter. (It went unanswered.)

My father dragged me along on several excursions to Albany, a four- or five-hour drive. I didn't like being alone with him and found these long car trips excruciating but was excited to trail through the halls of the state capitol as my father literally tugged on the sleeves of powerful passersby, introducing himself and the Committee to Control Obscenity by Constitutional Means, pressing his case and soliciting support. He befriended Mario Biaggi, our newly elected congressman, who, impressed with the lowly pizza man's grassroots efforts, vowed to help. Though Biaggi was a Democrat, akin to being a Satanist in my father's mind, the two men had much in common: they were about the same age, had both grown up in East Harlem, were both sons of poor Italian immigrants. The congressman was a frequent visitor to the capitol building and gamely introduced my father around, cheering him on, showing him the ropes. My father, immensely pleased, positively beamed in Biaggi's presence. (He returned the favor many years later, when Mario was convicted and jailed on bribery charges, by staunchly defending his mentor and insisting that he was being victimized because he was Italian-American.)

Cappi picked up other supporters along the way, a random assortment of wild-eyed right-wingers and Rosary-clutching fanatics, the same zealots who would later form local chapters of fringe groups like the Moral Majority and the Right to Life Party. He detested "bleeding heart liberals" and "knee-jerk liberals," spitting out the words like venomous darts. Al the cop, a regular at the pizza counter, a six-foot-four bruiser with a giant head and a hornlike voice, challenged my father between bites.

"Oh yeah, genius? And what about the First Amendment? We got freedom of speech in this country!"

But Cappi knew his Constitution and could recite the Bill of Rights by heart; he was adept at ensnaring his opponent in a web of tortured logic and legalistic mumbo jumbo . . . with footnotes. Al, like all other comers, eventually gave up.

My father began to see "filth" in everything and forbade us from partaking of most popular entertainment, especially movies. He railed against the likes of *Bonnie and Clyde*, *Barbarella*, and *The Grad-*

uate, and even against more frivolous fare like *Bob & Carol & Ted & Alice* or *Buona Sera, Mrs. Campbell.* There were, of course, exceptions: he took the whole family to see *Camelot, Doctor Dolittle,* and *2001: A Space Odyssey.* We even saw *The Heart Is a Lonely Hunter,* which rendered me inconsolable.

"But what about Mr. Singer?" I remember wailing about the character played by Alan Arkin, who commits suicide at the end.

I was equally wrecked, as were my sisters and mother, by *Ring of Bright Water,* a forgettable Disney feature about an unusual pet who gets killed by an overzealous gardener, chopped in half with a shovel.

"I thought it was just another otter," the gardener tearfully explains to his employers, the cute critter's human family. My father's were the only dry eyes in the house. "It's just a movie," he said, "it's not real."

Born Free had the same effect: Why oh why did the Adamsons have to return Elsa the lion to the wild? Why, if you loved a wild thing, did you have to set it free?

These movies were sad, but they were *chaste.* Anything with even a whisper of sex and modernity, "loose morals" my father called it, was verboten. I remember my parents' friends Luisa and Joe dropping by the shop after just having seen *The Secret of Santa Vittoria.* They loved it. My father mumbled disapproval.

"Oh, he'll never see that," my mother explained.

"What's not to see?" Luisa asked. "There's nothing in there. Maybe some kissing." And then she turned to me. "You've seen your parents kissing, right?" It occurred to me that I hadn't, ever.

Soon many of my favorite TV shows were off-limits as well, including *The Carol Burnett Show,* which my father deemed "too blue." I defied the ban, of course, willing to suffer lectures and petty punishments in exchange for a glimpse of my favorite brunette. How I loved Carol! Her warmth and humanity, her wild sense of fun, her vulnerability, her winning *gameness*—all flooded across the tube and filled my young heart with hope and aspiration. I thought I knew her, thought she knew me. She was a *friend.* And so was Harvey Korman. Vicki Lawrence and Tim Conway too. (Lyle Waggoner was more than a friend as he paraded across the screen in skimpy swimsuits.) But Carol was special, an active presence in my life. I sent her several fan letters and received highly personalized replies, always accompanied by an autographed eight-by-ten glossy.

When Uncle Frank (my mother's brother) died, I wrote Carol that her show made me laugh awhile, and feel less bad. She wrote back that she was sorry about my uncle's passing but happy that she could bring a little joy. She said that loss is a painful thing, but that laughter is the best medicine. I showed the crisply typed letter—always an exciting arrival in its ten-by-twelve coral gray clasp envelope with the official CBS logo in jet black—to my mother, and she was so touched by it that she sent Carol a note of thanks. Carol replied to that one too.

"I'm sure it's her secretaries doing it," I heard my mother telling a friend, "but still it's nice."

Even überconservative Barry Goldwater failed to pass my father's muster. Close, but no cigar—probably because Goldwater's brand of fundamentalist conservatism called for shrinking the reach of government in all areas, including the regulation of pornography. My father preferred a more dictatorial approach: right was right and wrong was wrong. And he was *right.* I don't remember his approving of any politician other than Richard M. Nixon. It was Cappi against the world. He disagreed even with people who agreed with him, like Bob Grant, the radical right-wing AM radio talk show host to whom my mother tuned in daily on WMCA. I don't know that she liked his politics exactly, but she found entertaining (and probably cathartic) his rolling river of rage and intolerance.

"You make me sick!" he'd bark at callers expressing an opposing viewpoint. "Get off the phone!"

"Just a showman," my father opined.

But my mother had a lot of trapped anger to vent, and Bob was a useful surrogate. Most of her other AM favorites were far less feral: There was Long John Nebel, a specialist in offbeat topics and occasional contests (I once called in when I was about ten years old, correctly identified the singer in a snippet of song as Tony Bennett, won a pair of tickets to see Tony live at Lincoln Center, took my mother as my date, got Tony's autograph after the show, and chatted briefly with a very friendly Pearl Bailey); the Fitzgeralds ("They broadcast from their apartment," my mother explained, "they're almost dead"); Joan Hamburg (*still* on the air as of this writing); Barry Farber (whose lazy southern drawl, paradoxically infused with great intensity, made his hyperconservative ramblings sound almost appealing—and who, in 1970, ran for Congress in New York's Nineteenth District on the Republican ticket, losing to Bella Abzug); and many others.

I could see in my mother's eyes that she was listening closely, engaged and entertained, as she went about the hard drill of her day. I was grateful to the little box for giving her pleasure. (As a young child, I assumed that tiny people lived inside it, performing live whenever we turned it on.) My favorite was the weekly comedy hour on WOR, featuring, among dozens, the routines of Nichols and May and Stiller and Meara. Their comedy was thrilling for its realism, its urgency, its contemporary flair. Stiller and Meara were to my child ears the funniest people on the planet:

"I hate you."

"I hate you too."

"I hate you more."

"I hate you more than that."

"I hate you with so much hate that if every grain of sand in the desert were a grain of hate, it would still be just a drop in the bucket of the hate I hate you with . . ." et cetera.

The routine, of course, wound up going full circle, so that at the end the couple were saying:

"I love you."

"I love you too."

"I love you more."

"I love you more than that."

"I love you with so much love . . ." et cetera.

For me, this material—and its delivery—was so funny that I couldn't even laugh. I just listened, wide-eyed and slack-jawed, in comedy overload.

My father had no apparent objections to AM radio (though he frowned upon all the new music on the FM dial). Broadway shows were another safe bet. It was he, after all, who started the tradition of keeping a coffee can in the hall closet into which we'd all deposit loose change (and occasionally paper money) until enough had been saved to buy Broadway tickets for the whole family. We saw *Fiddler on the Roof* this way (twice!), and *Man of La Mancha*. He could have flashes of fun-spiritedness, my father.

We ignored his TV ban with impunity (pretty easy since he was usually down in the shop), my older sisters getting all dolled up for weekly viewings of *The Man from U.N.C.L.E.*—just in case dreamy Napoleon Solo or Illya Kuryakin (Robert Vaughn and David McCallum) could see them through the tube. I secretly shared their crushes but also had a hot spot for Anne Francis on *Honey West,* which came as a great relief: it bothered me that most of my crushes were on men. It was Wrong. Something about the way Honey squinted her eyes and moved her mouth . . . and that mole. She turned me on. But so did Batman, in his leotard and mask, nubile, eager boy Robin at his hip. There were hunky dangers all over the dial, causing stirrings inside me that I tried hard to ignore: Chad Everett on *Medical Center,* Bobby Sherman on *Here Come the Brides,* Michael Landon on *Bonanza,* Bill Bixby on *My Favorite Martian* (so preppy and vulnerable). Tom Jones, Burt Reynolds. Even Ronnie Burns on old reruns of *The Burns and Allen Show,* a household favorite, turned me on a little. Eva used to throw kisses at the screen whenever David Selby appeared (as Quentin Collins) on *Dark Shadows.* I once followed her lead, relieved that my crush was shared, and she looked at me curiously.

"Boys aren't supposed to throw kisses at boys."

My mother's mother was hooked on *Dark Shadows.* I remember sitting in the living room of her apartment on 237th Street and White Plains Road, eating lupini beans and soaking in the turgid melodrama, Grandma squealing in horror and delight. My prepubescent attraction to the tall, dark Selby embarrassed me. I tried to quash it, wondered if Grandma could see it.

Eva and I tuned in as often as possible to *The David Susskind Show,* a constant source of amazement and cheap thrills, an unbroken parade of freaky guests and forbidden topics. I once heard a promo for an upcoming episode announcing that David's guest would be an "admitted homosexual." I decided that I had to see this episode and requested a sleepover at my adult cousin Marie's house. She and her husband, Ronnie, were young and open-minded . . . plus their place was big enough that I thought I could sneak in a viewing. As airtime approached, I made a big show of being tired and getting ready for bed. I settled into the guest room, waited until I heard my cousins close the door of the master bedroom, and then tiptoed back over to the TV and turned it on at low volume. Susskind had just finished introducing his guest when I heard someone approaching. I quickly changed the channel as Ronnie padded into the room to pick up a book he'd left there.

"I thought you were in bed," he said.

"Couldn't sleep" was my lame response.

"Okay, well, don't stay up too late."

I jerked the channel back to Susskind with a sweaty hand.

"I'm a schoolteacher," the admitted homosexual was saying, "and I always tell my students about who I am. I want them to know that they're seeing see a real, live one in front of them so that—" I heard Marie puttering around in the kitchen.

"Carl?" she called out. "You want a midnight snack?"

"Sure," I responded with a sigh. I turned the TV off and headed out to join her. Maybe I'd catch it in reruns.

Though my father objected hotly to most television programming, he was not above using the medium for his own purposes. He appeared on the tube himself several times, doing "Editorial Replies" on WPIX, our local TV station. The station manager had a policy of doing on-camera editorials about issues of the day, always ending his spots with "What's *your* opinion? We'd like to know." Cappi gave it to him—in response to an editorial against censorship. I remember watching hungrily, amazed and excited to see my father on television. Though I understood none of what he was saying, I do recall several uses of the phrase "utterly without redeeming social value." (Sadly, no tape or transcript exists, and WPIX does not seem to have archived this material.)

In the spot, my father, wearing his best blue polyester sports jacket and a shiny striped tie, speaks urgently into the camera, making an ironclad case for turning back the clock. But it is too late: the mighty river called the 1960s is at full swell, its fiercely raging tide already busting down our front door.

4.

FATHER AND DAUGHTER POSE IN FRONT OF CAPPI'S.
(A PORTION OF THE EL IS VISIBLE IN THE PLATE-
GLASS WINDOW BEHIND THEM.)

Rosette, smart and fiery, a born rebel living through the throes of the Psychedelic Revolution, departed radically from the smooth middle course Eva and I worked hard to chart. As the sixties progressed and hippiedom beckoned, my sister answered the call. She frizzed out her hair and wore torn hip-hugger jeans with little Indian print halter tops. She listened to rock 'n' roll and started smoking cigarettes . . . maybe even pot. She was willing to butt heads directly with my father, to *defy* him openly, which very nearly drove him mad. Many times he'd stalk out of the shop in his long white apron, spying to see if Rosette was hanging out on The Wall, a low stone structure running the length of Pelham Parkway, which served as a magnet for local hippies and love children. He'd often find her lounging there with the others and drag her, humiliated, back to Cappi's.

Eva used to do an impression of my father on these spy missions, which involved her donning a long white apron, miming the furious smoking of cigarettes (Kent 100s), and peering furtively through a newspaper into which two eyeholes had been cut. We'd howl with laughter. But it wasn't funny. My father's response to Rosette's rebelliousness was increasingly alarming. His methods were irrational, but he had legitimate reason to be concerned: free sex and drugs were everywhere. Many neighborhood teenagers were becoming pregnant or dying of heroin overdoses . . . or both.

Rosette would sometimes slip away in the afternoon and not surface again until well after midnight. On these dreaded occasions—which became hideously routine and whose patterns and rituals I came to know well—my father's fury ramped up steadily as the hour got later. My mother would send Eva home with Maria at some point. I'd stay behind at her urging as my father closed up shop and then started reeling around the place in a rage, screaming and thundering, leaving a trail of flung pizza pans, sauce pots, chairs, boxes, anything handy, in his wake. My mother would hover nearby, trying in vain to calm him, with me trailing a few steps behind. I think I was supposed to provide protection. Maybe she thought my very presence would force my father to control himself. It didn't. He didn't seem to notice me at all. Not even when I'd jump on his back, pound on his shoulders, and pull at his hair as he pounced at Rosette when she finally surfaced, pummeling her and tossing her around like a wet mop, screaming until his face went purple and his veins were popping out of his neck.

My poor mother would yell and shriek and try to pull him away from Rosette, taking more than one blow intended for her daughter. At some point she'd call out to me to phone the police. I remember getting change out of the cash register drawer—an activity I always enjoyed, even in this perverse setting—and slipping it into the large, round slots of the old pay phone. (A nickel, I guess. Maybe a dime by then.) I think I needed to stand on a chair to reach the coin slot. I don't remember ever actually dialing a number, or the police ever coming. Maybe they did, once or twice. I think my mother thought the threat itself would be enough. It wasn't. Nothing could quell my father when he was in this state. We got to know his hot, hard cycles and tried our best to dance around them. Except Rosette. She ran headlong at the bull and took a goring. Over and over again. She was a lot like him. She was fair-skinned like him, had his reddish hair and swaths of freckles. Whereas the rest of us resembled our swarthy, yielding mother, Rosette was very much her father's daughter in looks and temperament.

He was determined to break her. There was room in the den for only one Top Dog. It was a fight to the finish between these well-matched adversaries, the incessant roar of trains overhead providing a fitting sound track for the regular bouts of violence, sparks beating down upon our blighted little shop on a fixed schedule.

My mother tried her best to help us escape my father's wrath and megalomania. Her powers were limited, but she did manage to open up a few exits here and there. She could have used some help. I wondered where all the other adults in my world were. Couldn't they see that something was wrong? Was there nothing they could do? My aunt Diana and New Jersey Grandma, my father's sister and mother—we nicknamed our grandmothers by state, for some reason; my mother's mother was New York Grandma—sometimes tried to talk to him about his "temper," but he only blew up at them. (His younger brother, my uncle Danny, stayed out of it, as did my mother's side of the family.) Diana made excuses.

"He had a very rough life. He was beaten by his uncles. He was *trau*matized." (*Trau-* rhymed with *cow* in her pronunciation.)

All true, but cold comfort nonetheless.

"She doesn't have to live with him," Eva and I muttered. We knew the history:

New Jersey Grandma, born in Bari in 1896, had sailed to New York City as a young bride in 1918. After passing through Ellis Island, she and my grandfather lived briefly in Hell's Kitchen before moving up to East Harlem, then an Italian ghetto. They had four children, my father being the eldest, and eventually saved enough money to move up to Arthur Avenue in the Bronx. Soon after my father's thirteenth birthday, my grandfather dropped dead of a ruptured appendix. Grandma was suddenly alone in the Bronx with four young children, no money, and little English—all at the height of the Depression. She went on public assistance, took in piecework, and moved her family from one apartment to another every thirty days or so, making solid use of the "first month free" policy adopted by many Depression-era landlords.

The widow Rosa leaned on her oldest son to become man of the house, and my father, by all accounts, worked slavishly to fill that role. Concerned that he might become soft without a proper father figure, his uncles, my grandmother's brothers, three in all—Angelo, Victor, and Nick (a fourth, Leonardo, stayed in Italy)—dropped by on a weekly basis to beat him senseless. This was supposed to strengthen him, steel him, turn him into a *man*. These beatings continued for years, until Uncle Angelo boxed my father's right ear with such force that it bled profusely, probably busting his eardrum, causing permanent partial hearing loss. My grandmother took to throwing herself in front of her son whenever her brothers were near (much as my mother, years later, would do in another context) until the beatings finally stopped. My father was drafted into the Army at twenty-one—starting out as a medic but soon getting booted into the infantry in

MY FATHER, AS A
TEENAGER, HORSING AROUND WITH A
FRIEND—THE SAME SORT OF THEATRICS THAT WOULD LATER
GET HIM INTO TROUBLE WITH ARMY BRASS. HANDWRITTEN ON
THE BACK: KNIT NITE! OH COME ON NOW . . . I DON'T REALLY
LOOK LIKE LANA TURNER . . . SHE'S GOT *BLUE* EYES!

retaliation for a variety of offenses. The cocky soldier, stationed in England and the Netherlands, had appointed himself social director, organizing huge dances and parties, going AWOL for brief periods in order to procure supplies (and to recruit and transport truckloads of local young women), bending rules and stepping on toes everywhere he went. When he started staging little skits and shows parodying army life—and many of his superior officers—my father's new "theater" became the front line. He saw hard action with the 30th Infantry Division, General George S. Patton's Old Hickory, fighting in the Battle of the Bulge and the invasion of Normandy. In the combat zone, his job was to run ahead, alone, into enemy territory, and scope it out for the others. (He was being taught a lesson, and he knew it.) Uncle Danny assures me that this was not quite as dangerous as it sounds, since the enemy, if present, would not likely blow its cover so early in the game. Still, it must have been terrifying.

My father proved fearless, making the most of the rare quiet surrounding him on these solo expeditions by capturing live rabbits and ·chickens, later roasting them in pit fires and feeding them to his fellow soldiers—or to war-ravaged civilians.

"You can't imagine it," he'd murmur quietly, just once, decades later, about what it was like to hunker down in a foxhole with your best buddy . . . and watch his head get blown off. "You just can't imagine it."

When Aunt Diana said my father didn't really have a childhood, she meant it.

Still, as the beggar in *Fiddler on the Roof* quips to a deadbeat donor: "So if *you* had a bad week, why should *I* suffer?"

I wanted to leave, just run away with my mother and sisters, start another life somewhere, change our names maybe, reinvent ourselves, live free. Short of that, I wanted us to be surrounded by as many people possible. There was a measure of safety in the presence of others, and luckily the shop provided a steady flow. Customers, deliverymen, neighborhood regulars, relatives, and friends—Cappi's was a frequent whirl of activity, even as it yielded next to no profit. Over the years, my father hired a string of ragtag workers, virtually all of them new Italian immigrants willing to work for the pittance he could pay. (The sole exception was Jerry Lorenzo, a handsome local playboy with a mustache and sideburns. He didn't last long. "He's got bigger fish to fry," my mother said.) John and Nick were a father-son team fresh off the boat who worked the shop like it was their own, really putting their backs into it.

"You don't even have to tell him what to do," I remember my father saying about Nick, the son. "He just seems to know."

They learned the pizza trade from the ground up at Cappi's, eventually saving enough money to open a little shop of their own, brilliantly located at the entrance of the Burke Avenue station of the Number 2 line. It was an instant success. John, Nick, and their family—two teenage girls and a long-suffering mother, who worked the shop like my family worked Cappi's—became rich. Eventually, John was able to lease out the business for a healthy six-figure annual fee while kicking back in his newly purchased Italian villa. He bought a local television station there, and a few bars and restaurants. He had become a millionaire by learning from my father's mistakes: he chose an ideal location, kept the menu simple—pizza and heroes only—and welcomed customers instead of throwing them out.

"Look how he lets people get their own soda from the refrigerator case," my mother observed. "Can you imagine your father doing that?"

If my father was envious, he didn't let it show. He seemed genuinely proud of their success and was greeted like royalty whenever he visited—we all were. John's wife and daughters would fuss over us, making demitasse for my parents, bringing out special treats from the kitchen. Father and son would hail us from behind the counter and slide hot, bubbling pies our way, offering up soda and ices and heroes—everything and anything they sold. Our money was no good there. They sent us home with takeout.

I don't remember their ever having to intervene in our family madness while they worked at Cappi's. But that was the point: the very presence of others was a deterrent. Except when it wasn't. Like the day Rosette wandered into the shop after having snuck out the bedroom window the night before via the fire escape and disappeared for twelve hours or so. My father pulled her roughly into the kitchen when she surfaced and tossed her in a corner. My sister hovered there, wedged between the wall and the deep stainless steel sink, screaming for help as my father rained his rage upon her. Luckily, his childhood friend and army buddy Dino happened to be visiting.

"Whoa, whoa," he called, stepping in between them. "Take it easy there, Phil."

My father backed off. I think he saw himself for a moment through his friend's eyes. Dino was a hero to me that day. Could he move in with us? Anyone willing to challenge my father directly this way deserved a Purple Heart in my book.

Tessie DiResta once blasted him so hard that she rendered my father speechless. I nearly applauded at the sight of it. She was the mother of a good friend of Rosette's, in the habit of taking guff from nobody. Divorced and partial to plunging neckline displays of ample cleavage—and tight pants and skirts accentuating a formidable caboose—Tessie had taken Rosette out for the morning and returned her to the shop an hour or so later than promised. My father stepped outside to collect his daughter, telling her gruffly to "get inside."

Tessie apologized, explaining that they had stopped by Farenga Brothers Funeral Home to pay respects to Father Mannini, whose mother was laid out there.

"Yeah, right," sneered my father. Tessie drove away.

But then she came back. Her son Thomas had been sitting in the passenger seat the whole time. He was preparing for the priesthood. Was my father implying that this pious young man had been complicit in a lie? A lie about a *priest,* no less? Tessie marched into the shop with blazing eyes and a stream of hard insults.

"How dare you?" she shouted. "My son is a seminarian! What are *you*? Insult him like that again and I'll use your head like a mop right up and down the avenue!"

(And she could do it too. Tessie was a legendary figure on the handball courts of Orchard Beach, where she regularly challenged young men less than half her age, and whopped their little asses with the prowess and power of her game.)

"You're not fit to *wipe his boots!*" she shouted across the counter.

My father backed away, an odd smile on his face, not sure how to handle this woman. I think he was scared.

My mother and I stopped at the mailbox one day and found five plain envelopes, each marked in my sister's hand with the name of a family member. The letters had not been posted but had simply been slipped into the shiny brass box that morning. I remember Mom muttering "Oh no" as she opened the letter addressed to her. Suddenly she was crying. I opened and read the one addressed to me but recall nothing of what was written there, except that Rosette had run away. We rushed over to the shop. My mother pulled my father aside and handed him the bundle. My father got real quiet and focused. He might even have closed up shop for a few hours. He worked the phone calmly, calling neighbors and parents, inquiring about his daughter.

"She seems to have flown the coop," I remember him saying.

It made me think of pigeons. Cesar Impala kept a coop on the roof of a nearby building. He often dropped by the pizza shop, sometimes even helping out a little for no pay, brightening the place with his jolly presence, always a joke on his lips, a hand on your shoulder, a dance in his step (despite the limp). Where was he now? I sat quietly at the family table, folding pizza boxes, listening for clues to my sister's whereabouts.

She reappeared again a few nights later, her homecoming silent and anticlimactic. Only tense looks were exchanged between her and Cappi, no words, no blows, nothing more. It was late. We marched up into the apartment. I remember walking behind Rosette as she climbed the stairs ahead of me, relieved that she was back, anxious about what scenes might follow. She must have felt all this. She half-turned and said—very quickly, quietly, with tears in her voice—"I'm sorry, Carl."

Those words sliced into me with a piercing sadness. I wanted to tell her that it was okay, that I knew she was hurting, that I was glad she was home, that I would protect her the best I could. I wanted to hold her and stop her crying. I wanted to absolve her. But I was just her little brother.

I uttered a simple "It's okay," so softly that I don't think she heard.

Rosette was a passionate fan of the Beatles. She collected all their albums, swooned over their photographs, panicked during the "Paul is dead" hoax—frantically spinning records backward and studying album covers for clues alleged to be hiding there. We'd gathered around the tube to watch their first appearances on *The Ed Sullivan*

Show, and Rosette had gotten into big trouble for sneaking out to see *Help!* and *A Hard Day's Night.* She and her friend Peggy used to rock out to the band in our living room, teaching me dances like the Jerk, the Monkey, and the Swim (I never got the hang of them). One day while listening to Rosette's copy of the Beatles' *Sgt. Pepper's Lonely Hearts Club Band,* I became convinced that my sister had planned her flight in concert with the lyrics to "She's Leaving Home," in which a young girl awakens one morning at dawn, leaves a note for her sleeping parents, tiptoes out of the house, and disappears into the wide world forever. I was never able to listen to the song again without being overtaken by feelings of deep melancholia:

> *She's leaving home*
> *After living alone*
> *For so many years . . .*
> *(Bye, bye)*

5.

Except for those sickening bouts in the pizza shop (and sometimes at home—Eva and Maria witnessed their fair share too), my father's usual modes of punishment and abuse were verbal and psychological. He was prone to cornering and crazily lecturing his detainees (me, Eva, Rosette, or, more privately, Mom) for what felt like hours. He would grill and stab and poke and drown his victims in a crazy torrent of words, demanding ritualized responses and formal admissions of guilt as he led the accused through a complex web of self-incrimination, followed immediately by a sentencing stage— something like an enemy interrogation.

My mother always said that he was a frustrated lawyer. I think she meant *executioner*. Anything could set him off. He was never *not* in high dudgeon. We had always to be on our toes. Speaking of toes, he was paranoid about our damaging them in the shop.

"The toe is just a tomato with a bone in it," he'd say, warning us angrily not to drop heavy objects onto these fragile digits.

The shop teemed with danger: the great slicing machine with its exposed spinning blade; the giant dough mixer; the twin pizza oven raging at well over six hundred degrees for twelve hours a day; the six-burner stove going full blast in the narrow, bustling kitchen. But the gravest threat of all, apparently, was to our toes. A Freudian psychologist could have a field day here, I'm sure—something about castration anxiety, the toes representing penises (a total of sixty in our family of six). But I digress. He was known to hand down lighter sentences from time to time, almost quaint compared with his usual fare.

"Go get a pencil and paper, sit in the corner, and write 'I will not go outside without asking' five hundred times!"

Upon completion: "Get more paper! Write it a hundred more times!"

Or, my favorite: "You're grounded! Go to the storage room!"

Ahh. These were always welcome words. I often found myself actually *trying* to get into trouble just so I could do time. The room was a large cement holding area, windowless, where all the dry goods were kept. It was dark and cool and quiet, filled with great sacks of flour and well-stocked shelves of canned tomatoes, boxes of dry pasta, jars of green and black olives, anchovies, roasted peppers, maraschino cherries, pickled eggplant . . . a plethora of potential snacks. I'd lounge on the flour sacks and munch on the stock supply, luxuriating in the glorious quietude, sometimes sneaking in matches so I could "cook" long strands of dry spaghetti. (They curl into burnt, starchy semicircles, kind of tasty.) Sometimes I'd play store, a favorite pastime, ringing up items on a broken adding machine and packing them into brown paper bags or cardboard boxes, chatting cheerily with invisible customers. There were other entertaining distractions as well: the notorious porn stash (which for a while my father stowed here), stacks of the *Congressional Record* (Greek to me but fun to flip through), and a few pieces of industrial equipment.

Once, during an extra-long detention session, I got bored and maybe a little disoriented and started to see the giant pizza dough mixer as an attraction at Palisades Amusement Park. The machine, as tall as a man but much wider, was simple, consisting of a stand holding a giant hook that sat in a large metal basin; the hook would spin round and round, slowly kneading flour, yeast, and water into pizza dough. Why couldn't it double as a merry-go-round? I removed the basin, stood on the hook, leaned on the stand for support, and pressed the On button. The hook wound itself around my leg immediately, and with a couple of revolutions would simply have torn it off. To this day, I bless the manufacturer: right on top was a big red disk with the words EMERGENCY OFF BUTTON. (They must have anticipated this very scenario.) I pounded that chunk of plastic with all the force of my little fist. The machine stopped. Peeling myself carefully from around the hook, my leg convulsing violently, I crawled to the storage room door, cracked it open, and hissed out a desperate "Eva!" She was always my first line of defense, though she'd feign annoyance.

"What is it? What'd you do now?"

I told her. She looked at my leg, looked at the machine, looked at me, and whispered furiously before snapping the door shut in my face: "Do it again and you're dead. You *id-jit!*"

This pronunciation of the word *idiot* was one we both favored, having picked it up from Olivia de Havilland in a scene from *Hush . . . Hush, Sweet Charlotte,* a frequent, favorite offering on *The 4:30 Movie* or *Million Dollar Movie,* in which Cousin Miriam (de Havilland) bitch-slaps Charlotte (Bette Davis) in the front seat of a car and spits into her face a long, withering tirade that begins with the words "You *id-jit!* You wretched *id-jit!*" Similarly, we pronounced *stupid* "*stewe*-pid," borrowed from one of the side characters in *The Snake Pit,* in which de Havilland is confined to a mental asylum where a fellow inmate marches up and down the ward throughout the movie, haughty and delusional, taunting the others:

"You're all just jealous, that's what it is. You're *stewe*-pidly jealous of me because my lover is coming to take me away. You're *stewe*-pid with jealousy, look at you!"

I was too young to be put to work at Cappi's, having just turned six when it opened, but Rosette, seven years older than I, and Eva, five years older, were harnessed for peeling, pounding, slicing, egging, breading, and frying endless mounds of chicken, eggplant, and veal cutlets; rolling and frying thousands of meatballs (after grinding and seasoning the meat); pulverizing great logs of cheese; waiting on tables and counter customers; washing mountains of dishes and trays and pots and pans. They complained bitterly through the sweat and grease (no air-conditioning) but carried on dutifully. Refusal was not an option. I'd tag along with them on some of their Sunday morning fry sessions, just the three of us. They had to work their butts off, but I was free to putter about at will. I enjoyed the silence of the place at that hour, the stillness of its tableaux: a circus asleep. The shop belonged to *us* on those mornings. *We* were in charge. My sisters, I know, had an entirely different set of feelings, but I liked it. It made me feel all *grown-up*, a sensation greatly heightened the morning we arrived to find that Cappi's had been burglarized overnight.

Everything was normal as we unlocked the front door and entered the shop, but when we stepped into the dining room we discovered a giant, gaping hole in the wall, surrounded by debris. Someone had hacked his way right into the adjacent storefront, a small local branch of the Household Finance Corporation (a predatory lender that charged higher interest rates than the Mob). The burglars, neighborhood junkies turned criminals no doubt, stupidly assumed they'd find cash in the lending office. They had forced open a vent at the back of our kitchen, an aperture large enough for only a child or an emaciated addict to slip through, and hammered away at the wall with what must have been an ax. My sisters and I called home immediately; my father was there in minutes, the police arriving fast on his heels. We were asked to report exactly what we had seen and heard. This was pretty simple but felt important. No money was ever kept in Cappi's overnight, but the burglars had rifled around and stolen a few useless objects. The cops pointed out that they had taken their time, having kicked back with a few beers at some point, evidenced by the empty Löwenbräu bottles strewn about. "They couldn't drink the Schlitz?" my father wondered ironically. He took the whole thing in stride for some reason, quickly repairing the damages. Rosette and Eva did no frying that day.

When my father built Cappi's, the other structures in the burnt-out strip mall were still in ruins. But soon after he opened others followed, and eventually the entire strip became populated. Cappi's occupied the two northernmost storefronts, beyond which were empty lots stretching all the way up to Waring Avenue and beyond. The large southernmost storefront at the corner of White Plains Road and Thwaites Place, a location much more conducive to foot traffic, was occupied by a dry cleaner and, later, by Alanson's Appliance Shop; next to Alanson's was the Peppermint Stick, a candy-themed beauty parlor run by a pair of flamboyant queens named Kenny and Hank; then the Household branch; then Cappi's. The shop owners all patronized one another's establishments. My father even provided a baseball-shaped pizza for a promotional event at Alanson's, attended by Carl Yastrzemski. (He was fond of making novelty pizza, offering a green one in the shape of an Irish clover for St. Patrick's Day, and a

NEW YORK METS PLAYER ED KRANEPOOL, ACTOR JACK
WAKEFIELD, MY FATHER, AND AN UNIDENTIFIED
CHILD AT THE GRAND OPENING OF A NEIGHBORING
DRY CLEANER—ONE OF MANY PROMOTIONAL EVENTS
FOR WHICH CAPPI'S PROVIDED FREE PIZZA

red, heart-shaped one for Valentine's Day.) My mother got her hair
done at the Peppermint Stick; Hank and Kenny, in turn, dined frequently at Cappi's. I understood that they were gay even before I knew
what it meant. They were right out of *The Boys in the Band*: Kenny,
slender and sloped, his hair permed, was usually dressed in hip-
hugger bell-bottoms, flowing floral tops, and chunky rings and
medallions; Hank, taller, darker, and more handsome, shared his
partner's fashion sense but had hair like Chad Everett's, and long,
sexy sideburns. I had a child's crush on him and remember feeling my
earliest sexual rush when he picked me up and bounced me around
over his head, saying I was just the cutest, sweetest boy. I was maybe

six or seven at the time, a bit old, I guess, for this kind of baby play. But I didn't complain.

The Household Finance storefront changed hands a few times, and at one point became a mini-branch of Manufacturers Hanover Trust, the now-defunct commercial bank. One night while I was playing alone out front (I could entertain myself for hours by crushing soda cans under my heels and marching up and down the pavement, pretending to be wearing stilettos, scraping the ground with the cans to get that high-heel sound effect, a diversion of Eddie's invention). I absently tugged on the door of the bank. To my surprise and confusion, *it opened.* It was nighttime, well after business hours. All the other shops in the strip were closed. I stepped into the darkened bank, able to make out the outlines of a counter and three or four tidy desks beyond.

There's money here, I thought, a fleeting image of looting the bank flitting through my mind. It spooked me and I ducked out, running back into the pizza shop to file a report. After confirming the story, my father called the police. They arrived on the scene at once, having somehow summoned a bank employee, who drove over in a sweat and locked the place up, thanking everyone profusely.

Next day, the bank manager wanted to meet the boy hero. My father marched me into the bank proudly and presented me to a small, bookish man who rose from his desk as we approached. My head was racing with anticipation: surely there would be a reward, maybe a substantial one, maybe even enough to make me a real hero to my family. The little man thanked me heartily, joked with me stiffly . . . and handed me a *rain bonnet*. A rain bonnet! The cheap cellophane kind, factory-folded in a way that can never be duplicated, tucked into a little plastic case bearing the bank's logo. They were available by the handful in a basket perched at the door. This was my reward for saving the institution from certain ruin! Deflated, I walked back into the pizza shop and handed the useless thing to my mother. She pretended to be delighted.

She was sleep-deprived in those years. My father saved most of his verbal assaults upon her for bedtime. On a typical night in the apartment, after the ridiculous day had ended and my poor mother collapsed into bed in the living room—the ever-present train tracks just outside the window—my father would pace and smoke and pull at his hair, berating her and grilling her and doing his weird call-and-response routine, where he'd tell you the phrase he wanted to hear ("I was wrong" or "You were right" or "I should have asked first") and then have you repeat it to him over and over again in response to a series of shouted questions.

"You were late to the shop again today!"

"Phil, I had to clean the house and go grocery shopping. I was only five minutes late."

"*Only five minutes? Only five minutes?* How would you like to be hanging by your thumbs for 'only five minutes'? How would you like a hot fork on your tongue for 'only five minutes'? How would you like a splint under your fingernails for 'only five minutes'?!"

These were not threats of violence; the words themselves were the assault. My mother tried to reason with him, tried to resist, tried to give in, tried to remain silent, tried to speak—nothing worked. She'd end up sobbing and begging him to let her get a little sleep, something he didn't seem to need. I'd listen from my makeshift bedroom a few feet away, just off the adjoining foyer, and tell myself that my father was going to stop soon, that my mother was okay, that things wouldn't be like this forever. I comforted myself as if comforting another.

Eventually this habit evolved into the creation of a loving, beatific young woman named Theresa, who came to me in times of high distress to reassure me in soft, calm tones that my father didn't mean a lot of what he did and said; that it would be over soon; that she'd stay with me until it stopped; that I was safe. I saw Theresa clearly in my mind's eye. At the shop it became my habit, when my father started railing about one thing or another, to duck into the bathroom and look in the mirror—really just a pizza pan mounted on the wall, my father's idea, cute but nonfunctional—and summon Theresa. She always came when called, floating lightly into my space, appearing sweetly in the scratched aluminum surface of the pie pan, bringing instant calm with her presence.

Only many years later did I realize that my imagined Theresa bore a striking resemblance to the very real Theresa, my father's younger sister, his mother's second-born, who died at age twenty while my father was at war. The story goes that upon receiving the news of his sister's imminent death, my father went AWOL and journeyed home to see her one last time. He was court-martialed upon his return. Theresa was dead by this time. The charges were dropped. We had always been told that she died of leukemia, and that at the end of her life she was bleeding from every orifice, bleeding even through her pores.

Not too long ago, all these many years later, my aunt Diana accidentally mentioned the words "botched abortion" and suddenly the story made sense: Theresa had given herself to her fiancé before he set off for war, gotten pregnant, sought a back-alley abortion, and was killed by it. My grandmother never recovered from the death of her elder daughter. She keened and moaned and prayed and mourned Theresa at a small altar atop her pale bedroom dresser—sepia photograph in a gilded frame, single red rose in a white bud vase, white votive candle in a crimson cup—every night at bedtime for the rest of her life. All we kids knew of Theresa was the story of her death, the altar photo, and a few other faded, well-thumbed pictures that Grandma kept. She had a sweet, round face, Theresa did, soulful eyes, soft hair. She was said to have been kind and gentle, sensitive. Her picture confirmed this impression.

She was the woman in the pizza pan, *my* Theresa, either an unconscious, idealized "memory" of my long-dead aunt . . . or her gentle spirit returning to soothe and shield me.

It doesn't matter which. They're both the same.

6.

I took to school like a drunk to hooch. On my first day of kindergarten at P.S. 96, a prisonlike structure located just up the block from our building, my mother walked me into the classroom and lingered at the back with all the other mothers. Most kids were crying and craning their necks around, begging to be taken back home. But I appreciated the reassuringly ordered world of the classroom, comprehending at once that it would be *my* world. At lunchtime, I'd walk back down the block, stand across the street from our building, and yell up to the fourth-floor window for my mother to cross me. She'd pop her head out. "Okay, now!" she'd call when the coast was clear.

Upstairs, she'd serve tomato soup, or cream of mushroom, and grilled cheese or BLT sandwiches cut into quarters, plated decoratively and laid out on a miniature table (with matching chairs) in the foyer. I'd occasionally bring guests along, which was fine with her. I loved showing off the baby. Maria was less than a year old when I started school. I had not wanted a sister, had been wishing hard for a brother, but was immediately smitten with the writhing ball of flesh my parents installed in a frilly bassinet in the living room. Rosette and Eva no longer came home for their midday meals, so these luncheons were just Mommy, baby, sometimes a friend or two, and me.

The pleasing ritual ended just a few months into kindergarten, on the day Cappi's opened for business: I walked down the block and called for my mother, as usual. Instead of her head popping out of the window, New York Grandma's did. She filled in for her daughter sometimes, serving up buttery *pastina,* piping hot, always spooning some from a larger bowl into a smaller one to let it cool. In some of my earliest memories, she feeds me bites timed with the subway trains thundering by our living room window.

"Here come-a the train, here it come-a. Quicka-quicka pull inna tha station-a!"

Everything was a game with New York Grandma. I adored her. But today she steers me away from the building. "You MommyDaddy inna tha shoppa. Go enna say hallo."

Racing around the corner, I enter Cappi's to find my parents in fresh uniforms and aprons, standing proudly beside a shiny steam table filled with trays of meatballs, sausage and peppers, eggplant parmigiana, chicken parmigiana, baked ziti. My memory of that first day stops there, with that static image, a snapshot. (A year or two later I used this episode to open my autobiography, which I called *See-Saw* in a nod to the wild mood swings loping across our household, the first two lines of which were "A little boy in a blue coat and hat stands on a corner and calls up to his mother to cross him. That little boy is me." I never got much further, though I did design the cover art: a stick figure drawing of a boy child on an old wooden seesaw, like the ones in the playground at Bronx Park.)

I took great pleasure in the smell and feel of all my new tools—fresh, crisp books, used old ones, ink-stained mimeographed paper, newly sharpened No. 2 lead pencils—and copied lines from a reader into my black-and-white marbleized composition book with great gusto. "See Dick run." "See Spot jump." It was exhilarating, all of it.

Except for the teachers.

We had Miss Prendergast for first grade. First grade! We were only maybe seven years old, our growing bones chickenlike inside our child bodies, our little heads still creased and wrinkled from the forceps delivery so popular in our mothers' generation. How could anyone leave us alone in a room with this terrifying cross between Gloria Swanson as Norma Desmond in *Sunset Blvd.* and Bette Davis as Baby Jane Hudson in *What Ever Happened to Baby Jane?* . . . on *crack*? Miss Prendergast wore Kabuki white Pan-Cake makeup slathered on with a trowel, China red lips, heavy black eyeliner, and bright green eye shadow. Her hair was pulled back into a tight bun tied with lacy black ribbon. Giant lion's head earrings vibrated on both sides of her face, and she was always dressed in a baby blue or baby pink smock, her personal signature. Miss Prendergast's entire body trembled with madness.

"*You! Go close that door!*" she'd shriek like a horror movie sound effect.

Then she'd turn around, write a few words on the blackboard, turn back, see the closed door, and scream, "*Who told you to close that door?*"

We were confused, terrified.

"*All right, class. Line up for a fire drill.*"

Beat.

"*Who told you to line up for a fire drill?*"

I'd been hoping, I guess, for a lighter touch, having found myself an outcast and victim from very early on. "Faggot," some boy muttered in the first weeks of kindergarten, and others quickly followed suit. This hideous tag stayed fastened tight for the remainder of my school career. I didn't know what these boys saw exactly, but I knew they were right. That's what hurt most. I was the thing they said I was, the worst thing you could be. What had given me away so readily? Perhaps it was that I shunned boys' games right from the start (trucks and spikes and clubs and things), preferring instead the supermarket setup on the girls' side of the room, with little shopping carts, fake cans of peas and tuna fish, and cash registers with real play money inside. Who could resist?

"Faggot."

It was the same out in the school yard: boys' games seemed to consist of pushing each other against the chain-link fence and then dragging each other facedown across the cement and gravel recess pit. The girls, meanwhile, were playing patty-cake or leapfrog, or they were skipping rope or playing Giant Step—again, no competition. I floated over to their side.

"Faggot."

This all passed unnoticed by the teachers, who seemed to regard us as prisoners in a penal colony, constantly barking out commands and slamming their desks with their fists. (I guess we were difficult.) For third grade, we had Mrs. Pearlmutter, a skinny, wiry woman in her fifties, with tight pin curls and a bitter scowl. She was fond of musical discipline: in those days, each schoolroom contained an upright piano; when she wanted order, Mrs. P would rush over to the keyboard and slam out three harsh chords, having trained us that the first chord meant *silence,* the second meant *be seated,* the third meant *total attention.* Her facial expressions grew progressively threatening with each ascending chord. She never had to play them twice.

One day during a quiet lesson, a kid from another classroom entered and handed Mrs. Pearlmutter a note. She read it and called my name. "Go with this boy. Mrs. Seidelman wants to see you," she sniffed.

Mrs. Seidelman?! She was that mean teacher with the cat's-eye glasses, long, sharp teeth, and a reputation for being excessively strict. What could she possibly want with me? She wasn't even my teacher. I saw her only in the hallways and on our weekly Assembly Day, a paramilitary-style drill that she and fierce Miss Bello presided over like warrior women, with Miss B railing at us from the front of the auditorium while Mrs. S patrolled the perimeter, keeping law-breakers in line and occasionally cuing Mrs. Pearlmutter to head for the piano to sound out those warning chords. Miss B:

"If I don't have *total silence* in this hall in exactly *one second,* I am going to march each and every one of you into the *principal's* office, where you will be harshly *punished* and possibly *expelled*! Your *parents* will be called and *notes* will be made on your *permanent record,* which will follow you for *the rest of your life*!"

She'd sometimes target an individual student, always terrifying:

"You! In the white shirt and tie!"

But we *all* wore white shirts and ties, that was required attire on Assembly Day, so we never had any idea who she was referring to. It must have been part of Miss B's battle strategy to keep us off balance. She was a regular Chairman Mao, and now the stony chief of her elite guard was calling me into her classroom for a private audience. What could it possibly mean?

Mrs. Seidelman was marking papers at her desk when I entered, her students reading silently at theirs. She stood and beckoned for me to approach, grabbing a sheet of paper from her desk.

"Not a sound! Keep working!" she warned her students, many of whom looked up to see what was happening.

She shoved the paper into my hands.

"Take this home to your parents. Your artwork has been chosen for inclusion in an exhibit down the city." Her tone was so harsh that it took a moment to understand that this was good news.

"*My* artwork?" I asked, knowing full well that I had no aptitude in this area.

Rosette, Eva, and my father (Maria too, when she was old enough) were natural artists. I knew what good pictures were supposed to look like, and I knew I didn't draw them. But a gentle teacher named Mr. Izzo, frail and balding, probably gay, had entered my crayon rendering of three sailors from the *Niña*, the *Pinta,* and the *Santa Maria* in a citywide competition. I'm sure he was just as surprised as I when it won (along with several hundred others). The homoerotic subtext is probably what had caught the judges' eyes: the picture showed three boxily drawn sailors in color-coordinated outfits holding hands on the shore, as three triangular white sails float on waters behind them.

"Are you sure it's not a mistake?" I asked Mrs. Seidelman. "I really can't draw."

Sucking another bit of lemon, she testily assured me that "such a letter would not be in error." She congratulated me in the same tone she would have used to expel me, and then asked, "Did you brush your teeth this morning?"

"Yes," I lied. "Why?"

"Because there's a *putrid* odor emanating from your mouth."

My parents were delighted with the prize, and the whole family traveled by subway down to Park Avenue to see my work displayed in the lobby of Lever House. It was not hanging on the walls, like the best specimens, but was included in one of several book-style exhibits.

That was a little disappointing, but when we leafed through a massive binder and found my picture, I felt a momentary swell of pride. My drawing had been singled out of many by a panel of strangers who'd taken the time to write a letter to my school, mount my picture, and press it into this book.

But then Mrs. Seidelman's words came back to me: "There's a *putrid* odor emanating from your mouth." I may have been an award-winning artist, but I was still just another stank-breathed kid.

The only time she had anything nice to say was when I was bleeding. I was in third grade. Our regular teacher was absent. We had a young, insecure substitute, and I tried to win her favor by offering to close the windows when she commented that the room was cold. Ignoring the handy window pole, I jumped onto the wide wooden sill, reached my arm up under the shade, and hoisted the top half of the window into place. That's when I felt a funny, icy burn on my wrist, followed by the sensation of something wet running down my sleeve. I withdrew my arm to find a large, knife-shaped blade of glass—which had been hanging, jagged and unseen, from one of the windowpanes—skewered into my wrist, a fountain of blood gushing from the wound. I fell silent, in shock I guess, and wandered up to the front of the room.

The sub froze in horror, then screamed like she herself had been stabbed in the wrist with a dagger of glass. She opened the classroom door and yelled, "Help! Help!" (I remember thinking that she was being very unprofessional.) Mrs. Seidelman was the first to arrive on the scene, her heavy bust heaving in her print dress as she expertly took hold of my arm, placed two fingers firmly on the wound, deftly withdrew the glass, and then bandaged me tightly with her white handkerchief. She was always using that hankie to fuss with her nose. I knew there was snot on it, leaching into my veins. Other teachers arrived on the scene, and I heard Mrs. S say to them that "we should apply a tourniquet." Then she turned her attention to me and sort of smiled, which was unsettling on account of her long teeth. Her hands and arms were splattered with my blood, her hankie soaked with it. She rubbed her soiled fingers together as if assessing fabric.

"Your blood is nice and sticky. Bright red. Rich and thick. Good sign, means you're healthy." (Mrs. Seidelman was apparently a connoisseur of the blood of children.)

The school nurse managed to stop the bleeding, ignoring the teacher's continued entreaties to "apply a tourniquet." She was just dying to tie off my arm at the shoulder, even if it meant my losing it.

And so it continued, from grade to grade, with one exception: Mrs. Kirnon. She taught fifth grade, the only black teacher in a school where the student body was a mixed group, predominantly but by no means exclusively white. Mrs. Kirnon was petite yet strong-bodied, with a wide, sweet face and a soft, melodic speaking voice. She was a black woman from the previous generation, proud to call herself *Negro*. Her bearing was regal yet unpretentious, exuding warmth and decency. She reminded me of Maidie Norman, the wonderful character actress who plays the heroic but doomed Elvira Stitt in *Baby Jane* (who ends up taking it in the head with a hammer).

Mrs. Kirnon held me after class one day and talked to me about the teasing and taunting to which I was regularly subjected. She must have had me figured out for quite some time: I had responded to a class assignment to prepare a presentation on a public figure we admired, including pictures, biography, and a statement explaining our choice, with a lavish tribute to Miss Bette Davis. My mother had turned me on to the divine Davis, introducing me in early childhood to movies like *Dark Victory, The Letter, Mr. Skeffington, Jezebel, Beyond the Forest* . . . dozens of others. (We also loved Joan Crawford and *her* boatload of classics.) We tuned in regularly to Channels 9 and 11 to get our fix. My favorite memories of our apartment involve rainy afternoons spent in front of the television, Mom pressing clothes behind me as I lounge on the living room floor munching snacks, my eyes glued to an old classic, my ear half-tuned to the rhythmic hiss and thud of the heavy iron hitting the padded board, the light metallic tinkle as the iron is returned momentarily to its triangular aluminum tray, the soft shuffle of fabric as Mom shifts a garment, preparing to press another section.

Mrs. Kirnon smiled knowingly at my worshipful tribute to Miss Davis and displayed it on the bulletin board with all the others. Soon after that, we had our chat.

"You're a sponge," she said. "You absorb everything you see and hear, and you take it in and hold on to it. You don't have to do that all the time. Sometimes you can decide *not* to let things in, but just to let them roll off of you. Did you know that? *You don't have to let everything in.*"

This remains one of the best bits of advice, coming at just the right moment, I've received from any teacher, ever. I might have been a bit young to comprehend it completely, but I certainly got the gist. And I loved Mrs. Kirnon for delivering it so tenderly. I was proud of my special relationship with my teacher, and invited her several times to lunch at Cappi's, where a testament to her status was that she was allowed to eat slices at the table.

Mrs. Kirnon's sunlit fifth-grade classroom and her example of rectitude and kindness did nothing to prepare us for Mrs. Feldman, who ruled sixth grade. No one had alerted this broad, apparently, that she was no longer working in a roadside cathouse. She'd swagger into the classroom with her big old hair in a wildly teased-out do, her polyester dress clinging way too tightly to her bulbous form, her cheap, Technicolor makeup smeared and runny from a long night of prostitution (or so I imagined). A big, blowzy old bruiser, clearly unfit to be around children, she'd flop her fat ass down into the teacher's chair, kick off her shoes, slap her nylon-stockinged feet onto the desk, and start ordering us around. We were just starting to convulse our way through puberty—we didn't want Mrs. Feldman's big naked feet, wedge-shaped because of the bunions, in our faces. It was too much information. She thought of us as her harem.

"You—" (The teachers never knew our names. After all, they only saw us every day for a full year.) "Go get my pink puffy cha-cha slippers outta the teacher's closet. You. Go freshen my drink at the porta-bar. You. Get under the desk and recite the Gettysburg Address into Mama's panties."

I'm exaggerating, of course. But just a little. At least they knew to put her with the older kids. She was eventually removed from the school for passing out in an alcoholic haze during Assembly and nearly falling off the auditorium stage, not her first offense.

In my entire seven-year elementary school career, I managed to make a total of maybe five or six friends, all fellow freaks and outcasts. I couldn't play sports, was extremely bookish, and just generally stuck out like a sore thumb.

"*Faggot.*" The word followed me everywhere. But the truth is that I had a secret girlfriend named Violet, a chubby black girl in pressed pigtails with whom I used to sneak into the girls' bathroom for "sex." Our illicit affair started early, in first grade, and continued for several grades thereafter. I don't remember exactly how it began, but I do recall telling Violet that my doctor said my crotch was "too hot" and had to be held in the palm of a cool hand for several minutes each day. She was happy to oblige, and soon we had a standing appointment. We'd slip into a stall, I'd pull down my pants, and she'd hold my stuff in her hands for a while (they really *were* quite chilly). Then we'd rush back to class. Eventually I suggested that I return the favor. She demurred at first but soon took to dropping her drawers and letting me palm her vagina. Our hands were motionless as we touched each other, the white-tiled bathroom utterly silent around our hovering bodies. Still, it was more action than most boys my age were getting. So how was *I* the *faggot*? I should probably have bragged, but my thing with Violet was a terrifying secret. We were well aware that what we were doing was deeply forbidden.

Once, as we crept out of the bathroom and started back to class, a teacher came barreling down the hallway and spotted us.

"Hey! You two! What were you doing in the girls' bathroom?"

My stomach dropped into my hips. I think I shat my pants. But the teacher just kept marching on her way, never even breaking stride. This was typical of the distinct *remove* of most of our teachers . . . and of many other adults in our world.

It's a Saturday afternoon pre-tryout for Little League in Reiss Field, and I am up at bat. Pitch one: spastic strike. Pitch two: same. Pitch three: *very* spastic strike. This after fumbling every ball in the outfield, and throwing "like a girl." I haven't come here because I like to play ball, but because I am desperate to belong to something. I have already tried the Boy Scouts—Eva and Rosette are active Girl Scouts, earning badges, selling cookies, practicing survival skills—but find the first meeting in the auditorium of P.S. 96 so creepy and weird that I never go back: a disorganized and dictatorial troop leader with a hairy face and Coke-bottle lenses, "den fathers" wearing the too-small uniforms of little boys, dispirited Scouts slumped in their seats at the back of the room. ("It just wasn't for me," as Ann Lazerta would say.) Maybe Little League would be the ticket.

As I drop the bat and slump away amid gales of humiliating laughter and cruel taunts, from *both* teams, I look up hopefully at Mr. Fineman. His son Howie, a fat bully with crooked eyeglasses and matted hair, is hurling insults louder than anyone else. Maybe his father will intervene on my behalf. Instead, the grown man—a towering version of his lumpy son, a depressing vision of the child's future—sneers down at me.

"Maybe you oughta stick to makin' pizzas."

My best friend was Mitchell Blodnick, a funny-faced, much-teased prankster like me (we had both quickly learned the usefulness of being class clowns) whose family lived in reverse time order. Because her husband drove a taxi into the wee hours, Mitchell's mother routinely delayed dinner until then. The family would sit down to a nice meal of pot roast and chopped salad . . . at two-thirty in the morning. Then it was quality time and homework. Mitchell spent the first few hours of the school day with his head on the desk, fast asleep. Mrs. Blodnick slumbered until well into the afternoon, never brewing her morning coffee before four. She loved me.

"As big as he is, that's how good he is," she'd say. "Not like my lump of shit here, Mr. Good-for-nothing." I never knew how to respond to this type of praise, coming as it did at such cost to my friend.

"Did Mitchell tell you? He had an ingrown toenail, had to get surgery, the moron. He was laid up in bed for three weeks. I bought him some fuck books. Did he show you the fuck books? Show Carl the fuck books."

Again, I could think of no safe response.

Enid Blodnick could really lob one over the net when she wanted to. This is a woman who said to her brand-new son-in-law, in the midst of his wedding feast:

"Wipe your mouth. You look like an asshole after a shit."

My other good friend, Bruce Wasserstein (not the billionaire), eventually had to be caught in a net and carried away. His family had a history of troubled minds, but I liked their style: Mrs. Wasserstein once dragged a fully functioning fountain into the living room of their modern apartment, filling it with pots of water from the kitchen sink.

"Bruce! Plug in the fountain! Show your friend how it lights up! Hey, Bruce's friend, look at this!"

His older sister, Evelyn, unkempt and odiferous, tried from time to time to take her own life, never quite succeeding. She'd stuck her head in the oven, but Mrs. Wasserstein had gotten home in time to pull it out; she'd swallowed a bottle of prescription medication, but thrown it back up; she'd even jumped from the sixth-story balcony of their apartment . . . only to have her fall miraculously broken by a wooden bench. (The poor young woman suffered serious injuries but survived.)

Pear-shaped and clumsy, his huge teeth bound by heavy braces, Bruce was prone to loud fits of nonsensical yammering and random limb flailing. On our way home from school one day, while he was at the height of one such episode, the Wassersteins' car came tearing up the block, screeching to a halt beside us. His mother, wailing like a siren, jumped out of the passenger side, grabbed Bruce by the neck, and tried to hustle him into the car. He resisted hard.

"Come on, Brucie, get inside," his father muttered lifelessly from the driver's seat.

A third person, a mental health professional perhaps—male, I think, though possibly a large, masculine woman—emerged unhurriedly from the backseat and scooped Bruce into the car in one swift motion. The doors were slammed shut. The car sped away. I could still hear him screaming. When my friend resurfaced a few months later, he was strangely subdued, his eyes glassy, his mouth slack.

I even befriended the giant savant Harold Rointner. He was teased and tormented as much as I was, maybe more. I took pity. Harold stood at about six feet and must have weighed two hundred pounds by sixth grade. His body was an ungainly mess, all baby fat and loose flesh. He had facial tics and bodily tics, including one that involved lifting his arms and flicking his fingers around as if snapping them . . . but not snapping them. His parents, desperate for him to be accepted socially, threw expensive birthday parties at local catering halls, indiscriminately inviting all of his classmates. When he and I had the idea of building a clubhouse in the lots, his affable, corpulent father had blueprints made and constructed a deluxe model out of prefabricated lengths of two-by-fours and custom-cut plywood. The result was a proper two-room shack, such as you might see in a shantytown, only brand-spanking-new.

The clubhouse became a magnet for neighborhood boys, and Harold and I earned a modicum of social status for being its official owners and operators. (Still, most boys didn't hesitate to disrespect us in our very own lair. And neither of us had the guts to challenge them.) Eventually, spontaneously, a series of all-male soft-core sexcapades took place there: a bunch of boys would meet at the clubhouse in the late afternoon and someone would "dare" someone else to step inside, walk into the second room (which was quite dark), stand along the back wall, drop his pants, and let other boys enter, one by one, to cup and "feel up" his balls. I'm still amazed by the way nearly every single boy participated with open, gleeful curiosity. Reflecting upon them now, it occurs to me that these episodes were all about being a *boy,* not about being a *gay* boy. All boys learn more about sex from each other than they do from girls. Our clubhouse game was a *masculine* rite of passage. I understood this instinctively; it was part of the pleasure. "Sex" with other boys made me feel less like a *faggot.*

I don't remember Harold ever participating. I think he just stood off to the side, twitching and worrying. I was embarrassed by how much I liked him. He really was a *spaz,* but he was smart and articulate and could be very funny. Plus, he was an only child and had every toy ever made. We frequently played in each other's apartments.

I remember him walking out of my place one afternoon, his giant foot pausing on the stair.

"So . . . does this mean you're not mad at me anymore?"

I guess we'd been fighting. I felt a rush of emotion as I moved out into the hallway, riding a wave of genuine affection for my friend.

"I'm not mad at you, Harold," I answered. "I mean, if *we* can't get along, how is there any hope for *peace*?"

This moment stays in my mind because it's my first clear memory of *feeling* the fact of the Vietnam War. I was three years old when it started, in 1962, and though it raged on for the entire duration of my childhood, my comprehension remained muddy at best. *Silence* was the rule on the subject of Vietnam. It was simply not talked about in school or at home. I remember seeing body bags on the nightly news, and footage of wild peace protests, only half-understanding what I was watching. And I remember Jo Galotti saying that if her son Philip's number ever got called, she'd "dress him up in a wedding gown and high heels and take him down to the draft office just like that." The image of Philip—huge and hairy, a cross between Grizzly Adams and Charles Manson—as a blushing bride made me choke back a laugh. But choke it back I did: this was deadly serious, whatever it was. I remember *wanting* to understand the significance of this huge event in my world, *wanting* to feel its impact. That moment in the hallway with Harold was a start.

His apartment, a couple of buildings away, was our preferred meeting place. That was where all the better toys and goodies were. (Harold even had a real chemistry set, which we used to create tiny explosions in bubbling beakers.) Plus it was nice and *calm* there. The Rointner residence was a quiet zone, his parents padding around soundlessly in their underwear, his large, handsome mother always with a finger to her lips in a constant reminder.

"Shhh. Quietly."

His grandfather lived in a wheelchair in a back bedroom, also in his underwear. I never saw him move. He might have been dead. I knew these people were freaks, but still headed over to Harold's as often as possible.

"Would you boys like a malted milk?"

"Why yes, thank you, Mrs. Rointner."

"Shhhh."

7.

Every Tuesday afternoon during third and fourth grades, Mrs. Horowitz, a teacher's aide who had survived the Holocaust and bore a row of numbers tattooed onto the soft underside of her left arm, walked from classroom to classroom, gathered up all the little Catholic children, loaded us onto a yellow school bus, and shipped us over to St. Lucy's Church and School, where we received religious instruction in preparation for First Communion and, later, Confirmation.

Our Catechism instructor was Miss DelVecchio (Of the Ancient One). Short, round, and buxom, always with her hands tucked smugly under her bosom, Miss DelVecchio was one of those laywomen who aspires to nunhood but never joins the order. She dressed in boxy white cotton blouses, shapeless, ankle-length black skirts, and clunky buckled shoes.

"Raise your hand if you love your parents," she snipped at us on that first day.

I raised my hand. Seemed like the right answer.

"Very good. Now raise your hand if you *adore* your parents."

Hmm. Adore. I raised my hand again.

"No," she sniped. "You *love* your parents. You *adore* God."

And right there she lost me. I wasn't sure what *adore* was, but whatever it was, it was more than love. This woman was coldly instructing me to love someone more than my own parents. And who was she? *Miss DelVecchio*. I recoiled instinctively. Plus, her stories made no sense. She said that at the beginning of time there were only Adam and Eve, the first humans. They had children, and their children had children, and their children's children had children, and so on and so forth, until the entire Earth got populated. I had a question.

"Miss DelVecchio?"

I could see that she didn't want to call on me.

"Mm-yes?"

"If, like, Adam and Eve's children had children, and then, like, their children had children, and so on and so forth, until the whole world got populated . . . then wouldn't we all be *retarded*?" Because that was what they taught us in public school.

"No, no, no, children. You mustn't fuck your brother or your sister because then your children will come out *retarded*." I'm paraphrasing, of course, but they really let this point be known. (Perhaps they'd had a problem with it in previous classes.) Miss DelVecchio just harrumphed at my logic and mumbled vaguely about "the mystery and the wonder of the power of God." This was her stock response whenever she found herself backed into a corner.

"That's the mystery and the wonder of the power of God."

I had other questions too. About Original Sin, for example. Miss DelVecchio stopped calling on me, but I spoke up anyway. How, if you were just born, I wanted to know, could you possibly be *guilty* of *anything*? You were *just born*. But Miss DelVecchio insisted that we were born *dirty*, guilty of the sins committed by Adam and Eve. *Adam and Eve.* They had lived at the beginning of time. Why were we still paying for their transgressions? God sounded a little too much like my father.

"And then He sent Jesus Christ, His only begotten son, to be our Lord and Savior," she explained. "And Christ suffered and died on the cross for you, he *bled* for you and for all mankind, and now you must worship him and serve him and wash yourself clean in his blood—"

Whoa! Count me out! I'd rather be staring into Mrs. Feldman's bunion!

The Church's obsession with cannibalism repelled me. The holiest part of the Catholic Mass, we were taught, is the ritual of *transubstantiation*, wherein the priest magically transforms little round wafers (available for wholesale bulk purchase at Sunrise Religious Supply on Gun Hill Road) into the *actual flesh* of Jesus Christ. A cup of cheap port or sherry is similarly transformed into his actual *blood*. The flesh and blood are then fed to the congregation. This all sounded disturbingly like a plot from those B-movie horror flicks I watched regularly on *Chiller Theatre.* I knew even then that these people were being too *literal*. The Bible itself told me so: at the Last Supper, Jesus broke *bread*, gave it to his disciples, and said, "Take this, all of you, and eat it. This is my body." But it was *bread*. And then he took a cup of wine, gave it to his disciples, and said, "Take this, all of you, and drink it. This is the cup of my blood." But it was *wine*. These were *symbols*. Had he meant them literally, I reasoned, he would have held out his arm, offered it to his disciples, and said, "Take this, all of you, and . . . bite a chunk out of it. It's my *arm.*" Miss DelVecchio was not interested in such ruminations.

Still, I was drawn to the Church for its sheer grotesquerie and high theatrics. My memories of First Communion are vague, but I know I dug the props: the small white Bible with its hard plastic, marbleized cover, neat diary-style clasp lock, and smooth golden page edges; the pale blue crystal rosary beads in a white satin envelope; the fresh blue suit, white shirt, and white clip-on tie; new leather shoes with real brass buckles. On the big day, the girls were all in frilly white dresses and veils, the boys all in attire identical to my own. We lined up in separate rows down the center aisle of the church and approached the altar in boy-girl pairs to "receive." It had been drummed into our heads that to knowingly chew the communion wafer—*Christ's actual body*—was a mortal sin, punishable by an eternity of suffering in Hell. (Venial sins could be absolved through confession and penance, a twin ritual I disliked and resented.) But that first wafer stuck to the roof of my mouth. When I loosened it with my tongue, it fell into my teeth. I panicked as I felt my jaw reflexively masticating the flesh of our Lord and Savior. Though I didn't really believe most of what Miss DelVecchio had taught us, it was my policy to err on the side of caution.

Having received the blessed sacrament of Communion, I was ready to join the altar boy squad. This elite corps is composed chiefly of future theater queens. If you want to figure out who's gay in any parish, just look at the altar boys. Those long gowns and flouncy tops, the bells and incense, the all-male environment—it's a natural draw. You'll find these same twinks in the school play. Backstage in the sacristy, my comrades and I modeled the priests' fanciest robes and vestments, drank altar wine right out of the bottle, ate unconsecrated communion wafers like potato chips. (Turns out the body of Christ makes a decent snack. A little dry, but that's what the wine's for.) The priests would typically hole up in their quarters until just a few min-

ME, DAD, AND MARIA ON
THE MORNING OF MY FIRST COMMUNION.
THE STONE FAÇADE OF ST. LUCY'S CHURCH APPEARS BEHIND
US; THE RECESSED RECTORY, FRONTED BY GARDENS, CAN BE
GLIMPSED IMMEDIATELY TO ITS LEFT.

utes before curtain. For the record, none of them ever tried to molest
me. I don't know why. There ought to be a support group for former
altar boys who, like me, were *not* subjected to sexual advances. What
did the others have that we lacked? Truth is, I don't think anybody was
getting action at St. Lucy's. Our priests were deadbeats: Monsignor
DiNardo was pushing ninety and was no more approachable than the
Pope himself; Father Mannini was so shy and mousy that the nasal
drone of his voice was akin to silence; and Father Franco was simply
never around. We didn't know what his story was and speculated that
he might be an impostor. Or maybe a secret agent.

The shining exception was Father Oliverio, a swarthy, gutsy, soulful dream dad who brought enormous energy and a titanic sense of *fun* to everything. Just to be in Father Oliverio's presence was heartening: when you looked into his eyes, past the rolling laughter and high-flying antics, you saw genuine warmth and compassion; you saw a man who meant you nothing but good. This was not what I saw when I looked into the wild eyes of my own father. Kindly Father O was at once a helpful surrogate and a painful reminder of what I was missing.

But even he couldn't animate the lugubrious drone of Sunday Mass—the labored readings and recitations, dull prayers and hymns, constant commands to stand, sit, kneel. It all amounted to a kind of torture. I couldn't wait, *couldn't wait,* to hear the priest utter the words "The Mass is ended, go in peace."

"Thanks be to God" is the proper response from the pews.

I'd always leave out the "be to" part, profoundly relieved to hear the organ strike up a recessional and to feel a cool rush of air as ushers flung open the upstairs doors. The church proper, though lovely, was for some reason located on the basement level of the building, so airflow was limited. It has since been redesigned, but in those years the street entrance to St. Lucy's opened onto a large foyer containing some statues and a small gift shop, with doors on either end leading onto steep, narrow flights of stairs heading down into the underground hall. The reason for this architectural arrangement is unknown. Perhaps it's a symbol.

Altar boys, like theater folk, arrive well before showtime to prepare the set. The dark hall is cool and quiet then, and there is comfort in the highly ritualized chores and duties—lighting candles, filling cruets with wine and water, preparing incense, donning formal vestments. I served early morning Mass every day before school for a while, heading over to St. Lucy's at sunrise and groggily performing my duties as the same small group of old Italian ladies in black dresses and veils, the sole attendees at these ridiculously early services, gathered in a queue at the back of the church, pushing one by one into the hot darkness of the confessional booth, falling to their knees, and whispering their sins into the ear of a priest so close on the other side of a black metal screen that he could smell their breath.

"Say two Hail Marys and an Our Father."

Shoving back out of the confessional, the mournful old women would hobble down the center aisle of the church and collapse onto the cold marble steps of the altar to recite their penance, black wooden rosary beads trembling in their clenched fists. But they attended church *every day*. Why all this confession? Why not just do penance once a week, on Saturday, like everybody else? What sins, I remember wondering, could they possibly have committed since *yesterday*? And then I observed a typical post-Mass exchange:

"Hey. No you poosh-a me. I'm-a walk-a here."

"I no poosh-a you."

"You poosh-a me."

"Hey. Fock-a you."

"Fock-a you? Fock-a *you*!"

Suddenly I got it: confession freed you to sin. "I'll just confess it," I started telling myself whenever I wanted to tell a lie or steal candy or eat meat on a Friday. Miss DelVecchio knew this trick and said that God did too.

"No, no, no, children. Such antics are not tolerated. Sins committed in this fashion will *not* be forgiven." *Fock-a you.*

STANDING IN FRONT OF THE RECTORY
ON CONFIRMATION DAY

I was confirmed in 1968, at the age of nine. We were told that the sacrament of Confirmation enlisted us for life as soldiers in "God's Army," which we kids took to mean that we might be called upon at any time to kill or be killed in His name. But I didn't even like Him! God's love was unconditional, they said, yet any little misstep could land us in Hell. God made us in His own image, they said, yet our bodies were the Devil's domain. God had filled the world with abundant pleasures of every stripe and variety, they said, but only in order to *test* us. God was a sadistic bastard. He played too many mind games. He was my own father's supernatural doppelgänger—only worse, much, much worse. I wanted no part of it. Yet here I was, about to become His foot soldier. For *life*.

Rumors circulated that we would be slapped hard in the face by a bishop as part of the Confirmation ceremony, and that it would *hurt*. Miss DelVecchio assured us that it would just be a gentle tap, but who could trust her? Her God, like His nuns, was overly fond of physical punishment. I remember the terrifying mother superior—her Miss Gulch–like visage squashed into a starched white wimple, black robes flowing from her head and back, a gargantuan metal crucifix swinging from a thick braided cord slung around her waist—barreling up to my friend Johnny Sczepanski as he horsed around during a rehearsal, grabbing him by the arm, and whacking the underside of his wrist with a leather strap.

"Would you like another?" she bellowed.

Johnny, ever the wiseass: "Yeah."

She whacked him again with such force that silence fell all around us.

Johnny turned purple.

"And how about another?" she barked into his face, exactly like a dominatrix in the throes of a hard-core S & M scene. Johnny said nothing.

"I thought not," gloated the hooded victor, sweeping on down the aisle in search of another victim. The bishop's slap on Confirmation Day turned out to be nothing like this. It was exactly what Miss DelVecchio had described: a gentle pat. I was so numb that it wouldn't have mattered if he'd hit me on the head with a lump hammer.

I'd awakened that very morning to find New York Grandma slumped on the couch in our apartment, ashen and lifeless, the victim

NEW YORK GRANDMA

of a massive stroke. She'd slept over to help with party preparations, and when last I'd seen her she'd been buzzing around as usual, pitching in down at the pizza shop, dashing back up to the apartment, cooking, cleaning, running up to the roof to hang laundry, giving us kids piggyback rides. She was eighty-three years old at the time, but had the energy and physical stamina of a woman half her age. The corpselike figure perched on the couch was a stranger.

"Come here," she croaked. I approached timidly. She handed me an envelope with five dollars in it, my confirmation gift.

"Gremma's gonna die."

I'd chosen Joseph as my Confirmation name, not in honor of Jesus' father but after my beloved uncle Joe, Grandma's firstborn, so like her in looks and temperament. I'd kept this choice a secret from Grandma, planning to surprise her with it on the big day. Now she'd never know. Was this God's cruel idea of a joke? Was this what it would mean to be His soldier?

In the days and weeks that followed, Grandma had several smaller strokes. I remember staring down at her withered form in the hospital bed—tubes poking into her body, her ruddy olive complexion turned white, too white—heartbroken and lost. Where was my beloved mother's mother? Sometimes she seemed to recognize me and stared into my eyes intensely; other times, she thrashed around and tried to yank the tubes out of her body. When Aunt Virginia, her oldest daughter, came to visit, Grandma spat at her and hissed a string of guttural Sicilian curses into her face.

"*Puttana!*" she grunted, reaching up with both arms to pummel my aunt's face.

She tried the same move on a couple of nurses and was tethered to the mattress—a bizarre, funhouse mirror reflection of the opposite end of her life, when as a young girl in Sicily she was beaten and strapped into bed by a father determined to break her willful spirit. (She'd escaped him, and an arranged marriage to a similar man, by sailing alone to New York City in 1900, at the age of fifteen.)

Her violent outbursts were caused by the strokes, of course, but the flip side of Grandma's burning vitality had always been a hot temper. She never showed it to us kids directly, but I remember her and Aunt Virginia fighting bitterly from time to time, and I once caught a glimpse of New York Grandma throwing a fit in her sunny kitchen, shouting at my aunt and smashing teacups against the white porcelain sink, where they exploded into delicate shrapnel. As Grandma reached for her third or fourth cup, my mother led me down to Aunt Virginia and Uncle Frank's place. They lived one floor below with their adult children, my cousins Frankie and Marie, whom I adored. Aunt Virginia was fifteen years older than my mother, so my cousins were much older than my sisters and me. Frankie, the eldest, was already attending Iona College (he eventually became a T-man and ended up leading the bust of Studio 54) and had enough money of his own that he could buy me the neatest-ever gifts: a silver transistor radio in a white leather case, a fourteen-karat gold ring with a square-cut chunk of garnet, my birthstone, a steady flow of the latest issues of *MAD* magazine.

Marie, a few years younger than her brother, was a dark-haired beauty (my aunt and uncle were deep olive) with a toothy smile and music in her voice. She was a lot like Grandma, always crouching down to meet me at eye level, inventing games and diversions of all sorts, expressing amazement and delight at every stupid thing I did.

"I don't like Cousin Marie," I announced one night, padding into the kitchen in my footsy pajamas, eliciting a gasp from my mother.

"I *love* her."

In the waiting room of Our Lady of Mercy Hospital, my grown-up cousins tried to distract and entertain me. "She'll get better," they said of Grandma, but I knew it wasn't true. A burnt-out shell of her former self was eventually brought home to my grandmother's apartment, her once-dancing eyes utterly dead now, her newly slackened face a permanent mask of vacant despair. She couldn't walk unassisted and spent her days convalescing. Aunt Virginia and Uncle Frank became her caretakers.

"She made her own bed today," my aunt would report hopefully.

She made her own bed, I'd think.

Just days earlier, she could have *built* a bed, strapped it to her back, and carried it home to her native Sicily on foot, picking wild *gaduna* along the way. She'd often taken us to the park to collect mounds of the tender green in brown paper bags. At home, she'd clean them, chop them, and cook them into buttery omelets. (She picked *cicoria* too, wild chicory, which she'd prepare in a similar manner.) Uncle Frank, having been raised in an orphanage and on the street, knew how to cull a meal from nearly any patch of green and had taught Grandma all about wild mushrooms, identifying the sometimes subtle differences in appearance between the edible types and those that would kill you instantly. She became an expert, sautéing her wild harvests in garlic and butter, sprinkling fresh chopped parsley on top for a note of citric brightness in all that nutty depth of flavor. Her cooking was simple and hearty: pasta with white beans and bacon, *bacala* with tomato and onion, fava bean salad, escarole soup with chicken. Those days were over.

She made her own bed today.

"It's God's will" was all the Church had to say. Our Heavenly Father was too busy making rules and meting out punishments to provide much succor. Only in a phantasmagoria of blood and guts did the Church come truly alive: St. Lucy with her eyes gouged out, holding the bloody orbs on a white platter in her outstretched hands, blood trickling from open sockets where they'd been dissevered; sinners writhing in the fires of Hell, fanged serpents crawling into their bodies through every orifice, winged demons piercing their flesh with long black spades; Christ himself, crucified, blood pouring from hands and feet nailed mercilessly into the cross, blood flowing freely from a crown of thorns, blood running in long rivulets down his tormented body from horrid gashes on his torso and back.

All were on vivid, life-size display right outside the church building. St. Lucy's is famous for its replica of the Grotto at Lourdes (where the Virgin Mary is said to have appeared to Bernadette, thus inspiring her song) and, on an adjacent lot, its replica of the Scala Sancta, the Holy Steps in Rome. The curvy stone-and-slate stairway, dotted with painted plaster saints and trumpeting angels, winds higher and higher until it culminates in a larger-than-life diorama of Christ's crucifixion at Calvary. Beneath the steps is nestled a series of candlelit caves—an approximation of the Catacombs—cool, damp, and spooky, filled with the open tombs of dead saints and other eerie displays (including the aforementioned statue of the mangled St. Lucy, and the bas-relief depiction of Hell).

Pilgrims traveled from far and wide to seek miracles at the Grotto, often crawling on their knees or bellies along the stone path leading to the cove of the Blue Lady. Serene and beatific, the statue of Mary stood (and still stands) high atop a half-dome sanctuary of rough-hewn gray rocks, head bowed, hands folded in prayer. Water streams from beneath her feet, cascading down over the rocks and collecting in a pond below. (Because the plumbing and rocks have been blessed by priests, the water is considered *holy*.) Devotees drink greedily of Mary's spring, fill jugs and jars with it, bathe themselves in the tiny pond. Back in the day, neighborhood rumor had it that the water was recycled endlessly (which may well have been true, given that there were several drought emergencies in New York City at the time), and that we were drinking from the same flow in which others had just washed their feet or dunked their wounds.

"But the rocks purify it," we assured one another with dripping lips as we leaned in for another gulp.

Dozens of crutches and canes crowded the rocks leading up to the statue of Mary and were clustered down around her feet, placed there as testimony by those claiming to have experienced miracle healings at the site. Stories of such *miracoli* abounded, dating back from the Grotto's debut in 1939. Old-timers told the tale of the first miracle: In the wee hours of the morning, well before daybreak on the very Sunday that the Grotto was set to open, a great commotion was heard in the otherwise silent neighborhood. Lights flicked on in all the houses; people padded out to investigate. An old woman was running up and down the street, waving her crutches around wildly, screaming that she had just been cured of lifelong paralysis at the Grotto. From that moment on, the place was a Mecca. (It was whispered in some circles that the old woman had been a paid actress.)

"God works in mysterious ways," they said.

And He did: it was through church that I made my first set of true-blue friends . . . virtually all of whom turned out to be *gay*. We'd found one another as if by homing device at St. Lucy's Day Camp, which I started attending soon after First Communion. I knew a couple of kids from altar boy training, so I had a head start socially, and soon found myself in the warm embrace of a clique that would stay tight for years to come—all through high school and beyond. With my St. Lucy's friends, I had a sense of *belonging,* a feeling of *not being judged.* We knew intuitively that we were *alike* in some secret, elemental way, and we flocked together naturally. (Gay children are always relieved to find others like themselves, even long before they can put words to any of it.) Most of my new friends attended St. Lucy's School and lived in the immediate vicinity of the church in neat rows of attached brick houses. Their lives seemed calm and well ordered, right down to their tidy bedrooms and starched blue uniforms. My father had tried to send my sisters and me to St. Lucy's, but my mother had resisted. "I want you kids to be around all types of people, not just your own kind," she always said. The idea of being cooped up with a bunch of nuns all day was deeply unappealing, so I was grateful to Mom for choosing—and winning—this battle. My St. Lucy's friends dispelled any "outsider" feelings I may have had by making it abundantly clear that they considered public school totally hip.

"He goes to Ninety-Six," they'd announce when introducing me.

"Oh yeah?" the typical response. "What's it like?"

Even my spastic inability to play sports was put to good use at day camp. Dodgeball games on the rocky asphalt surface of the church parking lot were a popular—and, for me, dreaded—pastime. I couldn't throw for shit and was terrified of that speeding rubber ball, hurled with such impossible force by the heat-crazed boy campers that getting hit meant getting *hurt*. If the ball caught you in the face just right, it could break your nose. When it was my turn to throw, members of the opposing team would relax and saunter toward the chalk-drawn dividing line to taunt and tease me. They knew I "threw like a girl." Nothing was more humiliating than feeling that rubber orb leave my hand in the knowledge that it would just dribble limply over the line, barely in motion at all.

But then a star player—an oversize prankster named Joey Montecitto, whose throw was so lethal that the mere sight of him loping sideways toward the chalk line with ball in hand set even the toughest kids askitter—had a brainstorm: he would pick me for his team; when it was my turn to throw and all the opposing players had gathered at the line, I'd pass the ball to Joey and he'd take the shot. I loved watch-

ing their facial expressions go from mockery to terror as they witnessed the last-minute switcheroo. Joey and I worked out a series of
signals so that the other side could never be sure if we were going to
switch or not. Kept off balance this way, they were much more respectful. My friendship with Joey was a valuable asset.

Camp tuition was not much more than eight dollars a week per
child, so amenities were few. We were kept for much of the day either
in a shadeless cement recess yard or a stale, humid cafeteria. On rainy
days we were corralled into the school auditorium, mercifully dark
and cool, and shown god-awful films of stunning variety—everything
from religious educational reels to nasty grind-house features. (The
only one I remember was a low-budget, black-and-white B-movie
about a Marquis de Sade–like figure who tortures women and men,
mostly women, in his medieval dungeon. In one scene, the antihero
tethers a moist, buxom maiden to a leather chair, jerks her head back
by the hair, and forces over her face a cage full of rats. The rats are
contained in the upper part of the cage by a little gate, and the woman
is tortured with the threat for a while. Finally the gate is pulled open
and the rats fall onto her face, eating it hungrily as she screams in
agony. Fitting fare for a Roman Catholic day camp.)

St. Lucy's idea of a day trip was to load us like human cargo into
rented U-Haul vans and drive us up to Rye Playland or Heckscher
State Park. Inside the sweltering metal boxes, it was pitch-dark and
oxygen-free. Being packed body to body like that with my fellow
campers—a few of whom, invariably, would panic or pass out—made
me think of the slave ships I'd read about in a biography of Harriet
Tubman. I remember the profound gush of relief when, having arrived at our destination, the truck doors were opened from the outside and we'd tumble out into the sunshine like a load of wet clothes.
Even the most turgid summer air could feel like an arctic blast after

the ovenlike experience of the U-Haul van. (Camp management got some flack about these trips from parents and eventually started renting proper yellow school buses.)

Once in the water, we'd stay for hours, splashing and dunking and wrestling one another, finding any excuse to bang our slick bodies together, laughing wildly, with total abandon. Afterward we'd change into dry clothes, buy candy or ice cream, and sing camp songs on the bus ride home.

> *There once was a goat*
> *(There once was a goat)*
> *By the name of Billy Goat*
> *(By the name of Billy Goat) . . .*

We were banned from Rye Playland for a while because we'd dumped laundry powder into the water works at Ye Old Mill, raising an ocean of havoc-wreaking suds. Father Oliverio offered to make arrangements for us to return to the park under a different name, but only if we promised not to pull the prank. We promised, and then pulled the prank anyway. Back in the Bronx, we'd peel the skin off our sunburned noses, eat the last of our candy, play with whatever new trinkets we'd won or purchased, and then run off to our respective homes for dinner and bedtime, luxuriating all the while in the knowledge that tomorrow we would do it all again.

The mystery and the wonder of the power of God. Indeed.

8.

I don't remember the decision to sell Cappi's, but sold it was, for a handful of shekels, to a couple of suckers fresh from the Old Country. Suddenly, one sweltering day in August 1970, it was off our necks. Just like that. And not a moment too soon. Summers in the shop were brutal, with the massive steam table and twin pizza oven nudging the interior temperature up into the hundreds. The dining room was air-conditioned, grudgingly, but we were discouraged from spending time in there. A set of swinging doors near the kitchen that connected the chilly restaurant to the broiling pizza parlor was like a gateway between Hades and Paradise. I remember my body nearly convulsing as I moved between the two climate zones, but physical comfort was a luxury intended for paying customers only.

My father didn't believe in air-conditioning, nor did he put stock in fans, or even open windows. His theory was that you kept a place cool by sealing all the windows and doors. Fans, he said, actually *raised* the temperature by distributing hot air. He believed in eating hot soup during a heat wave. He said that if you heated up your insides, the outside air would feel cooler. The frail red line of mercury in the little thermometer hanging on the brick wall at the back of the shop, set into the belly of a two-dimensional plastic likeness of St. Anthony, practically burst into flames as it sailed above the one-hundred-degree mark and out of sight.

My parents had not discussed their intentions with my sisters and me, so the sale of Cappi's seemed to come out of the blue. My father sat listlessly at the kitchen table for weeks afterward, his head in hands. He was forty-eight years old, with a wife, four kids, and no money, his backbreaking six-year odyssey having ended in a total bust. Even the Committee to Control Obscenity by Constitutional Means had gone nowhere. I am the same age now, as I write these words, as he was then, and know well the heartbreak of defeat and the terror of looming poverty—especially in middle age. (I am, after all, his only son, and while I'm unlike him in many ways, I have duplicated some of his deepest patterns.) He eventually accepted a friend's offer of a job selling insurance, and I can still picture him heading out of the apartment in a slim, dark suit and slicked-back hair, a black leather binder tucked under his arm, looking like some other boy's dad. But my father quickly judged the insurance industry to be a scam and said he refused to go from house to house defrauding people. He tried a couple of other white-collar positions, but stuck to none of them. Pretense and perfidy peeved my father, precluding him from most professions.

To supplement our strapped family budget, my mother took a night job at Alexander's on Fordham Road, earning a dollar an hour as a salesgirl (for a total of twenty dollars a week). She was only a couple of years younger than my father and can't have been happy about our situation, but I know she was relieved to be free from the yoke of Cappi's. There was a new lightness about the woman as she showered and dressed in the late afternoon, slipping into sensible heels and hopping onto the Number 12 bus, riding away from the neighborhood and toward something that must have felt like freedom. (I hated her going and counted the minutes each night until her return.) My father put the kibosh on her budding retail career when he grew tired of feeding, bathing, and putting to bed two children and a pair of teen-agers by himself every night. His collisions with Rosette continued but were more infrequent now. Their last big blowout had happened about a year earlier, when she was denied a high school diploma for having cut gym class. My father's head exploded when he learned that Rosette would not be graduating with her class . . . yet he himself had been denied a high school diploma for the selfsame reason. Rosette went to summer school and got her diploma in the fall—something my father never did.

Aunt Diana was running the New York branch of a small interna-tional travel agency out of an office in Rockefeller Center at that time, and she hired my mother to be her sole employee. A crackerjack sec-retary with old-school typing and shorthand skills, Mom had worked for years before she got married (and for a short while afterward) for a senior editor at *Collier's* magazine. Photos from that period show a tall, dark beauty—slender and long-legged, with a slim waist, lustrous black hair, and a beaming smile—sporting sleek suits and gleaming purses, with matching hats and gloves. She'd left *Collier's* when she was pregnant with Rosette and reminisced with some melancholy about her days at the magazine and the farewell party her co-workers had thrown for her. Someone in the art department had worked up a cartoon in her honor, which my mother saved in the pages of a photo album.

'BYE 'BYE MARY it says, showing my mom—in red coat and blue

'BYE 'BYE MARY...

gloves, a pouf of auburn hair poking out from the front of a black ker-chief, her overall visage bearing a striking resemblance to Wilma Flintstone—pausing on the stairs to smile and wave as she descends into a subway entrance marked "Uptown—The Bronx."

'BYE 'BYE MARY.

That image had always saddened me. I was relieved to see my mother return to professional life—clean and dry, liberated from the sweat and grime of Cappi's kitchen. She loved going "downtown" every day, loved Rockefeller Center, loved even the express bus, happy to spring for the extra fare since it meant avoiding the subway crush. She brought me along with her on my days off from school, leading me through the hustle and bustle of midtown, pausing to point out the Art Deco murals and massive statues abounding. I was floored by the figure of Atlas carrying the world on his shoulders, his leg muscles alone stretching half as high as our building to my child's eye. At lunchtime we'd go to local coffee shops for shrimp salad sandwiches (my favorite), or to Zum Zum, a now-defunct chain of German counter restaurants, for sausage and sauerkraut. Back in the office I'd putter around while my mother worked, pretending to be working myself, once typing gibberish into the Teletype machine and somehow transmitting it to the head office in Europe. (When the big, clunky device set itself to clattering and wheezing as it wired a nonsensical message across the ocean, my mother nearly jumped out of her skin with panic.)

Like an offender drawn back to the scene of a crime, or like a victim having the same impulse, I kept floating back toward Cappi's (the new owners had retained the name), fascinated by the sight of these strange immigrant partners—one tall and slender, the other short and chubby, both bald—operating the place. They'd made a few minor physical changes but had otherwise left the place untouched. I purchased pizza and soda at the counter, reveling in the sensation of being a customer, relishing the fact that I could just walk away like anybody else. In an odd decision that I don't recall making, I asked the new owners for a job . . . and soon found myself working part-time at Cappi's for fifty cents an hour, feeling like a big shot because I knew the place so well, swelling with pride whenever the new owners asked questions about how my father accomplished this task or that.

My favorite feature of Cappi's had always been the cash register, and during downtime on the new job I toyed with it in my usual way. The owners thought I was either stealing or spying, or both, and fired me summarily.

My father returned to his roots: carpentry. He got himself into the union and took a job at the Saks Fifth Avenue warehouse down in Manhattan's old Meatpacking District. There were now two incomes streaming into the house, modest though they were, and things normalized a bit for our family. We returned more fully to the flow of life in the wider circle of our extended family. Our relatives on my father's side gathered every week for daylong Sunday dinners, which we'd missed out on for years because of Cappi's. In the old days before the pizza shop, New Jersey Grandma had hosted in her house in Union, but my memory of those gatherings consists chiefly of this single image: a table spanning the entire length of her wood-paneled finished basement, covered with white cotton tablecloths and laden with steaming platters of food.

"It's a Barese thing," my mother would say about the fact that Grandma's living and dining rooms were only for show, never for use.

And I remember Carlo—Charlie, as he was known—Grandma's second husband, whom she'd married in 1939 (when my father was seventeen years old). He was white-haired and Rubenesque, with rosy cheeks and a jolly laugh, and I can still picture him making wine in the garage, lifting me up onto a stool and feeding me sips of the scarlet brew from a jelly jar, laughing as I grimaced. "It's good," I'd say, trying to hide my distaste.

His death in 1963 was my first real encounter with grief. I loved my only Grandpa, my namesake, and missed him keenly. My mother often told the story about how Charlie had cried in the maternity ward of Misericordia Hospital when she and my father announced that their firstborn son would bear his name.

"No, no," he protested. "You must name him Domenico, for your real father."

"*You're* my real father," Dad said. And the two men wept.

(Years after his death, Grandma had Charlie's body exhumed so it could be transferred into an aboveground unit beside her own planned burial site. In such cases, cemetery officials will arrange a viewing of the body upon request. Grandma requested. "He look-a good!" she later enthused about a man who'd been dead for more than a decade.)

By the time Cappi's was sold, Grandma had moved into a two-family brick house in Fort Lee, maintaining only a modest residence for herself while renting out everything else. Uncle Danny and Aunt Terry had become the new hosts of our regular family gatherings.

Sunday at their navy blue shingled ranch house in Paramus, New Jersey, was the highlight of my week. Danny was my father's younger brother, the baby of the family, whom Dad idolized and adored. His wife, Terry, a spitfire in deep olive, with jet-black hair and big brown eyes, ruled the house with authority and bore a passing resemblance to Maria Callas—only softer, prettier. (Or maybe I'm thinking of Callas because Enrico DiGiuseppe, the Italian tenor, was Terry's first cousin and joined our Sunday table several times.) Their kids, my cousins—Daniel, Christine, David, and Carla, in age order—were a matched set with my sisters and me, corresponding in age just about exactly, the only difference being that they were two boys and two girls instead of three girls and a boy. We formed a tight gang of eight, each matched with our age partner but also reveling in the pleasure of being one big troupe.

To my sisters and me, Paramus was "the country." Our cousins'

EVA, ME, ROSETTE, DANIEL, AND CHRISTINE—
AN EARLY PHOTO

house sat on the edge of a golf course, itself on the edge of a woods. We caught all manner of critters and insects in the surrounding "wilderness," building custom-made habitats for our wild pets, killing them with kindness. The house had a sizable attic that Uncle Danny had converted into two jazzy bedrooms with slanted walls and funny little windows. From the girls' room, you could crawl through the closet into the unfinished part of the attic, the floor of which consisted only of beams and fiberglass insulation, fitted from below with Sheetrock ceilings. My cousin Carla, Maria's age partner, maintained a doll "hospital" in there. She was a tiny, pretty thing, quick to laugh but painfully shy, with long purple-black hair, her mother's wide, limpid eyes, and a heart-shaped mouth. We'd enter Carla's secret lair to find naked Barbie dolls in various stages of vivisection, hanging by their necks from short lengths of laundry line tacked into the ceiling beams.

"They're sick," she'd explain.

These rough areas held great allure, and one Sunday, David and I wandered alone deep into their darkest recesses. He was my frequent partner in crime. A year younger than I, slender and petite, all floppy black hair, dark freckles, and two front teeth, David was shy and quiet, probably an outcast like me though we never compared notes. We crawled together far beyond Carla's doll hospital, balancing on the beams, heading blindly into blackness, searching for I don't know what. As we crept along, I lost my footing, slipped off the beam, and went crashing through the thin Sheetrock underfoot, remaining in the attic only from the waist up, my bottom half wriggling around somewhere below. I hoisted myself back onto the beams and crawled desperately to safety. Trembling, David and I tiptoed downstairs to survey the damage, taking care to appear nonchalant.

"What are you boys up to?"

"Oh, nothin'."

We both went ashen as we slipped into the master bedroom, opened the door of the walk-in closet, and found neat rows of shirts, dresses, suits, jackets, coats, shoes—all covered in dust and debris, a gaping hole in the ceiling above them, chalky crumbs of rubble still trickling down. We snapped the door shut and immediately agreed to forget the whole thing, planning to just feign ignorance when confronted with it later.

I usually luxuriated in the car ride back home to the Bronx: the George Washington Bridge lit up against the night, looking for all the world like an open jewelry box in the Land of the Giants; the fascinating marker at the state line between New York and New Jersey, which my father had pointed out several times but the concept of which remained perplexing and abstract; the sight of my mother gazing contentedly out the window; the delicious aroma of each of my father's freshly lit Kent cigarettes (yes, *delicious*). My sisters would either fall asleep or gaze off dreamily. I'd struggle to stay awake, enjoying the quiet rattle of our cozy rolling cabin, marveling at the way the moon stayed fixed in the car window the whole way home. How did it do that? But on this night I was tense as I waited for the other shoe to drop: the Paramus debacle would soon be discovered. There would be consequences.

By the time we got to the apartment, the phone was ringing. My father picked it up. I could hear Uncle Danny yelling on the other end. He was usually mild-mannered and jovial with us kids, if a little distant, so I knew my troubles were deep. David had made a full confession. My father hung up the phone and asked for my version of the story. I blamed it all on my cousin. Though I might normally have felt guilty about diming out a peer, I felt justified in this case because David had so readily cracked and pointed the finger at me.

"I didn't even know where he was taking me," I lied through my teeth in a sweat. "How would I even get back there if David didn't show me the way? He said he plays there all the time! He was the one who slipped through the ceiling!" Miraculously, my father just mumbled a limp reprimand and sent me off to bed. I scampered away, grateful for the reprieve and drunk on the power of my wiles.

Daniel, my oldest cousin, Rosette's age partner and a total nature buff, kept a six-foot boa constrictor in a giant aquarium on the shag-carpeted floor of his and David's attic bedroom. Rosette and Maria were horrified at the very mention of Dino, but Eva and I were held in thrall by the fat, pendulous reptile, especially when Daniel lifted it out of its tank, wrapped it around his neck, and invited us to stroke it.

He explained that it killed by crushing the life out of its prey as Eva and I took turns draping Dino around our shoulders. I loved the feel of his silky, leathery skin, gently scaled, smooth and cool and luxurious; loved, too, the weight of his intense musculature flexing just beneath the skin's surface as he slithered around my neck and shoulders. There is obvious sexual subtext here, of course, but Dino was genuinely fascinating. Plus, I was eager to impress Daniel in every way possible.

It was hard not to have a crush on my older cousin. He had a natural, easy masculinity about him, smooth and sexy without trying. Daniel was a bodybuilder and nature enthusiast long before either was fashionable. Having been a hunter since boyhood, he was frequently in full camouflage, including face paint, a bow and arrows lashed across his muscular chest. During his high school years, he took up amateur taxidermy and was constantly killing and stuffing small game from the woods abutting their house.

He once took me out on a hunt, stressing that we had to move as soundlessly as possible, so as not to scare off our prey. As we closed in on a raccoon and Daniel aimed his weapon at the helpless animal, bringing his finger to his lips in a reminder of the importance of silence, I purposely rustled some leaves and snapped a few twigs. The raccoon scurried away. Daniel quietly banned me from future expeditions. This was how it was with my cousins. We didn't fight. When tensions arose, we'd instinctively adjust our behavior in order to maintain maximum conviviality. (Good cousins are like siblings with no downside.)

"The pirates," as Terry referred to her brood, kept a host of other pets—a dog, several birds, a cat . . . and a fluffy white rabbit fittingly named Snowball. Oh, how we loved that bunny! On Sunday afternoons before dinner, we'd race over to the chicken-wire cage in the

side yard to take turns feeding, holding, and petting the poor, terrified animal. One day we arrived at the cage and found it empty. Where
was Snowball? My cousins had gone to church in the morning and remembered seeing him in his cage on their way out. My grandmother
had been the only one home during the time he seemed to have disappeared. We ran into the house and gathered at the stove, where she
was stirring the Sunday gravy.

"Hey, Grandma. Have you seen Snowball?"

"Hah? What's-a Snobollo?"

"*Snowball*. The rabbit. Did you see him?"

"I no-no. I no see no-ting-eh."

We raced back outside.

"Here, Snowball," we called, confident that we'd find him happily
hopping about nearby. "Here, pretty rabbit . . ."

Eva and her age partner, our cousin Christine, formed a trail of
vegetable pieces leading into and out of the yard, hoping Snowball
would pick up the scent. They were always a busy pair, those two.
Whether weaving sit-upons (seat "cushions") out of newspaper,
building nature preserves, or rescuing and nursing wounded animals, they could always be counted on for an industrious swirl of activity. Christine was a page from her mother's book—high-spirited
and beautiful, homegrown, a real "can-do" gal. But even her and Eva's
best efforts proved futile: dinnertime arrived with still no sign of
Snowball. We washed up and went to table. Over the pasta course, as
we chomped on scrumptious chunks of "gravy meat" (any of a variety
of succulent animal parts stewed in the Sunday gravy), we plotted with
our mouths full.

"After dinner we'll go search some more. Maybe he hopped into
the golf course."

That night, in the car on the way home, my father chuckled qui-

NEW JERSEY GRANDMA

etly to my mother about how funny it was that we kids were still planning to search for the lost rabbit while we were actually in the process
of eating him. I thought I would hurl. We had chewed and swallowed
our beloved pet! And he was delicious! While my cousins were away
at church, Grandma had snatched Snowball from his cage, slit his
throat, skinned him, boned him, and browned him for her sauce.

Though horrifying, Snowball's murder had been a crime of opportunity. Grandma's Sunday cooking routines were well known to us,
reassuringly consistent, and didn't usually involve the slaughter of
family pets. No matter whose house she was staying in (sleeping over
on Saturday night was part of the deal), Grandma would awaken with
the sun, make her bed immediately upon rising, wash and dress herself, and march into the kitchen. There she'd brew a pot of coffee and
dump a five-pound bag of flour onto a wooden board (which she traveled with always). She'd divide the flour into roughly two halves: One
half would become a risen dough for making bread, *focaccia* (*fugatch'*
in our butchered pronunciation), and *pizza fritta*—chunks of dough
smacked and pulled into pancakes, deep-fried in vegetable oil,
drained and patted dry, then sprinkled with powdered sugar—an exquisite treat, especially for breakfast. The other half would become
pasta dough.

Grandma's specialty was *cavatelli* (we pronounced it *gavadel'*),
"little caves" of pasta with rolled edges, made from white flour and
water, no egg or other ingredients. She would knead the dough briefly
but with muscle, form it into a couple of perfect globes, cover them
with damp dish towels, and put them aside to set at room temperature
for half an hour or so. When the dough was ready to be worked,
Grandma would knead it again for a minute, slice off a modest slab,
roll the slab briskly between her palms to form a tubular shape about
a foot in length, slice the tube into small chunks (each less than a half

inch square), and then use her fingers to drag each little chunk toward her along the floured board before flicking it away again, creating the cave shape. *Toward and away, toward and away.* Grandma used the middle fingers and forefingers of both hands, working at great speed, forming at least four *cavatelli* with each swipe. (Don't try this at home. It's a technique reserved for masters.) She'd periodically collect the formed shapes and spread them out to dry on clean white sheets sprinkled with flour and draped over every available surface. (We kids loved to pop the raw pasta into our mouths as we passed, especially when they'd begun to harden.)

Once she'd filled the house with fields of drying pasta, Grandma would get started on the "gravy." (Most Italian-Americans refer to Bolognese sauce, or *ragù*, as "Sunday gravy." I don't know how or when that started.) Here again, her movements were as regular as clockwork: She'd pour a couple of inches of olive oil into a giant pot and heat it over a medium flame. She'd toss in some chopped garlic and start browning meats: freshly rolled meatballs (usually made of seasoned chopped beef, but sometimes containing chopped pork and veal as well), sweet sausage, hot sausage, *bragioli* (flat sheets of thin-pounded beef, seasoned and rolled tightly into log shapes, and fastened with string or toothpicks—we pronounced it *bragiol'*), ribs, rolled pork fat (I forget what they call it, but it's basically *bragiol'* using butter-soft pigskin instead of beef), pig knuckles, bits of steak, maybe even a few chicken legs and thighs. Once all the meat was well browned (in batches), Grandma would pile it onto a platter and set it aside, covering it lightly with "tinfoil" or a pot lid. Then she'd strain and refresh the oil, throw in some more chopped garlic and a few good handfuls of chopped onion, sauté them well. She'd open eight or ten cans of whole peeled tomatoes—the only store-bought ingredient, preferred to fresh tomatoes for their consistency—and push them through a sieve right into the pot.

The first batch of raw tomato to hit the oil always made a satisfying hiss and released an aromatic cloud of fragrance that floated throughout the house. (The bouquet of a properly prepared Sunday gravy lingers well into Monday night.) When all the tomatoes were in, she'd add a few cans of tomato paste, stir it smooth, and season the young sauce with salt, pepper, fresh and dried basil, parsley, and oregano. A couple of bay leaves were added at the end. Upon starting to bubble nicely, the gravy would be set to simmer atop a low flame for four or five hours, maybe longer, stirred gently at regular intervals. During the final thirty minutes or so of cooking, the browned gravy meat would be added to the pot and allowed to stew luxuriously. Sometimes Grandma would throw in a few shelled hard-boiled eggs. Along the way she might have added a tablespoon of sugar, a chunk of carrot, or a splash of milk to reduce acidity. I'm sure she had other tricks too, but they're lost to me. We kids would visit her in the kitchen once in a while, hungry for a treat of fresh, crusty bread dipped into the bubbling sauce and handed to us over a napkin. Or better yet, a fried meatball on a fork. (They're a different kind of delicious before they go into the gravy.)

She'd boil the *gavadel'* in calm batches, pounds of it, and present it to the table in two huge, steaming bowls: one tossed in the glorious Sunday gravy; the other in a ricotta sauce, adored by us kids and utterly simple: Grandma would just spoon ricotta into a heated pasta bowl, swish some boiling pasta water around in it, season it mildly, and add some fresh-grated Parmesan. Nothing more. (The gravy meat, of course, would have been pulled out of the pot prior to serving, and presented to the table on triumphant platters toward the end of the pasta course.) The taste of Grandma's *gavadel'* (some families, not ours, pronounce it *gavadeel'* or *gavadeels*) is the sort of powerful sense memory that instantly conjures the past in all its fullness. It is inimitable. It died when Grandma did. I haven't tasted it in decades. Yet I taste it as I write.

The meal surrounding the pasta was sprawling but simple. There would have been *antipasto*—serving platters groaning with olives, roasted peppers, quartered fennel bulbs (*finocchio* or *finoik'*), *soprasatta* and other dried meats, a few cheeses and breads—before we sat down. And there would usually have been trays of *fugatch'* lying about (the sole ingredients of which were bread dough, olive oil, crushed tomatoes, salt, pepper, oregano, and rosemary), which Grandma served in fat, savory squares, cakelike, stacked high on a platter. At table—including a kids' table, which the adults took care to make an exact replica of the adult table, an enchanting touch—pasta would be served first, gravy meat on its heels. Then there'd be a break. Then a roast or two, usually chicken or pork, would be served, along with a few kinds of vegetables and potatoes and a giant salad (fresh from Grandma's garden whenever possible) sprinkled with raw minced garlic. Following another leisurely break, coffee would appear on the table (demitasse and American, the former served in tiny china cups and saucers with tiny spoons, a sliver of lemon rind for a touch of brightness, and a healthy splash of anisette), along with bowls of warm nuts (in their shells), fresh and dried fruit, and Grandma's *biscotti*. Slowly, other desserts would arrive, like homemade cheesecake (both Italian and American), bakery-bought *cannoli, sfogliatelle, pasticiotti* (cheese and custard varieties), rum babas, butter cookies, dried dates and figs, boxed *torrone*.

The family would gather around the table at two in the afternoon, maybe earlier, and not push away for the final time until at least eight o'clock. Dinner was a six- or seven-hour affair. We kids would jump away between courses, and disappear after we'd eaten dessert. The women would be up and down a lot, helping to produce the event. The men were stalwart, rising occasionally from the table to stretch their legs, use the john, take a snooze, or check sports scores—loosening their belts and saying "oof" as they rose heavily, food swelling their bellies—but otherwise remaining in place for the entire time. During the spring and summer months, there might be a bocce ball game after dinner, or a game of horseshoes. We might take the dessert course outside, where the proliferation of fireflies was utterly fantastic to me. We didn't have those in the Bronx.

Eventually, the good-byes would begin. More than forty minutes later they'd still be in progress, the entire family gathered and chattering at the door. This would continue for another ten or fifteen minutes outside at the car. Finally we'd load in and drive off, begging one last time for a sleepover even though we had school the next morning. My father would honk his horn as we pulled away, and everyone would wave and call out to one another as if we were heading cross-country and not planning to gather again the following week.

Maybe in some part of us we understood that these moments were fleeting, incandescent, and would someday soon—sooner than we knew—exist only in memory.

Part Two

— — — — — — — — — — — — —

THE HOUSE

YEARS

9.

In November 1971, less than two years after selling Cappi's, my father boldly moved us out of our one-bedroom apartment and into a big old house a block away. Perched high atop a winding stone staircase on an excessively rocky plot—its gray asphalt tiles giving it the appearance of being the biggest boulder on a great pile of smaller ones—the ramshackle mock Victorian was the sole private residence in a grid dense with apartment buildings. It had been abandoned for years and was said to be haunted. Every Halloween for as long as I could remember, neighborhood kids would dare one another other to run up the spooky stone stairs and knock at the heavy wooden door, fully expecting Vincent Price (as Dr. Phibes) to slither out of the darkness and snatch us into his lair. The old man who owned the place had once owned all the property around it. He'd made a bundle selling off parcels to developers but had never been able to part with the house. His daughter, Adele, a former pizza shop customer and den mother in my sisters' Girl Scout troop, stopped my mother in the street one day and tipped her off that he was finally ready to let go. She said she thought the old place would make a great home for our family, especially since my father was handy, and the price would be reasonable.

Mr. Marxson lived in a small brick house, newly built, on Bronx Park East (the next street over, heading west). My mother walked me up to his front gate one afternoon in late summer. She told me to go ring the bell and say that my father was interested in buying the property. (I don't think she even consulted my father about it beforehand, so desperate was she to move out of our apartment.)

"So tell him to come see me," grumbled Mr. Marxson.

That night, my parents had a private conversation at bedtime. I could hear their muffled tones but could not make out the words. Next day, I took the same walk with my father, only this time *he* did the talking. The old man named a price. My father countered with an offer of seventy percent less. "Sold," said Mr. Marxson, later regretting his decision and trying too late, after a binder had been signed, to back out of the deal. "Don't worry. He doesn't need the money," Adele assured my mother sweetly. New Jersey Grandma donated some cash to help with the down payment, and before I knew it we were packing up and moving in.

I remember walking through the house for the first time. It had been freshly whitewashed, the odor of cheap paint suspended in a musty stillness. Old wooden doors creaked as they opened into gracious, ample rooms dappled with sunlight filtering in through streaky windows. A lovely oak staircase graced an entrance foyer at the back of the house, which, earlier in the century, long before the development boom, when the area was all rolling hills and pastures, had been the front. (A backward-facing house—too conspicuously metaphorical.)

"You're moving into the *haunted house*?" gasped the neighbor children, too spooked to make fun of us.

And haunted it was: over the course of our first few months there, I spotted a tall old man in the military uniform of a bygone era, medals crowding his chest, sitting quietly in a wingback chair, rising softly and disappearing whenever I approached. I never mentioned it to anyone, but many years later my sister Maria asked me out of nowhere if I'd ever had such sightings. She had seen him too. He faded away after the first few months. (Who could blame him?)

We were drunk with pleasure over all this new space: ten rooms on three floors (counting the two separate halves of the attic), plus a basement, a yard, a wraparound porch. There were crawl spaces and hidden alcoves—and windows, windows everywhere, windows of every size and description. I counted them: thirty-two. ("Some job to wash them," my mother noted anxiously.) Best of all was my private bedroom, a first, just in time for adolescence. It was the smallest room in the house—a tight rectangle of space, about a hundred square feet, on the second floor, at the front—but I loved it like a castle, decorating and redecorating constantly, buying colorful throw rugs and appropriating items from around the house, keeping my little nest well ordered and squeaky clean.

"I'll be in my room if you need me." How I loved the sound of that. I saved up for months to buy a Lloyd's quadraphonic stereo sound system with built-in eight-track cassette player and space-age flip clock at Sears on Fordham Road, mounting one speaker on each of the four walls and blasting my favorite music—especially Melanie—until my eardrums throbbed. I had a major obsession with the singer and pasted pictures of her all over my closet door. When my father had had enough of her moaning and keening, he blasted into my room one night, ripped the needle off the record, and tore her pictures down, shredding them with his big hands and threatening to trash my brand-new Lloyd's quadraphonic stereo sound system with built-in eight-track cassette player and space-age flip clock. (That's when I discovered headphones.)

Our newly acquired staircase inspired Eva and me to act out scenes from our beloved *Hush . . . Hush, Sweet Charlotte*: "Okay, you be Bette Davis crawling up the stairs after her and Olivia de Havilland just dumped Drew's body in the swamp, and I'll be Joseph Cotten at the top of the stairs waiting for you. You climb up, see me, tumble down, and then I'll jump down over you and be Olivia de Havilland at the bottom of the stairs going, 'Hush, hush, sweet Charlotte.' "

We continued to share an intense love of classic movies, with a special affection for the overripe and campy. We adored *Charlotte* and *What Ever Happened to Baby Jane?* of course, twin masterworks by the director Robert Aldrich, but also embraced lesser expressions of the genre, like *Die! Die! My Darling!* (Tallulah Bankhead), *What's the Matter with Helen?* (Debbie Reynolds and Shelley Winters), *The Nanny* (Bette Davis), *The Baby* (Ruth Roman), *Berserk* and *Strait-Jacket* (Joan Crawford), *Dead Ringer* (Bette Davis as twins), the prison movies of Ida Lupino, and others of this ilk. They played constantly on our favorite movie channels. We memorized dialogue and blocking and broke into scenes at the drop of a hat.

When New York Grandma came to visit, we commandeered her wheelchair and acted out our favorite scenes from *Baby Jane,* taking turns in both roles. Grandma's condition had deteriorated to the point where it was no longer possible for my aunt and uncle to care for her at home. She had been installed at the very lovely (but still depressing) Providence Rest Nursing Home, a rolling estate on the waters of Pelham Bay. We visited her often (my aunt and uncle visited daily), wheeling her around the property in nice weather or collecting her from the sunroom—where she sat like a withered branch, staring at nothing, surrounded by others just like her—to lounge with her down in the lobby or to sip tea in the tiny "café," a room I found especially dismal for its insistently cheery décor. Grandma said nothing, seeming barely to register our presence.

"How do you feel, Grandma?" I'd ask awkwardly, not knowing how to talk to her now that she was a ghost.

"Lu'stess," she'd mumble in her Sicilian dialect: "The same."

The rest was silence.

Every few months or so, my father and I would bring her to the house for a weekend visit. I remember feeling unusually connected to my father on these Grandma-collecting missions. We were both unnerved by her condition and had to work closely in order to maneuver her lifeless form safely. (She was pretty much paralyzed by then.) My father encouraged me gently as we went, so unlike his usual style.

"Careful, Carl. Got a firm grip? Good going. Gently, now. Almost there. Nice job." We'd carry her, chair and all, up the stone steps and into the house, keeping her snugly wrapped in cold weather. Once inside, we'd lay her down on the couch, where she'd stay for the remainder of her visit, on her back, staring at the ceiling, motionless and silent as a clam, stirring only to eat, take medicine, or be carried to the bathroom. When it was time to bring her back, we'd reverse the process.

"Did you have a nice visit?" a kindly nun would ask, taking the chair from us to guide Grandma away. (The Sisters of St. John the Baptist owned and operated the home.)

"Yes, very nice," we'd say, Grandma staring vacantly.

"Good-bye, Grandma. Good to see you. Love you."

No response; just the sound of the rubber wheelchair rims rolling away across polished tiles, the soft shuffle of the nun's feet, the whoosh of her copious blue robes.

Though she seemed to be semicatatonic, the horrifying truth is that Grandma was fully alert: when you looked into her eyes you could see beneath their glazed surface a burning intensity. She knew exactly who and where she was, understood fully what was happening to her. I was her caretaker when she visited, and slept on an old recliner at the head of the couch in order to keep an eye on her overnight, rising when she moaned to lift her onto the wheelchair and into the bathroom. I'd transfer her gently to the toilet seat—hiking up her nightgown just slightly, pressing its worn cotton edges into her arthritic fingers, encouraging her to do the rest—and quietly recede while she did her business, lifting her off the bowl when she moaned again, and returning her to the couch. The intimacy of these nights and my role as her guardian pleased me deeply despite their inherent sadness. I still treasured Grandma, still remembered her as a force of nature, still saw in the watery depths of her eyes a spark of the special thing we once had. Sometimes she'd call me over to the couch, her voice the rasp of a rusty hinge.

"Cahllo."

"What is it, Grandma? Bathroom?"

She'd shake her head feebly and lift her arms, reaching for my hand.

"Come-a," she'd wheeze.

And then she'd grab hold of my hand with surprising strength and squeeze so hard that it actually hurt, pulling me toward her and staring into my eyes with candent ardor, her pupils pulsating, her eyelids frozen, her mouth a crooked gash. When I tried to pull away, she tightened her grip. The old gal had life in her yet!

"You're scaring me, Grandma," I told her during one such episode.

Her eyes died down then, her hand fell away.

He doesn't understand, she might have been thinking to her her-self. And I didn't. But I do now.

"You played Blanche last time! It's my turn!"

Eva and I fight over the wheelchair while Grandma vegetates in the next room. Long-suffering Blanche Hudson is the preferred role in our *Baby Jane* reenactments—especially for the rats in the cellar scene, into which Eva always injects real production value by digging out an old tray, improvising a fancy lid (usually made out of cardboard and aluminum foil, which my aunt Virginia called "alludian furl"), finding or creating a suitable something to play the dead rat, rear-ranging furniture, and just generally going that extra mile to set the scene. I love playing feeble, fallen Miss Hudson, tucked anxiously into my wheelchair, hungry and frightened. I hear Jane's demented shuffle approaching my room. The door opens and Jane enters, car-rying a tray and setting it down in front of me.

"Who was that at the door earlier?" I ask hopefully.

"Elvira" is Jane's flat response.

"Where is she now? In the kitchen?"

"No. I gave her the day off. She has a pretty hard time, consider-ing. Told her to come back next week."

My anxiety ratchets up a few notches. I twist my skeletal digits into the fringe of the threadbare blanket draped across my knees. Jane turns to leave. Then she turns back.

"Oh, Blanche, you know we got rats in the cellar?"

I cringe. Could it be? No, it couldn't. Yes, it could. But I'm so *hun-gry*! I must lift the lid! I reach for it. Cue suspense chord (supplied by Eva). Can't do it. Try again. Suspense chord. No go. Try one more time. Suspense chord. I tear the lid off the tray—to reveal a dead rat lying on a bed of lettuce, slices of tomato as garnish! I freak out in Blanche's particular way, making little, choked grunting sounds, pushing at the wheelchair in shock and confusion, ultimately driving myself around and around in mad circles as Jane howls with laughter just outside the door.

And cut. We switch roles.

Living in the haunted house was a badge of honor in the street. Other kids wanted to know what it looked like inside, and whether I'd encountered any ghosts. I regaled them with tales of terror, spoke of my fearlessness in the face of paranormal activity, invited a select few to come and see for themselves. I had always been embarrassed by our apartment building, frequently lying about where I lived. "Right there," I'd say when asked, pointing to one of the modern elevator buildings on our block with "fancy" lobbies and terraces off every apartment. I realize now that our old building was far lovelier, but at the time I considered its age a liability. Moving into the house changed all that—I lived someplace special now, someplace I could brag about. All was well. Things were looking up.

And then one Saturday afternoon when I was innocently going about my business, my father summoned me with six words that would change everything:

"*Bub*," he yelled, "gimme a hand with this."

Bub. He'd never called me that before. It wasn't a good sign.

I don't remember what he wanted help with that day—maybe ripping out an old radiator or tearing a window out of its socket or hacking up a chunk of the floor. I've purposely forgotten. All I know is that, whatever it was, I *hated it.* And it ended up taking *all day.* The next day my father called out the same words, again referring to me as *Bub,* again recruiting me into another nasty, daylong project. Soon, I was given a set of work clothes. It was then I realized that *Bub* was my slave name: Without ever formally announcing his intentions or articulat-ing a master plan of any kind, my father had apparently decided that he and I were going to gut this house while we were living in it—I mean gut it *completely*: walls, floors, ceilings, windows, plumbing, electricity, *everything,* down to the bare beams, down to the *bones*—and then build it back up again inch by inch, foot by foot, room by room. All ten rooms. All three floors. From that first Saturday afternoon for-ward, every weekend for the rest of my teenage years was spent in an endless cycle of hard labor.

On weekdays, I'd come home from school and find to-do lists waiting for me on the kitchen table, written in carpenter pencil on ragged scraps of brown paper:

BUB
DEMOLISH REAR AND SIDE WALLS OF YOUR BEDROOM
RIG ROPE AND BUCKET PULLEY SYSTEM
USE PULLEY SYSTEM TO LOWER RUBBLE INTO SIDE YARD
FORM RUBBLE INTO PILE
DIG 6' X 6' TRENCH
BURY RUBBLE IN TRENCH

"He's gonna bury *me* in that trench," my mother would say. "That's what it's really for." I got angry when she talked liked this, which she did quite often. I scolded her freely about it, but she'd just smile and assure me that it was true.

"Ooh, if I only had the strength!" she'd often moan while we were still living in the apartment. "I'd go up to that roof and throw myself off, I really would!"

Or: "Every night I pray to God that I won't wake up in the morning. But every morning, there I am."

Her dream of home ownership had quickly become a turbid nightmare of demolition and chaos. She tried desperately to keep a semblance of order, dusting and mopping constantly against a tide of pulverized plaster, biting back sobs and muttering about how other women did not have to endure this. She had stopped working for Aunt Diana months earlier, when the travel agency moved its field office to New Jersey, and took a full-time job at TNT Appliances, a dirty, messy repair shop and appliance parts supplier located directly under the El on White Plains Road. My mother occupied a cluttered booth at the back of the long, narrow shop, answering phones, scheduling appointments, dispatching workmen, balancing books, and generally running the place for nine hours a day in exchange for a miserly sum that was insulting even then. When she came home at the end of the workday, it was to a house being ripped apart. (She'd remain at TNT for eighteen years.)

Demolition was the easy bit. On Saturdays and Sundays we'd do the really heavy work, like ripping out, rerouting, and replacing plumbing and electrical lines; displacing and replacing wall beams and floor beams; dropping and hoisting ceilings; drywalling and spackling and sanding and priming and painting; mixing and pouring thousands of pounds of cement; cutting and threading miles of pipe and tubing; slicing lumber; carrying loads and loads and loads of raw material into and out of the house . . . the list is endless.

"Up and at 'em, Bub," were the horrid words I'd wake up to on Saturday mornings. (I thought he was saying "Up and Adam," which made no sense. But then, none of this made any sense.) I'd linger under the sheets for as long as possible, until my father started screaming my name madly or marched into my room to dump a glass of water into my sleeping face. I started counting time from the moment my feet hit the floor.

"Let's see, if I drag my ass as hard as I can and don't start working until ten and we break for lunch at one, that's three hours. If we're back to work at two and we break for dinner at six, that's just four more hours, seven hours total. And already, just figuring this out, ten minutes have passed, so that's six hours and fifty minutes. And if I go to the bathroom a couple of extra times, that's another ten minutes, so we're down to almost just six hours total," and on and on. And on.

My poor mother would see me sometimes all covered from head to toe in plaster dust, streaked with sweat, blistered and sore and impossibly miserable, and say, "This is your penance. You'll do this only once in your life. You'll never have to do this again." Saturdays were no picnic for her either. She'd start the day by going grocery shopping with Josie, her old friend from Cappi's, who had a car and took her around to the markets and specialty shops on Allerton Avenue. Josie would arrive in the morning and have breakfast at the kitchen table with us before she and my mother headed out for the day.

"Just some tea and dry toast, Mary," she'd say, still unable to eat like a normal person. (Her son Eddie and I remained friends but hung out a lot less often these days . . . perhaps to avoid getting into the kind of sexual horseplay his friend Gene and I engaged in regularly.) Josie loved to gross us out with breathless tales of her weekly mishaps, most of which involved bodily functions gone wrong.

"So I was sitting on the bus and this man was standing in front of me and he sneezed really hard and I felt something wet land on my cheek and I knew it was snot but I didn't wanna say anything so I just covered it with my glove and when I got home I ran into the bathroom and there was a loogie the size of a giant oyster hanging down from my chin all green and yellow and—"

"So I was driving home from the doctor and all of a sudden I realized that I hadda take a diarrhea and I says oh my God I gotta take a diarrhea but I'm on the Cross Bronx over here there's no place to pull over what the hell am I gonna do and then I felt something funny and I says wait a minute I think it's coming out and oh my God I started to panic and the next thing you know I emptied out my pocketbook the good one with the silver handle that my cousin Brenda Ann gave me you know the one and I pushed it under me and I says I'm just gonna have to go in here. And I did! So now I had a pocketbook fulla fresh diarrhea and the car was all stinked up and my underwear was tangled around my knees and—"

"Ew, Josie! Stop! Enough!" we'd shout, at once delighted and repulsed.

I lingered at the breakfast table for as long as I could, desperate not to begin the workday. My father would storm in and out of the kitchen in a cloud of cigarette smoke, already dirty from an early morning work session, gruffly telling me it was "time to get started."

"I'm still eating breakfast," I'd say, sluggardly spooning cereal into my mouth.

"Oh, hi, Cappi," Josie would chirp. His response was a grunt. "I don't think he likes me," she'd fret. And he didn't. My father approved of none of the people any of us brought into the house, approved only of his own friends and associates.

Stepping into Bub's theater of operations always filled me with grief and panic. How I hated this! My father never told me what we were doing or what to expect. He never stopped to teach or train me. He just barked orders and exploded when I didn't do things correctly, expecting that I would somehow know my way around this type of skilled labor. The sound of my mother and Josie returning home just before lunchtime was the sweetest music: I'd leap like an antelope out the front door and down to the car, carrying bundles of groceries inside, breathing great gulps of fresh air, poking my head into the bags to see what treats my mother had picked up—maybe Chips Ahoy! cookies or Triscuits and Laughing Cow cheese or Gino's pizza rolls. After putting the groceries away, my mother would go out to a nearby diner for lunch with Josie while my father and I took our only break of the day.

"Don't knock it till you've tried it," Dad would say as I moaned in disgust over his favorite sandwich: half a loaf of Italian bread scooped out and filled with a pile of salami, a pile of provolone . . . and a fistful of raw chopped beef.

We didn't talk much during lunch, my father and I, but just quietly devoured our sandwiches while gazing into the tiny screen of the kitchen TV (always on). Classic westerns were typical Saturday afternoon fare on the local movie channels, and we'd sometimes sit for a few extra minutes to catch more of the action. I didn't care for westerns but would gladly have watched every one ever made if it meant not returning to the killing fields.

"They don't make 'em like this anymore," Dad would comment wistfully. "*That's* the way to make a movie."

"It's great," I'd agree.

I remember thinking in these quiet moments that this was what Saturday afternoons could be like, free like this, easy, spending a couple of hours watching a western with your dad, cleaning your room, maybe, and then running out to find your friends in the street.

"All right, Bub. Back to work."

By the time my mother returned from lunch an hour or so later, my father would have worked himself into a rage. What was taking her so long? Why did she think she could go gallivanting around with her friend while he was left to labor miserably?

"Where were you?" he'd bark when she walked back in.

"I had more shopping to do."

"Oh yeah? Where are the packages?"

"They're outside."

"You're *lying*!"

"Phil—please."

And they were off, my father berating my mother about wasting time and money with "that woman," my mother whimpering, eventually crying, saying she wished she were dead. Her Saturday lunches with Josie were the only real break in Mom's week, the only little slivers of time that didn't belong to somebody else. She was willing to pay this price for them, willing to exchange a full pound of pain for each paltry ounce of pleasure.

My sisters weren't off the hook either. The proper Twisted Head home is a brutal workplace for all. My father had them working in the yard, running errands, even doing some light demolition. Eva got the brunt of it. Maria was still too young—eight years old when we moved into the house—and Rosette had ways of making herself scarce. She had taken a full-time secretarial job at Union Carbide ("down the city") and was now more like a boarder than a family member. My father kept a close eye on her but had otherwise backed off considerably, realizing, I think, that my sister, nearly twenty, would soon be out of his clutches anyway.

"Ho! How's the Taj Mahal coming over here, hah?" Dino's voice at the back door was always a welcome noise. He'd drop by once in a while, just for quick minute. Other friends of my father's would do the same. (Men love to watch other men work.)

Dino smelled like the sea—or the bay, anyway—living, as he did, in a one-bedroom beach bungalow on City Island with his wife and four children. Their family was another mirror reflection of my own:

three girls and a boy roughly the same ages as my sisters and me, tight living quarters, strained budget. Dino and my father had met during the war, and it was easy to see how much Dad loved him. He'd always brighten in his buddy's presence, suddenly becoming playful and light, and often packed us into the car for spontaneous spins "to the island." I remember all-night poker games at Dino's kitchen table (his chain-smoking, highly charismatic, somewhat mannish wife, Esther, Jewish, the only woman in attendance), we kids flopping on bunk beds and floor pallets, giggling and laughing until we drifted off to sleep to the reassuring sound of occasional roars rising from the next room.

Daytimes, we'd picnic on the cement patio—strung with party lights for nighttime affairs—stairs from which led right onto the sands of the beach. There was a little shack packed with fins, rafts, tubes, snorkeling gear, and other such necessities. We'd grab a few pieces and head into the surf (notoriously polluted at the time). I nearly drowned when I attempted to breathe through a snorkel tube underwater, inhaling a good half gallon or so before realizing that the simple hose was not a magical source of oxygen. When my father took me out on a rowboat and tried to teach me how to handle a fishing rod, I very nearly ripped his eye out with my awkward line-casting technique. Luckily, he was wearing a visor cap; my hook snatched it handily, swung the cap wildly above our heads for a moment, and then dropped it into the soup. My father glared at me long and hard. He said nothing, but I could hear his words clearly: What on God's green earth is *wrong with you*? He rowed us back to shore in a lather, muttering Barese curses the whole way.

I bet you wish Angelo was your son, I remember thinking. Dino's boy was a bronze, sandy, beach jock, slinging gear and working the water like he was born to it. He and my father traded fishing stories and other adventure tales. Sorry, Dad, I thought self-pityingly. I know I'm not the son you wanted.

"Feel good, Carli?" Dino would ask on his Saturday afternoon drop-ins.

"Not really," I'd say, neck-deep in one gruesome task or another.

"Sure, not yet. 'Cause you're doing inside the walls. You can't *see* your work at the end of the day. But wait till you start Sheetrocking and painting—that's when you can *see* the progress. *That* part you'll like." I loved Dino, so funny and gentle—Art Carney to my father's Jackie Gleason—but this was not the kind of hope I sought. Sheetrocking and painting would be my salvation? I wanted to pull him aside and beg him to make my father stop—or at least leave me out of it.

"He trusts you, Dino," I imagined saying. "He listens to you. Tell him this is crazy. Tell him I'm too young to do this. Tell him I'm living in hell. Can't you see I'm living in hell?" Instead, I smiled and tried to allow his encouraging tones to work on me, having learned by then to take solace where I found it.

Ann Lazerta, another holdover from the halcyon days of Cappi's and the Villa Reda, visited our house often and always had a sympathetic word for me. She once saw me walk by the table fresh from a hellish scene of demolition, coated and caked with dust and debris.

"Ooh, Carl honey, that's no good, sweetheart. That's no good for your lungs. Drink a glass of milk, it'll clean them out." I was grateful for any advice. I drank the milk. If it had gone through my lungs, I would have drowned. But she believed in milk, Ann did. *Scotch* and milk, actually. That was her drink. "Because the ulcer." But that's another story. Ann loved stories. She loved *one main* story, actually, which she told all the time. It changed slightly, depending on the day, but always went pretty much like this:

"So, I got up about seven. I made my coffee, you know. I drank it. And then I says, Let me take my shower. So I took my shower. And while I was in there I says, I'm gonna wash out my panties. So I washed out my panties, you know, just in the shower like. And then I hung 'em up to dry on the shower bar, you know, the rod, and then I came outta the shower and I says, Let me get dressed. And so I dried off, you know, with a towel, and I got dressed—"

And on it went from there, her story. Every moment of her day, every meaningless detail. For hours. She'd be dolled up for it too, her hair meticulously coiffed, dressed in a velour designer maxi lounging gown with jewel-encrusted slippers and matching accessories. She took little mincing steps like a geisha . . . only Sicilian. She lived in a building just across the street, and we could see her heading over. My mother, my poor mother, dreaded these visits and panicked as Ann approached.

"Oh God, she's coming over again, I can't take it. I'd rather pull my eyes out with a poker. I'd rather set my hair on fire. I'm gonna put a bullet in my head—"

Ding-dong. "Oh hi, Ann. Come in. You want a drink?"

There were times when Mom really couldn't bear a visit and she'd turn off all the lights and have us scatter throughout the house in hiding so Ann would think no one was home. It would have been within her rights (but it was not in her power) to put a stop to these visits, since Ann was just using my mother as a kind of beard . . . and a source of free booze.

She had a boyfriend, Ann did, and twice a week, sometimes

more, he'd tell his wife he was "taking the dog out" and she'd tell her husband she was "going to Mary's" and the secret lovers would meet in Bronx Park. (Now that I think of it, Ann was probably naked under all that velour.) At some point during each of her visits, the phone would ring. If anyone other than my mother answered, a meek, nasally man's voice would ask, "Is Mary there?" This was code, and we kids knew it.

"Ann, it's for you." She always acted surprised.

"Really? For me?" She'd stay on the phone for a few minutes and then announce that she was going to "take a walk," as if this were normal for a visitor. Off she'd go to meet Nicky-Nack (his name was Nick, but she insisted on this affectation), returning after an hour or so with not a hair out of place. She'd down another drink or two, smoke a few more cigarettes, and finally leave for the night. By that point my poor mother would be hunched over the kitchen table, exhausted and furious, her fist planted firmly in her teeth to keep from belting Ann in the mouth. It never occurred to her to express her displeasure directly, and Ann seemed oblivious to her suffering. Indeed, she seemed oblivious to much of what went on around her. Maybe that's one reason I liked her and found her presence comforting: she was a model of disengagement, tranquil and pristine amid the chaos. My father didn't like Ann and didn't approve of these visits. He knew what was going on with Nicky-Nack in the park at night, knew my mother was a beard for it, knew we kids knew the whole deal—and liked none of it. But he held his tongue, a rare exercise of restraint, perhaps out of a sense of loyalty from the Cappi's years. Ann sailed glacially along—impervious, well accessorized, and nicely pickled.

And what of the house itself? What had the poor old place done to deserve this violent assault? It wasn't really in such bad shape when we moved in. A little neglected and moldy, definitely in need of freshening up. But it didn't need its guts ripped out, its face torn off. Only my father could explain (though he never did) why it was necessary to attack with hammers and claws the twelve-foot molded tin ceilings, ripping them open here and there, and then build frames nearly five feet lower than the original height so we could nail up Sheetrock ceilings that barely cleared the tops of our heads. Only he could explain (but again, did not) why we needed to attack the soaring, graceful archways that connected one room to another, hacking them up, squaring them off, and shrinking them down to hobbit size.

How about the stunning array of old sash windows and bay windows and cabinet windows, and even a couple of stained-glass windows? Why was it necessary to rip out every single one of them, trash them, and replace them with . . . well, *wall,* in most cases, or tiny little crank windows set ridiculously high, like on a ship or in a prison cell? There was no answer. There was not, in fact, even a question. It just *was.* The living room wound up with no windows at all. It originally had four of them, sunlight dancing in through oversize panes of watery glass, plus an old country door leading out to a pillared wraparound porch—all junked. Our renovation rendered the room squared off, shrunken down, and pitch-black, opening now onto an enclosed cement box, uselessly L-shaped, with Styrofoam drop ceilings and fluorescent lighting. Tara's back parlor and veranda had successfully been transformed into the horrifying dayroom of a state asylum. Why?

The house vomited out of its windows and doors a steady stream of demolished plaster and heavy debris, which amassed itself into piles all around the little property. Piles and piles. And these piles, my father sometimes decided, had to be moved. I'd get a series of to-do lists instructing me to move a certain pile of rubble to various points all around the house until it had made a complete rotation—just like in *Bent,* the play and then the movie. But *Bent* takes place in a Nazi concentration camp in Poland. And I was supposedly in the middle of my childhood in the Bronx. I think in *Bent,* actually, it's rock piles that the prisoners are forced to move back and forth, not mounds of demolition debris. Of the two, the latter is more difficult to handle. I can say this with some authority because I've had experience with both.

The rock piles were a consequence of my father's conviction that the property around our house was too *rocky* and needed a thorough *sifting.* Producing a huge, industrial-strength screen he'd built at work, he instructed Eva and me to sift the entire contents of the back and side yards. It took months, but we finally finished the job. When it was over, and after Bub had gotten a good workout moving the resulting rock pile all around the perimeter of the house, there were heavy rains. We ended up knee-deep in mud. Not to worry. Cappi had a solution: put them back. Dig the rocks back *into* the ground. (A new twist for Martin Sherman, author of *Bent,* should he wish to write a sequel.)

I missed out on dozens of Bar Mitzvahs. My Jewish friends and I were turning thirteen when we first moved into the house. I had many invitations. And I loved a Bar Mitzvah. To me, it was like a wedding but for just one kid. The really fancy ones were at Leonard's of Great Neck or Terrace on the Park in Flushing (it revolves), where they'd serve stuffed derma and chopped liver and other exotic treats. There would be live bands and floral centerpieces and matchbooks with your friend's name embossed in gold. "Barry" in fancy script on a satin matchbook. Loved it.

"Dad, it's Eric Golub's Bar Mitzvah next Saturday and they're having it at—"

"Not on *my* time, Bub."

That was his stock answer. Not on *my* time.

And all my time was his.

10.

I had started attending Junior High School 135, named for the number of ways you could get killed before lunch, just a couple of months
before we moved into the house. The cramped, ugly schoolhouse was
a dead ringer for an outbuilding in a Siberian penal colony, replete
with razor wire and heavy gates barring the windows. "Race riots"
were daily occurrences: Kill Whitey Day, Kill Blackey Day, Kill Rican
Day, and Kill . . . just *Kill* Day. A kid I knew was stabbed to death in
the school yard for his banana-seat bicycle. You'd expect a little
school-sponsored counseling for the student body after a tragedy like
this, but none was forthcoming. We heard not a word from our teachers or administrators on this or any related topic. They simply were
not equipped.

Take Miss Terrance, our math teacher (please): tall and skinny as
a pole, a tuft of white hair poking up from the top of her head, oversize horn-rimmed spectacles magnifying her soggy eyeballs. Poor
Miss T was only nominally functional, her black dresses turning gray
before our very eyes as she choked on clouds of chalk dust while use-

lessly sounding out commands in a voice trapped inside her head and sinus cavity, like the speaking voice of a deaf-mute ("Ghlass, ghum do order now, ghlass"), her classroom teeming with scenes of near-fornication, glue sniffing, switchblade practice, and worse. That's an exaggeration: outright criminal activity was less common in classrooms than in public areas . . . unless you happened to be in one of the "special" sections. The school's tier system grouped kids according to academic aptitude: 7–1 was the most advanced class, 7–2 the next most advanced, 7–3 the next, et cetera—the numbers continuing all the way up to 7–17. The double-digit tiers were where the roughest action happened. I didn't catch much of it firsthand, since nerds like me were grouped into the highest level of the caste system, the "SPs." I forget what "SP" stood for—"special placement" I think, not to be confused with "Special Ed"—but I started out in 7SP-1, the school's intellectual elite, scheduled to skip eighth grade. I guess it made me cocky.

My childhood friend Mitchell Blodnick had matriculated into 7SP-1 right alongside me, and we quickly built a reputation for being inspired class clowns, hooked on hearing a steady stream of laughter, our increasingly bold antics getting us sent to the dean's office on a regular basis. One of our many offenses had been the moronic mocking of a classmate's surname: *Muñez*. Victor *Mucous* we dubbed him, repeating it at every opportunity, making up little skits and stories about the Mucous family.

"Happy birthday, Victor Mucous. Here's your gift—a box of tissues and a handkerchief. Ah-ha-ha-ha." I'm not proud of it. Dean Zizzo, fierce and swarthy, barked at Mitchell and me from behind her desk, a tangle of keys jangling in her cleavage.

"What's your last name?"

"Capotorto."

"*Crap*otorto, *Clap*otorto, *Crack*otorto—you like that?"

"No."

"And how 'bout you? What's your last name?"

"Blodnick."

"*Blob*nick, *Slob*nick, *Glob*nick—you like that?"

"Nope."

"THEN STOP DOING IT! BOTH OF YOU! NOW GET BACK TO CLASS!"

But we didn't stop. We were both demoted in the spring, dumped with a thud into 7–2, a dizzying reproach. I begged my teachers for mercy, but the decision was final. Stung by the summary ejection, I was terrified about what my father's reaction might be. But his response to the whole affair turned out to be oddly muted. He seemed more hurt than anything else, saying little, just staring at me with genuine disappointment and sadness in his eyes. Same with my mother. It wasn't discussed at school either: the demotion was announced and that was that. No stern talking-to, no visit to the guidance counselor, nothing. All this silence was deafening. I buckled down and got serious, applying myself with new focus and vigor. Mitchell and I started spending less time together, like two drunks trying not to tempt each other off the wagon. Enid Blodnick tried to have Mitchell's demotion reversed, and I remember overhearing her confront a school official in the hallway.

"Well, that's just not good enough," she was saying. Then she turned to her husband, the cauliflower-eared, mutton-nosed, heavily bespectacled Mr. Blodnick.

"What do you think, Shulie? Should we go over his head?"

"Anything you say, Enid," was his beaten-down reply.

"Ghlass, now, ghlass, blease—" poor Miss Terrance continued droning endlessly, to absolutely no avail. As minutes passed and chaos mounted, she'd crack, hopping suddenly onto the windowsill, half-clambering out onto the ledge, and screaming:

"I'm gonna JUMMMMP!"

The room would fall silent.

She had our attention. She'd climb back down.

"Okay. Now. Turn to page forty-six and work on exercises one through . . ." and chaos would erupt anew.

"Shit, she ain't gonna jump. So anyway I called my cousin Pooni and I tole her Tuni said Suki is going with Pooki and Tino and I could go with them, but she said no because then I can't go with Coco and Pito like my mother said! No because my mother said!"

All the kids in school, especially the girls, spoke in a Nuyorican accent. It was just the hip way to sound. Didn't matter whether you were Jewish or Italian or Irish. Even little Gita Polaski got in on the action: "No *pero* because why you gotta be like that?" Her people hailed from *Krakow,* a long way from the islands. What was up? The teachers seemed not to notice, consumed as they were by their own disorders. The ones who weren't completely nuts had simply checked out . . . like Mrs. Balbos, our typing instructor, a kind of somnambulant Cro-Magnon woman, with giant head and hairy arms.

"All right, class, put your paper in the roller and roll it up until you get to the top of the page," she'd intone monotonously through thick, fleshy lips.

"Very good. Now type four x's. Now type three spaces. Now type twelve x's. And hit return. Very good. Now type six spaces. Now type eight x's. Now type four spaces. Now type twenty x's." And so on, until finally: "Now roll your paper out of the carriage and take a look. It's a portrait of Spiro T. Agnew."

Mr. Bonzitti was supposed to be teaching us Italian. Instead, we learned how to decorate the room like a Roman garden using paper cutouts and water paint, and how to make eggs in paradise and other humble dishes from the Old Country.

"The first thing you'll need is a nice marinara sauce"—and out would come a tub of it, homemade, along with a hot plate, cookware, utensils.

"You just heat up the sauce nice-nice in a little skillet, and when it's good and hot, gently bubbling, you crack two eggs into it. Cover the pan and let the eggs poach for a while, nice-nice. When they're all white and congealed, spoon them out just like this, with plenty of sauce, onto a slice of crusty bread. Grate some cheese over it, eat and enjoy. Delicious. Class dismissed."

We had learned one Italian word: *marinara.* But at least the man was fun, alive, engaging. (And if truth be told, he *did* teach us Italian. I still retain the basic vocabulary and essential rules of grammar he gave us.)

While walking around the room checking homework one day, Mr. B came upon Grace Delgado, a gussied-up, gum-snapping princess.

"I forgot," she muttered casually, inspecting her manicure.

"You forgot?" the teacher pressed. "Really? Did you forget ya hair spray? Did you forget ya nail polish? Did you forget ya makeup? Did you forget ya gold chains, ya tight pants, that little top ya wearing—did you forget those? No. Those you remembered. Your *homework,* though, *that* you forgot. Nice, very nice. *Zero!*"

He meant it, but he was also being campy. Mr. Bonzitti was flamboyantly gay . . . and it didn't seem to matter. I considered his classroom a safe zone.

The death of my mother's older brother, my cherished uncle Joe, hit me hard. I wasn't ready to return to the rough-and-tumble of the fray and lingered after Italian class, my last period before lunch, to ask Mr. Bonzitti if I could eat my sandwich in the empty classroom.

"Why?" he wondered, comforting me when he heard the answer, confiding in me about his father's frail health (Mr. B lived with him and was his caretaker), turning off the overhead lights and letting me sit quietly at the back of the room while he busied himself at his desk.

Toward the end of the period, he ambled over and asked how I was doing. I felt better now, calmer. The room was chill and dark. My teacher looked down at me kindly, taking in my obvious fondness for early seventies bling: several chunky silver rings made from cutlery handles, wide silver cuff and POW/MIA bracelets, and a huge cross-shaped medallion festooned with sparkly stones in various shades of blue.

"So," he said meaningfully, "you like *jewlary,* hah?"

"Yeah," I answered softly, looking back at him with candor, trying to show myself to him, knowing full well what we were saying to each other.

"You're gonna be fine," he said after a moment. "Better get ready for class." I thanked him, gathered myself, and exited into the teeming hallway as a bell clanged hard above my head, signaling the end of lunch period. Students started streaming into Mr. Bonzitti's room, now brightly lit, as I walked away. I don't think he had time to eat lunch that day.

In the hallways and bathrooms and stairwells, it wasn't unusual to be set upon by gangs of ruffians demanding money. When you said you didn't have any, they'd answer, "Oh yeah? All I fin', all I keep?" which meant you were about to be frisked and mugged. It was fight or flight at that point; I usually chose flight. My sister Eva spoke of a veritable organized crime ring operating out of the girls' bathroom, composed of hard young vixens demanding a steady flow of cash from their weaker or unprotected peers, beating to a pulp those who failed to pay up, stuffing their victims' heads into dirty toilet bowls—and flushing. Eva had wisely chummed up to one of the tough girls, and so was safe. She had started hanging out in the Eastchester projects, and was dating a Puerto Rican kid named Hector. My mother was unhappy about the fact of Hector but helped hide it from my father. ("Birds of a feather flock together, Eva," whispered Aunt Diana unhelpfully.)

In an effort to be more "fly," Eva started ironing her hair—literally bending her head over my mother's ironing board and dragging the old steam appliance across her poor, tortured mane, sometimes pinning an artificial Afro poof to the top or back. She ironed her jeans to a crisp, pressing a tight crease down the center of each leg, and wore hoop earrings and a two-tone, maxi-length leather jacket. She began to speak in Nuyorican cadences and brought thrilling new music into the house—by Marvin Gaye, Donny Hathaway, Isaac Hayes, Curtis Mayfield, Bobby Womack, Aretha Franklin, Minnie Riperton, Barry White and the Love Unlimited Orchestra, New Birth, First Choice, the Emotions, and so many others (all of it leading inexorably to the imminent birth of disco). I loved this music immediately, just as I'd loved the music she'd brought home years earlier—James Brown, the Supremes, the Jackson 5, the Stylistics, the Delfonics, the Spinners—and tried to imitate the laid-back, salsa-inflected dance style of Eva and her friends.

She let me tag along with her to the projects occasionally, but only once I'd been properly styled and attired: she ironed my jeans and somehow frayed the outside seams into fringe—a popular ghetto effect at the time—and directed me to buy nylon T-shirts in dark colors, a three-quarter-length Shaft-style jacket in brown leather (on sale at Alexander's), and black-on-black Playboy shoes. I completed the look by slicking back my hair and wearing a single silver bangle bracelet. I liked the flyboy effect and thought I wore it well, but my preferred personal style was more on the mod side—print shirts and bell-bottoms, hair blown back and sprayed. When one day I wore a slender belt covered in bright green sequins, my favorite accessory, a boy pointed at me and said, "Look! He really *is* a fag!" But I went right on dressing to the nines, despite the cost. My cream-colored, pre-platform shoes with dangling fake brass coins instead of buckles were to me the height of fashion, but made me a laughingstock among the tough kids.

"Hey, yo! I used to had a pair a' shoes like that . . . but then my father got a job! Ha-ha-ha-ha-ha!"

This particular boy considered me too ridiculous to bother attacking, finding me much more useful as comic fodder, but that was not generally the case: a few fearsome bullies tormented me throughout my entire three-year career at 135.

Carmine Colaci, an overdeveloped, overly hairy thug in training, was fond of striding up to me in the school yard, surrounded by his crew, taunting me and calling me "faggot," knocking books and food out of my hand, punching me to the ground. I was terrified of him . . . and also secretly attracted. Perhaps it was mutual; perhaps he just wanted to be intimate with me, for intimate he made us: fear of Carmine ruled my world. One day, finally, I could take no more and just broke on him, suddenly shouting words I still remember:

"What do you want from me? Do you want to know that you can beat me up? Is that what you want? Okay: you can beat me up! You're a better fighter than me. Okay? So now you know it. So why don't you just leave me alone now, hunh?"

Carmine blinked and backed up a few paces, waving me off with his arm as if I weren't worth a moment more of his time, summoning his crew and stalking away. He never bothered me again. The same technique failed to work as effectively with slim, sexy Fernando, a rough-trade heartthrob who'd been victimizing me since grade school. He was more violent than Carmine (hotter too, which complicated matters), and put a real hurting on me many times. Here, again, there was a clear homoerotic subtext: Fernando was fond of getting his boys to hold my arms and legs, stepping back to take a good look at me all restrained and struggling, then sauntering forward with sex in his eyes, leaning erotically over my mouth, forcing it open with his hand, and spitting down my throat, long and slow. Then he'd punch me in the stomach and walk away. (If Fernando is still alive, he's a gay dungeon master.) The fact that I was secretly attracted to my tormentors did nothing to make their attacks more palatable. I still rushed home to scrub Fernando's spit out of my mouth, gargling with Listerine so hard that I'd end up vomiting, still lay awake at night nursing violent revenge fantasies, still sent away for the Charles Atlas brochure, determined to transform myself from a ninety-eight-pound weakling into a mighty muscleman capable of vanquishing all enemies with a single blow (an effort hindered by my keen and immediate disdain for weight lifting).

Maurice Wilson was another hunky scourge upon my back, a muscular, handsome kid in need of a good bath and some mouthwash. He was fond of pushing me into hallway corners and demanding cash.

"Gimme whatcha got, gimme whatcha got, gimme whatcha got . . ."

I gave him money the first time he accosted me, a mistake, but quickly learned to wriggle out of any hold he put me in, and eventually he gave up trying.

I dreaded navigating all common areas, especially the gymnasium and locker room. At these times, I became unnaturally aware of every movement I made with my body, each changing expression on my face, the appearance of my clothes and hair. My profound discomfort was itself an invitation to ridicule and mock me, which my cocky peers accepted with glee. I remember once having to walk down a long hallway past a group of boys who started heckling me from a good distance away. I happened to be carrying an old Decca record in a paper sleeve—my mother's treasured recording of "One Meat Ball" by the Andrews Sisters—that I'd brought in for a show-and-tell history assignment. As I approached the boys and their taunts crescendoed, I began banging the record against my leg rhythmically, not realizing what I was doing until I heard an awful *crack* and felt the old 78 collapse into pieces inside its brittle sleeve. My heart sank. My mother had owned this record since the 1940s! Panic rose.

"See what you made me do?" I shouted.

"See what you made me doooo?" they mimicked in the whiny strains of a girlie-boy. After school, I raced to Harry's Hardware under the El, broken record in hand.

"How do I fix it?" I asked desperately. "Can I glue it?"

"Not really," offered tall meek Harry. "It's just broken."

I bought two tubes of epoxy and frantically reassembled the pieces, creating a sticky, lumpy mess. I tucked my Frankenstein creation carefully into its yellowed paper sleeve and buried it in a box deep in the recesses of the attic, where it remains to this day.

Who were these boys so confident of their youthful masculinity, their *coolness,* their sense of entitlement? What did they recognize in one another that allowed them to bond so readily? And what was it that they *didn't* see in me? I knew the painful answer: I was a *faggot.* Not necessarily effeminate, but ethereal, a dreamer. Sensitive and soft-spoken. Shy. Quiet.

Faggot.

I hated being alone with other boys (the presence of girls softened and equalized the atmosphere for me) and tried everything I could think of to get out of gym class—regularly faking chronic knee problems, shortness of breath, bouts of dizziness and nausea. My excuses usually sufficed to keep me tucked into the bleachers, but occasionally I'd be forced to join a game of basketball or volleyball. I had no natural affinity or affection for these activities, and no one had taught me anything about them. I guess I was just supposed to know how to play sports by virtue of being a boy. As I humiliated myself on the gym floor—always picked last for any team ("Naw, man! Not fair! We hadda have him last time!")—I could hear girls taking class on the other side of the divider. A cute little ditty was playing on a record player and the girls were all singing along, presumably dancing a dainty little step.

Go, you chicken fat, go away!

Why couldn't the boys dance and sing? Why did every social interaction between us have to be a scene from *Lord of the Flies*? The best part of gym class was the bell signaling its end, at which point we'd scurry down to the locker room, pull our pants up over our gym shorts, and race off to the next class before the next bell rang. No extra time was provided, so it was a game of Beat the Clock. I was grateful for the lack of nudity and the overall brevity of the locker room experience. Any class immediately following gym period was my favorite class of the day.

I started smoking pot in eighth grade. Serena Tibbins, a friend and soul mate who I'm sure turned out to be a lesbian, rolled a joint one day after school and asked if I wanted to try it. We were already smoking cigarettes, having started a year earlier. (I regularly swiped cigarettes from my father's packs of Kent 100s, eventually switching to menthol and buying my own packs of Kool.) But pot was different. I hesitated. I thought about my father.

"I have chores to do when I go home."

"Oh, you'll be able to do your chores," enthused Serena. "Not only that—you'll *love* doing them!"

We slipped into a hidden corner and toked up. The effect was subtle, but Serena was right: I moved through my afternoon chores with greater ease than usual. Digging ditches was actually engrossing, and the work felt good in my body. I was a little spacey and hungry afterward, but content. The next day, Serena and I toked up again . . . and we were off and running. Pot put me more comfortably in touch with myself, helped hold my general discomfort at a safe remove; it *insulated* me.

My St. Lucy's friends continued to be a lifeline. How I longed for them at my side, sometimes imagining them there, as I negotiated the perils of 135, but they were still attending St. Lucy's School and would soon disperse to various local Catholic high schools. We met as frequently as possible, hanging out for hours on "the corner" (the intersection of Bronxwood and Mace avenues, on opposite sides of which sat St. Lucy's Church and St. Lucy's School), imitating our ridiculous teachers (the nuns were even more whacked out than the teachers in public school—and had the option of using physical force), reenacting scenes from our favorite B-horror movies ("Dr. Cushing, Dr. Cushing come quickly! Mrs. Cushing is growing, she's, she's becoming huge—she's—she's—ARGGHHHHH!"), and dancing the Pony at the drop of a hat to new music by Carole King, Carly Simon, Seals & Crofts, Melanie, Cat Stevens, and others of the era. We joined the St. Lucy's Catholic Youth Organization (CYO), which sponsored rap sessions and dances and occasional day trips.

The CYO was "run by radicals," according to my father. He had taken sides in a parish rift over the embattled Monsignor Rosetti, who'd been brought in to replace the newly deceased founding monsignor. Rosetti, cold and strict in the extreme, possessed all the charm of a Nazi dentist. He even looked the part: tall, pinch-faced, and silver-haired, with supererect posture and a forward-thrusting chest. The haughty high priest made some unpopular changes right away, like replacing all the church's lovely old votive stands—black wrought-iron tiers hugging the perimeter of the room, holding dozens of crimson cups aglow with candlelight—with ugly new electric-light units in a garish shade of red. At the same time, he resisted many popular changes already under way, like folk masses held in the humble school auditorium (with scraggly-haired singers strumming acoustic guitars and hunks of brown bread in place of communion wafers), a proposed lay dress code for nuns, and so on. If a baby cried while he was saying Mass, Monsignor Rosetti would stop, clear his throat, and announce testily that services would not continue until the baby had either been quieted or removed (. . . or *shot*).

There was a movement afoot to oust him, and some of its most vocal proponents—twenty-something young adults who'd grown up in the parish—were also active in CYO leadership. I began having to lie to my father about my whereabouts and got into huge trouble one Christmas Eve for attending midnight folk Mass. How could I dare skip the formal church service for "that hippie convention" across the street? I understood that getting verbally pounded and harshly punished for attending church was far beyond the pale, even for my father.

He insisted that I start attending weekly meetings of a grassroots, right-wing Christian youth group called Just Evangelical Students United in Spirit, or J.E.S.U.S. This band of zealots, three in all, was led by a brother-and-sister team, Len and Linda, college-age children of some religious fanatics whose attention my father had attracted in his fight against smut. (The third member, Ned, a soft-spoken young man with a degenerative muscular disease, who moved with great difficulty on metal crutches, seemed to be in love with Linda.) The four of us met in the basement of Len and Linda's parents' house, where no refreshments were served. The group was dour and perversely square. They dressed like 1950s suburbanites, and spoke only in religious dogma. Once, when I prattled on excitedly about some expansive ideas I'd heard from older kids at the CYO—restatements of the sentiments summed up in "Imagine," the new hit single by John Lennon—Linda and Len became visibly agitated.

"That's *communism*," the sister hissed.

"Who said this to you?" her brother wanted to know, grabbing pen and paper. "What's his name? Where does he live?"

I knew exactly who'd said it to me—Andy Arliss, a gentle older teen who'd been my counselor at St. Lucy's Day Camp—but feigned amnesia.

"Oh, I don't know," I responded to my interrogators with burning face and ringing ears, picturing poor Andy being descended upon by a SWAT team in riot gear. "I just heard it around."

Meeting of J.E.S.U.S. consisted chiefly of discussing ways to inspire "Christian renewal in America," especially among the nation's youth, and planning various antiabortion protests. These involved meeting at the crack of dawn on Sunday mornings, traveling to area churches, and accosting parishioners with grisly images of aborted fetuses and heated rhetoric about the "murder of unborn babies." Our theatrics occasionally attracted a few sympathetic ears, but most often we were vilified. I remember one spirited young lady yelling in Linda's face.

"It's *my* body! I am free to do what I want with *my body*!"

"Not to kill" was Linda's creepily disassociated, singsong response. "You are not free to kill."

At one point, J.E.S.U.S. encouraged me to write an antiabortion essay for a boroughwide antiabortion essay-writing contest. I had by then discovered that writing came naturally to me, an easy source of approval and praise. I enjoyed tackling a good writing assignment and threw myself into the task like a pro, restating and dramatizing in my essay the talking points of the many pamphlets my mentors had supplied. A trained seal barking for fish, I waxed macabre about the barbaric nature of most methods of abortion—burning up the fetus from the inside out by injecting it with saline solution; dismembering the fetus inside the womb and drawing it out limb by limb; making a hole in the fetus's head, sucking its brains out with a vacuum hose, collapsing the skull, and then sucking the entire body out through an even larger hose—and cataloged the long-term physical, psychological, and spiritual effects of abortion on the mother, including infertility, insomnia, depression, and isolation from God.

I won second prize, which came with a cash award of fifty bucks. It was the first time I had made money as a writer. (I'd have to wait a good twenty years to repeat this trick.) At a dinner honoring the winning essayists, I collected my booty and checked out the first-placer, a tall, wan girl of maybe fourteen, with long blond hair and bookish spectacles. What could she *possibly* have written that had surpassed my inflamed prose?

Sometimes we were joined on our antiabortion outings by the rest of the club's membership, consisting solely of an Irish woman named Nellie, in her fifties, who clutched rosary beads in her fidgety hands at all times and was prone to loudly leading the group in prayer at the slightest provocation. She saw the Devil in everything, warning me that he could assume any form.

"That pavement could be the Devil. Or that building. Or that old woman. Or that little child. The Devil is everywhere!"

Traveling by car one hot Sunday morning to a targeted protest site, we saw another car broken down at the side of the road, over-heated, steam pouring out of its open hood. Nellie raised her voice and rosary beads:

"It's the Devil. Let us pray that he does not take our car as well. Hail Mary, full of grace. The Lord is with thee . . ."

I hadn't brought my rosary beads along. Nellie, not missing a beat, slipped me one of several spares she carried. I begged my father to stop pushing me into the arms of J.E.S.U.S. He eventually relented, but still insisted that my sisters and I attend formal church services every Sunday morning—*not folk Mass.* (My mother got a pass so she could tend house. She said she didn't need a church or a priest in order to talk to God. "I can talk to Him from right here," she'd say, rag in hand.) Eva and I frequently claimed to be attending Mass when in reality we were eating kosher franks and potato knishes at the Hebrew National Deli on Allerton Avenue. We'd finish up in time to get to church for the very end of the service (". . . the Mass is ended, go in peace"), so we could see which priest was serving and pick up a couple of bulletins. At home, flashing our paperwork: "Yeah, we went to ten o'clock Mass. Father Mannini served."

Junior high school graduation was held in Loew's (which we pro-nounced "Low-ees") Paradise on Fordham Road, a then-ruined movie palace with a mighty organ blowing dust, a sea of faded, fraying crimson seats, sumptuous but flaking scenes of Heaven frescoed onto vaulted ceilings, rats running underfoot. (The Art Deco masterpiece, built in 1929, has since been restored and declared a landmark.) We sang the school anthem, changing the words a bit: *"Cheer, cheer for 135 / Our school's more dead than alive."* I won two award pins, for attendance and spelling, and was twice called to the stage to receive applause.

So they'd been paying attention, after all.

11.

It's a suffocating Saturday afternoon at the crest of summer. My father has instructed me to demolish the walk-in closet in the master bedroom while he works elsewhere in the house. (I don't remember where my parents are sleeping while their room is being bulldozed.) Sweating inside my too-big work clothes, I step into the closet and use a crowbar to pound a hole into the ceiling, pulling at the plaster until I've loosened it enough to break it off in big chunks. (I still have not learned how to avoid getting showered and pummeled from above when taking down a ceiling.) Soon I am ankle-deep in rubble. Next, I tear away a couple of strips of lathing and slip a length of two-by-four into the opening, using the slender beam like a lever to rip the rest of them down. They make a sound like machine-gun fire as they snap and tumble, releasing a shower of soot, splinters, and other debris. This is one of my least favorite tasks. After today, I will approach it with a new level of dread.

As I pull down on the makeshift lever and fir strips explode above, *a family of dead squirrels* collapses onto my head and shoulders.

It takes a moment to figure out what has happened. The first thing I notice is the stench—not of rotting corpses but of something deeper, older—rotting *bones.* The squirrels are skeletons, their sharp, skinny remains cracking in foul fragments into my hair, down my shirt, all over me. The mommy or daddy squirrel skeleton has landed at my feet, pretty much intact. I scream and race out of the bedroom like a boy on fire. My father rushes upstairs, laughs when he sees what all the fuss is about.

"They're dead," he observes. "They won't bite."

I had long fantasized about finding treasure inside the walls, sealed as they'd been for more than half a century. Maybe the original owners had buried chests of gold coins or precious gems there, and then forgotten. Indeed, I'd recovered from inside the living room walls a nest of small bottles and decanters dating back to the late nineteenth century . . . but they and the squirrel skeletons were the only booty the house ever yielded. All the rest was rubble.

"Best thing to do is get back on the horse," said my father, sending me back into the closet graveyard after I'd cleaned myself up.

Still shaky, I swept the bones into a far corner of the bedroom, covered them with a box, and continued working, demolishing the rest of the closet cautiously, one foot firmly outside the doorway. The procedure was identical in every room of the house: Once all the plaster, lathing, moldings, doors, and resulting wreckage had been removed—and all the grand windows, with their hidden lead-weight pulley systems, had been torn out and replaced with tiny portholes or closed up with plywood—I'd "clean the beams," scanning them with the claw end of a hammer or cat's-paw to locate and remove any remaining nails (of which there were always thousands), prepping the beams for insulation and drywalling (following any necessary plumbing and electrical work, of course, of which there was always plenty). Then came spackling, sanding, and painting. It's hard to say which stage of the work I hated the most, but a few come to mind:

Standing on a ladder or a platform improvised from a few layers of plywood propped across a pair of homemade sawhorses, holding a sheet of half-inch drywall (about four feet by eight, weighing about ninety pounds) above my head, pressing the sheet with all my might into the beams above—while also keeping its borders snug—as my father twists his body around mine, nailing the ceiling into place.

"Don't move!" he barks, pounding his hammer desperately, fumbling a nail here—"Shit!"—bending another there—"Dammit!" I strain and strain; dropping the ceiling would mean serious injury for us both, yet I feel my muscles giving out, saying nothing as I grunt and push, grunt and push. Eight or ten nails or more have to be sunk before it's safe for me to relax. "All right," my father says at long last, "you can let go." The primordial physical relief I feel as I release my grip and hop down to floor level almost justifies the pain. I drop to my knees. When I stand up again, it's time for another sheet. Or:

Downstairs in the basement, at the massive old table saw my father dragged home from work one day—its shark-tooth blade unsheathed and prone to sparking—manipulating one end of a sheet of plywood (again about four by eight, but weighing less than Sheetrock) while my father works the other, straining to hear his shouted directions above the high-pitched whine of the motor and the terrible roar of blade against wood. "No, no!" he bellows, sparks bouncing as the plywood pops off the blade. "Hold it straight, pull it up, push it down! No! No, no! *Ho!*" And periodically: "Lift the motor, lift the motor!" The well-worn device slowed down with heavy use and literally had to be tilted upward to get it going at full pace again. Somehow, I was to keep the motor lifted while at the same time guiding my end of the acre of plywood through the *Pit and the Pendulum*–like spinning blade, the air growing thick with exhaust, sawdust, and the acrid odor of burnt steel (blades burn as they rip). Or:

Unfurling great rolls of pink and yellow fiberglass insulation (its deadly fluff a demonic variant of cotton candy), the skin on every inch of my body immediately starting to prickle as it gets covered in a dust of tiny, sharp particles, my eyes throbbing with a million little stab wounds—slicing off great lengths of it with a box cutter and stuffing them into the wells between the beams, fastening the strips on both sides all up and down with a ten-pound staple gun.

The miasmic heat slowed our labors, blighted them. My father continued to reject the very idea of air-conditioning, so the house was a stagnant hotbox of unbearable intensity. Our whole family was flushed, woozy, and on the verge of vomiting for three months a year. We each devised our own method of staying cool, aided mainly by a few antiquated fans smuggled in by sympathetic relatives. Aunt Virginia donated a couple of specimens from the 1920s, with open steel blades that could dice a man into bite-size chunks. Eva liked to take a cold shower, soak a sheet in ice water, drape the sheet over her damp body, and lie in front of a fan overnight (a formula, I now realize, for developing pneumonia, which fortunately she never did). Whenever possible, we sought the blessed frigidity of department stores and movie theaters—Alexander's and Loew's Paradise, of course, but also the RKO Fordham, the Valentine, and Woolworth's on Westchester Square, where you could get a sandwich and soda at the lunch counter for about a buck. When we came home, it was not uncommon to find my father boiling a great kettle of bone stew, his original recipe, filling the already stifling air with musky, beefy clouds of steam.

My family never vacationed or traveled, especially now that we had the house. In earlier years, my father had occasionally loaded us into the car for jaunts to Jones Beach. I have only dim memories of the beach itself but remember enjoying the shows in the amphitheater at night. We saw *South Pacific* that way, though all I really cared about was the breeze coming off the ocean from behind the stage. I was never a fan of direct sunlight and routinely got burnt to a crisp. Sunblock was not popular at the time. Our preferred tanning solution was baby oil, which I'd smear all over my body and then fry like a pancake, later to watch the first few layers of skin peel away in stiff sheets. There had been a few other family day trips, as well—to Washington, D.C., for example, where I was blinded by the sunlight bouncing up from all that white pavement as we traversed seemingly endless expanses, climbing shadeless stone steps to gawk pointlessly at one sun-drenched monument after another—but even such minor diversions were now things of the past. Many families in the neighborhood (Jewish, mainly) rented little summer cottages up in the Catskills or down at the beach, or belonged to Shore Haven, a working-class Bronx "resort" consisting mainly of an overcrowded outdoor pool, a clubhouse, and tables full of rotund ladies in inappropriate bathing suits playing mah-jongg beneath beach umbrellas. My equivalent was standing in front of an open fire hydrant (I was too old now to frolic in the sprinklers at Bronx Park).

But then Aunt Diana and Uncle Aldo bought a summer house on the Jersey shore, and a whole new world opened up to me: suddenly my cousins and sisters and I were children of leisure for a week or so every summer.

I thought Diana and Aldo were rich. I thought they were jet-setters. I considered their main residence (a lovely but modest brick house in Fort Lee) a place of great elegance and refinement, a notion buttressed by my aunt at every opportunity.

"No, no, no, kids, don't sit on that chair! Aunt Diana paid a lot of money for that chair. No, no, no, don't walk on the carpet, kids. That's a *very* expensive carpet. Stay on the plastic runner. No, no, no! Don't go near that desk, that desk cost Aunt Diana a *fortune.* No, no, no, don't sit on the down comforter, you'll crush it. No, no, no, kids! No, no, no, no, no!"

"No, no, no kids," my sisters and cousins and I secretly mocked. "Don't breathe that air! That's *very* good air! Don't enter the house, kids, no, no, no! Aunt Diana paid a lot of money for that house! Oh no, no, no, don't put that food in your mouth, kids. That food is *very* expensive! No, no, no, kids! No, no, no, no, no, no!"

Driven and highly successful (soon to make a small fortune in real estate but still working as an international travel agent at the time), Diana was very much the breadwinner. Aldo dabbled at various jobs but clearly preferred the life of a playboy. The couple, childless, trotted the globe regularly, shipping home treasures of every variety. When my aunt bagged a giant sailfish on a boating expedition somewhere in the tropical Atlantic, she had her catch stuffed, mounted, and installed on the wall of my grandmother's knotty pine-paneled den; from China, she and Aldo shipped home a triptych of black-lacquered screens, richly engraved, and a formal dining room set for twelve, handcrafted in rosewood, a thing of eternal beauty (Aldo's taste was flawless); in Africa, they traded cotton clothes for masks and beads and ceremonial objects; they won skiing trophies in the Swiss and Italian Alps; purchased glorious silk carpets from Persia and other exotic ports of call; wore mile-high mink hats they'd picked up in Russia and the Ukraine.

MY AUNT, HER MONSTER CATCH . . . AND THE FISHING ROD
THAT BROUGHT THEM TOGETHER

Once in a while we kids would get little trinkets. I recall a couple of rag dolls from Mexico, a string of beads and bones from Africa, and some random airline giveaways—white vinyl carry-on bags stamped with the Alitalia logo in sky blue, miniature wooden barrels containing single servings of scotch whiskey (we still have a few of those), sleep masks and slippers bearing the names of various carriers. These objects were talismans. I held them and stared at them and carried them around, trying to coax from them a sense of the glamour and excitement they betokened.

The summer house was a simple cabin that had been built upon over the years. It was warm and cozy inside, with knotty pine paneling and old-fashioned nautical-themed fixtures. My aunt had spruced it up a bit, papering the walls in the guest bedrooms in coordinated jungle prints with matching linens. Our favorite was a tiny bedroom at the back, with a bunk bed and electric lanterns instead of lamps. Two walls were leopard, two were tiger; the bedding was zebra-striped. The house sat on a narrow strip of land in the town of Harvey Cedars, near the southern tip of Long Beach Island, where the beach and bay front are just across the road from each other. Diana considered the area "very fancy" and never let us forget it.

"Oh no, no, no, kids! Don't drape your towel over your shoulders like that! That's *very* Jones Beach. We don't do that here. Just carry it on your arm."

"Oh no, no, no, kids! Don't lay your wet towels over the railing like that! It's not that kind of house!"

"Is that the only bathing suit you have? Maybe you can borrow one of mine."

In the evenings, we'd often go to Bay Village, a typical beach tourist spot in nearby Surf City, the streets of which were lined with fudge and taffy shops, surf shops, novelty boutiques, and the like.

When Diana treated us to ice cream, we'd get one cone for each pair of kids. I always demurred, finding the idea of licking a licked-over scoop of ice cream revolting. Eva and I would pool our money together and stop in to Surf City Bakery to buy piles of elephant ears—big crispy pancakes coated with sugar and cinnamon. "Oh no, no, no, Aunt Diana! Don't touch those elephant ears! Those are our elephant ears!" we'd mutter under our breath as Diana reached over to snap off a hunk. "You kids are eating me out of house and home!" she'd say, despite the fact that my mother always sent us there with bags and bags of groceries.

Uncle Aldo—our own Marcello Mastroianni, handsome and dashing, with brown wavy hair, Italian movie star sunglasses, and worldly panache—provided a perfect foil for Diana, bringing a sense of fun and fascination to every activity. The mellifluous tones of his accented voice we mimicked lovingly:

"Let's-a fly-a theese kite-a. What eeza theese, a kite-a? How does-a theese work? Who invent-a theese? Well, the way the kite-a work eeza theese—"

And he'd launch into a lively explication of kiting and aerodynamics, the history of the toy, its scientific and industrial applications.

"Let's-a tie-a this kite to the porch-a rail, and-a een the morning-a we see where itta go. Okay?" And then in the morning: "Come-a let's see where the kite-a go. Oh my Godda look a theese. The kite eeza in-a the tree. What-a happen-a here? Well, what-a happen-a was-a theese: Last-a night the kite-a was-a fly over-a the bay. But, overnight-a, the wind-a change direction-a, and what-a happen-a? The kite-a change-a course, it blow around-a over-a the land-a, and then it-a get caught inna theesa tree. Okay. We get another kite-a. Now . . . who wanna go to the ocean-a?"

We'd grab our towels and trail behind him like ducklings, our rubber flip-flops slapping our heels in unified rhythm.

"You sure you don't want to wear sneakers instead?" Aunt Diana would call as we disappeared into the cool sea grass.

Uncle Aldo had grown up in Venice and on the Mediterranean seashore, and taught us how to deal with ocean currents. You had to have courage, he said, in that famously elegant accent, but you mustn't be stupid. You had to run out into the sea and swim beyond the terrifying crashing of the waves to where it was calm, just before they broke. If you were about to get caught in a wave bearing down upon you, you had to dive deep underneath and let it pass overhead. Once you were safely past the crash zone, even the fiercest wave could be friendly and playful. You mustn't go too far out. But you mustn't stay close enough to shore to get tangled up. There was a right place to be, and Uncle Aldo showed it to us. He didn't favor rafts or floats or boogie boards. Our bodies were our instruments. Eva and I frolicked in the surf for hours on end, until we were pruned and waterlogged, riding the waves like Aldo taught us. (Maria was too young and small for this depth, and Rosette was one for short dips.)

Eva invented games like Grecian Columns, which involved various types of spinning jumps and complex underwater landings. We shouted phrases underwater to see who could hear whom, and kept our eyes open as we dove down to the ocean floor, scouting for treasure. We tried to terrify each other with mock shark attacks. (Poor Maria, when she was old enough to venture more fully into the surf, was on the receiving end of many of my most cunning underwater attacks. I found irresistibly thrilling the screaming, laughing hysteria they elicited.) When we could stand the water no longer, we'd busy ourselves along the shoreline, building elaborate structures of wet sand, burying one another up to our waists and sculpting lower bod-

ies in the shapes of mermaids and mermen and other mythical creatures. (Eva was in charge of design and engineering. Her plans were
always wildly detailed and ambitious.) Or we'd head over to the bay
and catch some dinner.

Our industrious uncle taught us how to clam, crab, catch shiners,
and pick mussels. (He taught us to set lobster traps too, but we never
got lucky.) I loved skipping out into the bay on his little rowboat during low tide, occasionally attaching an outboard motor, parking in the
middle of nowhere, and dropping lines tied at their ends with fish
heads (which the fish store supplied free of charge). The idea was to
let the bait sit on or near the bay floor for a while, and then raise it
slowly, almost imperceptibly, hand over hand, to the surface. If we
were lucky, several crabs would be feasting upon the rotting head.
We'd scoop them up in a net and dump them into a bucket containing
a few inches of seawater. Uncle Aldo taught us that, if after a while you
got no bites, you should move on. You had to try many places, he said,
before you found "a bedda," which, once located, could easily yield a
couple dozen crabs.

One time my cousin David and I rowed out alone and caught so
many blue crabs that we ran out of buckets. We started just loading
them right into the boat and kept on crabbing. That day is legendary
in the annals of our family fishing stories. Aunt Diana still loves to
talk about it. She fails to mention that we were rewarded with barely
an ounce of crabmeat for our labors. Drunk with pleasure over a boatload of blues, Diana set her lobster pot upon the stove. When the water reached a rolling boil, she and New Jersey Grandma tossed the
writhing, snapping creatures, a few at a time, into the bath. (They
knew how to handle the angry crustaceans without getting bitten.)
The poor things thrashed about wildly under the lid for a moment,
then quickly fell silent. After a few minutes, they turned from blue to

pinkish red. That's how you knew they were done. They were removed from the pot with tongs and set aside to cool. The process was repeated over and over until all the crabs were cooked.

Next, the long pine dining table was laid with newspaper, and every kid in the house, eight of us including my four cousins, was called to production-line duty. To get meat, you had to rip the hard shell off the crab, cut the crab in half, and pick at it with tiny forks. Diana made sure to toss back to us any carcasses she felt had more to give. Spent shells and claws were piled off to the side; meat was tossed into a large bowl in the middle of the table. When all the crabs had been eviscerated and all their meat harvested, Diana whisked the bowl from the table, divided the meat into several small plastic containers, lidded them, labeled them, and stored them in the freezer. We'd eat pasta that night.

At least she'd saved a few live crabs for the sauce. These were the unluckiest. The manner of their preparation was this: Holding a crab deftly between thumb and forefinger, keeping out of the way of its snapping claws, Aunt Diana would turn it upside down and stun it into stillness by letting hot tap water beat down on its soft white underside. Then she'd flip the prone but living crab back into an upright position, toss it onto a cutting board, and use a fork to rip the shell off its body—which produced a horrible sound and seemed unnecessarily cruel. (Being tossed into a vat of boiling water was no picnic for the crabs either, but we were told that they went into shock the moment they hit the brew, and therefore felt no pain.) The deshelled, but perhaps still living, crabs were then tossed into a pan sizzling with olive oil and chopped garlic. This slowed them down pretty good.

"Not so lively now, eh?" Aunt Diana would say. After searing them on both sides, she'd add some crushed tomatoes, fresh basil, and more fresh garlic. Then she'd cover the pan and let it simmer. After a while, she'd remove the crabs, now quite dead, of course, adjust the seasoning, and let it continue to simmer. Eventually the sauce would be served over pasta, with crabs on the side to be picked at in between mouthfuls. The dish was delicious, but the brutality involved in its preparation dampened the pleasure. Plus, what we really wanted were crab cakes! But by the time we sat down to dinner, the great mound of delicate white meat we had so painstakingly extracted from the crabs we caught ourselves—pulpy and salty and fresh from the bay—was already frozen hard in a series of plastic containers.

Once in a while we'd find a soft-shell crab hiding beneath a regular one. This was a special treat, utterly delicious when dredged in seasoned flour and fried in garlic and oil, or else grilled on the barbecue. (Grandma also loved to use them in a marinara sauce.) Aldo explained that crabs shed their shells every season and were shielded by other crabs until their shells grew back. The idea of crabs working together like this, protecting and aiding each other, made them a little too personable for the treatment we gave them. It was different with clams. They seemed like rocks. I couldn't imagine their feeling pain. Here again, you had to search around for "a bedda" if you wanted to yield results. Uncle Aldo taught us to read the tide tables, and at low tide, in the late afternoon, about sunset, we'd wade out into the bay and dig around with our feet until we felt something hard under the sand. Then we'd reach under and pull up whatever it was, hopefully a clam.

We collected our harvest in green net bags Aldo kept for just this purpose. He had clam rakes we could use, but his and our preferred method was au naturel. I was always amazed by how far out into the bay we could wade and still have our heads remain above water. (Despite Aldo's patient coaching and gentle coaxing, I never learned to like being in water over my head. Luckily, clamming *required* that your feet remain planted and wriggling on the bay floor at all times.) Aunt Diana's job during our clamming outings was to stand on the shore and shout unwanted advice.

"You're not going out far enough! Go out further! No, further!"

No matter that we were already up to our chins. How much further did she want us to go? Uncle Aldo had warned us about areas of the bay that were channels to the open ocean. We were to avoid them at all costs, whether on foot or aboat. Aunt Diana seemed to be sending us in their direction. Maybe she was trying to drown us.

We had no need of coaching, anyway. Our clamming expeditions always ended in success. Eva and I got good enough at it that we were allowed to go out unaccompanied. I savored the serenity of being in the middle of the quiet bay at sunset, wading slowly, digging gently, bending and rising again, calmly collecting dinner as the sun prepared to melt into the horizon. Back at the house, smaller clams would be rinsed, chilled, forced open, and loosened in the shell with a clam knife, squirted with lemon, and slurped down just like that. The rest of the clams usually ended up in *linguini con vongole,* which New Jersey Grandma prepared to exquisite perfection. There were many tricks to this dish: She'd let the clams sit for a while in fresh water, forcing them open ever so slightly to release their sand. Then she'd steam them even more briefly in a couple of inches of water. As they opened more fully, she'd pull them from the pot and set them aside. The clam juice was strained through cheesecloth to remove any remaining sand. Pasta water was then set on the stove to boil. At the same moment that the pasta was thrown in to cook, Grandma would sear a handful of fresh chopped garlic in a skillet containing an inch or so of olive oil. Then she'd toss in the chopped clams, along with the clam juice and some fresh chopped basil and parsley. By the time the pasta was cooked (al dente, always), the sauce was ready.

Grandma always heated the pasta bowl by swishing hot pasta water around in it and then dumping the water out again. She'd throw a little sauce into the bottom of the warm bowl before turning the strained pasta in to it. Then she'd pour the rest of the sauce over the pasta and toss it thoroughly with a pair of forks. She'd pour a little more olive oil over the piping hot pasta, maybe even toss a little raw minced garlic into it—*a cruda,* they call this technique. A few extra clams were scattered on top, shell and all. After dinner, many of the clamshells were washed, dried, and stored for future use as ashtrays or spoon rests, or for stuffing and baking.

Mussels we simply plucked off the jetty when the ocean had receded enough to allow access—a dangerous activity, as the rocks were slippery and sharp, but easy pickin's. Grandma would amble out onto the jetty in her housecoat and apron and bend into the rocks to pick fat, healthy specimens for her sauce, the wind flapping at her backside.

"Cover up, Ma!" Aunt Diana would call. "We can see everything you own!"

Grandma prepared the mussels two ways: steamed, and tossed into *al'ogl'* (sautéed garlic and olive oil) with a little butter, an appetizer; and cooked into a briny, zesty marinara—made from fresh tomatoes when they were in season—served over pasta, the main course.

We caught bucketfuls of shiners (silvery little fish that dart around in very shallow bay water during low tide) by simply dragging a net just below the surface of knee-deep water. Uncle Aldo said we had to rush them home so they could be rinsed and cooked just moments after dying. Grandma would dredge them in seasoned flour, fry them in a sizzling mix of olive and vegetable oils, drain them on brown paper or paper towel, and sprinkle them lightly with salt. They were eaten whole, like French fries, which bothered me because they had little faces. Eyes and heads. They were so cute in life, so seemingly hopeful as they darted about athletically. Pretty too—iridescent and shiny, late day sunlight bouncing off their backs from beneath the surface of the water. The crispy brown things they became were disturbing. Little black eyes, fried, stared at you if you looked hard enough. Plus they had a distinctive and slightly bitter aftertaste. I imagined this to be the flavor of their tiny organs and waste deposits; the taste of their bones and teeth and fins. I ate them quietly, without gusto.

Same with eels. Uncle Aldo's eeling excursions were the least popular of his nautical offerings. I forget the eeling process—I think it was similar to crabbing, except that you had to bash the eel's head against the side of the boat in order to kill it, and it had to be gutted and cleaned right away. My grandmother usually sautéed the meat in garlic and oil, sprinkled with fresh chopped basil and parsley. She might have broiled it sometimes. Or dressed it and thrown it on the barbecue. We kids were grossed out completely. Eels were snakes. And snakes were not food.

An expert gamesman, Aldo had been known to spontaneously gut, skin, and carve up roadkill (deer especially) if it was fresh enough. In the backyard of his and Diana's house in Fort Lee, he used a BB gun to hunt squirrels, rabbits, and other small game. Sparrows were a favorite treat. He'd shoot the little birds right from the kitchen window, feather and poach them, and serve them at room temperature—head, beak, feet, and all—with a mayonnaise dressing on the side. That was breakfast. Lunch might be squirrel meat sautéed with onions and vegetables. (He was always daring us kids to try some.)

In true Renaissance fashion, he also happened to be an excellent photographer, and built a darkroom in the finished basement of their house, where he developed marvelous black-and-white portraits and gag shots. Using wigs and hats and other props, he did my grandmother up in several poses over the years: Indian chieftess, 1960s swinger, Dutch milkmaid. New Jersey Grandma, dark and heavy of body and head, somber of spirit, wears the same deadpan expression in every shot, staring directly into the lens. The pictures are a riot. He made one of himself done up as a Roman soldier, wearing an authentic silver helmet, one of many antique novelties he'd acquired at auction or on his travels abroad.

One Sunday when I was maybe four or five, we were having dinner at my grandmother's house and I stepped away from the table to use the bathroom. It was my habit to leave the bathroom door ajar as I sat on the john. (This slang term for "toilet," used commonly in our family, always confused me. Who was John? I preferred *bacaos*, which my father explained was just "back house" with an Italian accent.) Aldo approached in his friendly way and asked me something, I wasn't sure what. I thought he was asking if I wanted the door left open. I said yes. This seemed to please him greatly. He scurried away. A moment later he was back, carrying a tripod and a 35 mm camera. I hunkered down onto the bowl, too timid to tell him that I'd prefer he didn't take my picture just then. "Say *formaggio*!" Snap. The picture became for me an iconic image of my youth. (Years later, Aldo made an ten-by-twelve print of that shot and gave it to me for my birthday, a gift I treasure.)

He even set up a BB gun shooting range in his suburban basement by sectioning off a long, narrow hallway and installing some kind of bullet-absorbing material and a target on the far wall. He'd gather up the kids, herd us downstairs, and invite us to take turns. Of course

MY BELOVED UNCLE

he'd first coach us in his usual way. We'd learn the history of the BB gun, its design and construction, common uses, and proper handling. I remember trembling with a sense of danger and foreboding as, with a reassuring smile, Aldo handed me the firearm. I was shy as I took it, shy as I shot. I dreaded the whole affair . . . but liked it too.

Aldo was gentle with us kids, and kind. He seemed genuinely to enjoy spending time with us. Yet he always maintained a certain distance. It might have been simple Old World formality, warm though it was, or it might have been a form of respect (or something else) for my father, who couldn't stand his brother-in-law and didn't hide it. He always said Aldo was a fake, a phony, a freeloader, a user of my aunt and grandmother. He felt Aldo was making fun of him all the time, mocking and deriding him behind his back, which might have been true. I know my uncle found my father ridiculous and insufferable in many ways. But he was also just a natural prankster and provocateur.

When he decorated a bunch of my aunt's Styrofoam hat forms with faces made from cut-up photographs and a variety of buttons, and lined them up on a shelf inside the hall closet, my father insisted that they were intended to leer exclusively at *him.*

"That guy knows exactly what he's doing," he complained bitterly. I don't think the heads were intended especially for my father, but I do think Aldo enjoyed getting his goat. At family dinners during the saying of grace, my father would grumble and moan as Aldo bowed his head theatrically and screwed his face up into an exaggerated expression of piety, earnestly mumbling gibberish, lingering in his melodramatic pose a moment too long, crossing himself broadly in a mockery of fervid devotion. My father started every meal at their house with a knot in his stomach; we kids, with a giggle. For some reason the two of them were usually seated together. Aldo liked to push the envelope with scatological jokes, "off-color" references, and political comments that he knew would irk my überconservative father. When the teasing had gone far enough, Diana would put an end to it.

"Aldo! Basta! A tavola no!" (She spoke only the cleanest Italian

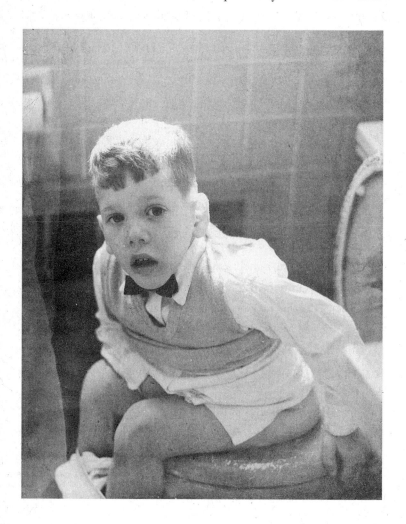

with her well-born husband, reserving the rougher-sounding dialect for her mother and brothers.)

My father refused ever to step foot in the beach house.

"Over my dead body will I go down there," he declared, even before the closing.

He was at constant sword's point with his younger sister. Everything she did and said was *wrong*. Diana didn't help matters by constantly correcting my father, "advising" him, pleading with him to find a white-collar job. She hated the fact that we lived in the Bronx. It was an embarrassment, a misadventure, "*trau*matic for the children."

"Diana, *please!*" was my father's usual response. Their visits often ended in screaming fights, with poor Grandma trying uselessly to defuse the tension.

"*Ma no, no. Bebe l'aqua fresca, bebe.*" Eva and I would later laugh, not unkindly, about Grandma's faith in the calming power of fresh water.

I was grateful that my father did not block our visits to the shore, even allowing my mother to join us once in a while, a special treat.

"Mary, are you comfortable? Use this pillow. Mary, you look cold. Wear this sweater. Mary, are you warm? Open that window. Mary, Mary—"

"She doesn't give me one moment of peace," Mom would complain.

But I found Diana's concern for her sister-in-law's comfort endearing. And I liked seeing my mother at leisure, a rarity. She wouldn't go in the water, never even wearing a bathing suit (she sometimes referred vaguely to a near-drowning incident in her early twenties), but she'd sit in a beach chair at the water's edge, her cotton pants rolled up to the knees, her feet resting in the water, a floppy borrowed sunhat on her head. I remember studying her in this pose, soaking in the image of the woman completely at ease.

Sometimes Grandma would toddle across the road and join her in a similar pose and getup. They seemed more relaxed than usual as they chatted there, gazing contentedly into the roiling surf.

12.

It was upon my return home from one of these trips to the shore that I decided to kill my father. It would be easy: potential accidents were everywhere.

Now! I thought. Do it now! as I stood at the base of a mile-high ladder propped against the side of the house. The old extender was creaky and rusted in spots, and supported my father's weight just barely as he boarded up yet another large rectangle of space that had once been a window. The ballast I provided by pressing my entire body against the base was critical: without it, the bald feet of the ladder would surely slip, and my father would come crashing down from three stories high. If the wreck didn't kill him, it would certainly slow him down.

The voice grew louder: "Just step away," it said. "Step. Away."

I looked down at my sneakers on the cracked pavement, looked into the dirty cuffs of my work pants, looked at my white-knuckled grip on the ladder. I pictured myself stepping away, the ladder slipping, my father falling. These images did not sicken me or make me feel guilty, nor did they thrill me or fill me with glee. Instead, they just played out in my head in a coldly assessive sequence. I was weighing my options. In the end, I decided against patricide, realizing intuitively that killing my father would damn my existence.

Suicide was the next best option. I considered it seriously. Of all available methods, jumping from the roof of a building seemed the most desirable—mainly because it featured a thrill ride on the way to oblivion. I gazed appraisingly at the tops of the tallest buildings in the neighborhood, scouted various jumping-off points, imagined chaos in the street after I'd landed. (Was it true that if I jumped from high enough I'd go right through the pavement? How far down? To China? We'd tried to tunnel there as children through the sandboxes in Bronx Park.)

Or I could overdose on sleeping pills, which sounded pleasantly painless. Sominex was available at Fair Drugs on the avenue ("Take Sominex tonight and sleep / Safe and restful / Sleep, sleep, sleep . . ."), but I knew something stronger was required and had no means of procurement.

Stabbing myself in the heart was my least favorite idea, but the one I came closest to acting out. Eva, at whose shoulder I weathered the torrential storm of family life, had said some silly, hurtful thing. My response was all out of proportion. I felt *betrayed.* And utterly *alone.* I marched into the empty kitchen, scribbled a simple suicide note ("This is *your* fault!"), opened the knife drawer, withdrew the biggest blade I could find, skewered the note onto it, and prepared to fall on my sword, hari-kari style. But then Linc barked at me and I snapped to. Either he was trying to save my life . . . or he just had to pee. I put the knife down, destroyed the note, grabbed the leash, and headed for the park.

That dog, our family's first, was a friend to me a thousand times over. We'd gotten him as a puppy after our first year or so in the house, and he eventually grew to the size, nearly, of a Shetland pony. (His parents were a German shepherd and an Irish wolfhound.) My father at first resisted the name Linc because it brought to mind the street-strutting, hip-hugger-wearing, vaguely Black Pantheresque character of the same name from TV's *The Mod Squad,* but he relented when my sisters and I explained that the moniker was a nod to the dog's birthday, which he happened to share with America's sixteenth president. Linc was my loyal protector inside the house and on the street. He'd growl and bark during my father's screaming fits and push his body against my legs to form a canine barrier between my attacker and me. I'd let my hand dangle down and settle gently in the wiry tuft atop his head, sometimes whispering to him to quiet down, telling him that everything was okay. My father seemed to ignore Linc's presence, but I knew he knew the dog was watching.

It's Halloween night, and I am walking home from a hangout session on "the corner" with my St. Lucy's friends. A gang of boys is marauding around the neighborhood, armed with cartons of eggs and sacks of flour. They see me walking alone down a darkened street and whoop at one another to cue an attack. I break into a trot . . . and it's then that they spot Linc in powerful stride beside me, his back rising nearly as high as my waist, his spiky black coat giving him the appearance of a hellhound, its silver flecks aglint in moonlight.

"Oh shit, hold up, hold up! He got a big dog!" yells one of the gang.

"Shit!" the others exclaim as they catch sight of him.

The boys hold their fire, withdraw, and lope off in search of another victim. Linc is my bodyguard, helper, big brother. When I take him into the depths of Bronx Park, he points out things I've never noticed before—a half-buried animal corpse, a hidden tunnel—and pulls me up the steepest hills by forging on ahead, digging his claws into the hillside and straining to support my weight as I use his leash like climbing rope. When we get to level ground, he jumps and barks and licks my hand. He knows he's done well. I reward him by letting him off the leash, and he's usually pretty good about it.

But sometimes he runs away, runs far into other neighborhoods, runs and stops just long enough to let me get within half an inch of his collar before running off again. It's a game to him but a horror for me, exhausting, unnerving, humiliating. When finally I snag him and drag him home, I tie him to a pillar in the cellar, yell at him, slap his hindquarters with the leash. He yelps and growls, bares his teeth and makes as if to bite me. I dare him to try, sticking my wrist into his jaw, taunting him. (He never so much as nibbles.) This is a contest for alpha status. I win. The victory is hollow. I feel guilty afterward, guilty as I'm doing it, guilty now as I remember. Linc always forgives me, wagging his tail and licking my hand when it's over. In spite of our struggles, he knows what I know: that I would never really hurt him. I might scare the shit out of him—and I did—but I would never, ever bring him real harm, nor let any come to him on my watch.

Our beloved canine once ate an entire tray of fried meatballs fresh from the pan. New Jersey Grandma screamed as if under physical attack when she turned from the stove to place the last meatball on the steaming platter behind her and found it empty, Linc licking his chops nearby. He ate about a dozen one-pound boxes of candy that I was supposed to be selling for school—Turtles they were called, little clusters of nuts and caramel coated in chocolate; ate four huge globes of raw bread dough, which Eva had set out to rise during her bread-making phase ("Try this—it's whole wheat apple cinnamon raisin nut date bread with oats and seeds"); ate the rotting corpse of the lower half of a squirrel (the upper half having already been gotten to by some other animal), swallowing the thing whole as I tried desperately to yank it out of his mouth by the tail (Eva fed him Maalox afterward); ate used tampons out of the bathroom trash, and chunks of cat shit coated in Kitty Litter, Turtles from hell ("*turdles*" we dubbed them, screaming in horror whenever we caught him with one). He ate my actual turtle, Romeo—or Juliet, I could never tell them apart. I flushed the masticated remains, bright green, down the toilet, weeping and feeling like a terrible father.

It wasn't the first time I had exposed my turtles to danger. The previous pair, Abbott and Costello (I could never tell them apart either), were accidentally drowned in hot water and bleach when, while I was cleaning out their tank in the bathtub, they somehow climbed out of their little holding dish and spilled into the soup, perhaps a double suicide.

This was typical of the kind of luck we had with most of our smaller pets.

Pino the parakeet had survived a near-fatal attack by Niffi while we were still living in the apartment, only to die months later from a cancerous tumor that grew so large it ended up nearly doubling the size of the little bird. Named for Uncle Aldo's brother, who lived in Milan and whom we'd met only once or twice, Pino was Eva's special charge, her precious baby. She bought a beautiful white cage and fancy perches, swings, and treats. She bought a record album called *Teach Your Parakeet to Talk,* and played it for the bird over and over again on our portable phonograph. (Side One: "Good morning birdie; good morning birdie; good morning birdie." Side Two: "Good night birdie; good night birdie; good night birdie." Pino never made a peep.) After he died, we heard that his favorite brand of birdseed was coated in shellac and was causing an outbreak of fatal tumors in parakeets and other birds all over the country. Eva was outraged, vowing through her tears to sue the Hartz Mountain Corporation as she nestled poor Pino into a white corsage box and carried him off into the lots to be buried alongside all the other dead.

"MURDERER!! LOOK IN YOUR TANK!" I woke up one morning to find Eva's note taped to the front of my aquarium, scrawled on loose-leaf paper in squiggly red letters dripping blood. I tore the note away and looked inside to find my pet fish floating upside down at the top of the tank, steam rising gently from the water. I had cranked the temperature way high the night before to heat the water after cleaning the tank but forgotten to turn it down again, literally simmering my pets to death. (When I told Uncle Aldo about the accident, he said the fish would probably be delicious skinned, boned, and squirted with a wedge of lemon.) The aquarium had been a particular point of pride for me. With Eva's help, I'd amassed an unusual and colorful collection of freshwater specimens and created a charming underwater habitat for them. It made me sick to flush the whole boiled lot down the toilet; made me feel like a flop and a failure.

I even managed to kill Mikey, my Venus flytrap, which had grown nicely for several months on a steady diet of bits of chopped meat, but then withered and collapsed inexplicably. Obesity was probably the cause. I never stopped feeding that plant, so fascinated was I by its delicate little pods, each about the size of a lima bean, opening like a mouth to accept a meal, and then closing again to swallow it, the soft tendrils along the "lips" of each pod suggesting facial hair.

I'd found Mikey (named for the kid in the Life cereal commercial: "Mikey likes it!") through the back pages of *Archie* comic books, from which I regularly ordered gag items, even into my teen years: itching powder (ground horsehair), hand buzzers, fake vomit, fake dog poop, 3-D specs (they just made everything fuzzy), various voice-throwing devices (they didn't work at all), whoopee cushions, garlic "candies" (my mother loved them), squirting rings, nail-through-the-nose tricks, severed-finger tricks, packets of fake blood, and loads of other such gear—all of which I found to be useful social lubricants. Sea monkeys, the only other living things sold by mail order, turned out to be teensy freeze-dried brine shrimp, which, when "given life," darted about aimlessly in still, murky water. The full-page ad in *Life with Archie* promised a veritable underwater civilization: mommy monkeys in pert *That Girl* flip-dos and strands of pearls stood in doorways of neat suburban homes handing lunch pails to little ones boarding school buses as daddy monkeys, dressed in natty suits and carrying briefcases, hopped into late model cars and drove off to work, waving warmly to their kids and adoring wives. In real life, after a few days, the stagnant bowl of spermlike organisms began to stink. Even Linc stopped wanting to lap it up (he'd drunk nearly half the population already). I flushed the foul soup without remorse.

The most tragic of all our smaller pets was little Missy, a truly adorable apricot toy poodle Eva brought home from Le Chien, the chic Upper East Side dog-grooming salon she'd started working at a few months after graduating from high school. Planning to save money for college and eventually become a veterinarian, Eva had started her animal-care career at K-9 Sentry on Burke Avenue, purveyor of attack dogs, but had quit after a just few weeks, recounting chilling tales of brutal training sessions and a rat infestation so severe that the poor caged mongrels sported fresh bite marks on their backs and bellies every morning.

Le Chien was at the polar opposite end of the spectrum. A sweet little storefront done up like a French patisserie, on First Avenue in the seventies, with miniature perfumed pedigrees dancing in the plate-glass window and gemstone-encrusted pastel leather collars for sale in a beveled case, the shop was owned and operated by a former southern belle of a certain age—a slender bleached blonde in pale designer pantsuits whose high-rise apartment was uniformly white and gold and whose neurotic Lhasa apso, Frou-Frou, could be surprisingly vicious. Le Chien's client list overflowed with celebrities, so the shop turned up frequently in gossip and society pages.

"Who was spotted popping her pooch into chic Le Chien for a wash and fluff? None other than the Divine Callas herself!"

Or, less tastefully: "Stevie Wonder 'sees' to it that his precious pet gets the royal treatment at Le Chien, dog grooming salon to the stars."

(The savvy shop owner must have had an excellent publicist.)

Eva labored in the back, doing the actual bathing and grooming alongside a hearty German woman named Laura, hidden behind a set of white louver doors framed by elegant drapery.

Missy had been dropped off at the shop for boarding but never picked up again, having been purchased only months earlier by the operator of an upscale brothel for the purpose of "entertaining the girls" during downtime. Apparently, the girls were not entertained. Missy arrived back at the shop dehydrated and underfed, with matted coat and filmy eyes. Eva and Laura took an instant shine to the poor little rich girl, plumping her up and letting her out of the cage more often than the others. The little dog returned their kindness with ebullient affection and absolute obedience. When no one claimed her after a few weeks, and after several calls to the owner went unanswered, Eva's boss let Eva adopt the dog with the caveat that she'd have to be returned if the owner resurfaced. (He never did.)

She came home to us in an elegant powder blue carrier. We installed our sloe-eyed secret in Rosette's attic bedroom (my father knew nothing of her existence), laying blankets on the floor to absorb the sound of her little paws skittering across the old linoleum, taking turns spending time with her to keep her from yapping. Linc picked up the scent right away, almost giving us away by whining and pawing at the bedroom door incessantly. When finally we introduced them, it was love at first whiff. Linc was supremely gentle with his new baby sister; she, bold and delighted to make his acquaintance, stood up on her hind legs and sniffed his nose, ran around in tight circles, made goo-goo eyes at him. The unlikely duo (Eva did them up as a lion and a lamb at Christmastime) quickly invented a game that became their signature: Missy would jump up and grab ahold of his scruffy beard with her teeth while Linc tossed his head around gently. You could practically hear them laughing.

When we broke the news of Missy's adoption to my father, we emphasized the natural kinship between the dogs. He objected mildly . . . but couldn't resist. Who could? Missy was the happiest, fluffiest, sweetest pup ever, with an exhaustive capacity for soaking up and doling out affection. Eva gussied her up in little rhinestone collars and fleece-lined coats and booties, all purchased with earnings from the shop. She was very disciplined with her salary, saving and spending in proper measure. She'd sometimes bring me to work with her, splurging on lunch at Ray's Pizza (I can attest here and now, thus settling the perennial debate, that the original Ray's was located on the Upper East Side, in the seventies); candlelight dinners in the cave-like atmosphere of the Monks' Inn—a theme restaurant featuring waiters in long, brown robes serving French country fare, rough loaves of black bread on well-worn cutting boards, and fresh-churned butter in earthenware bowls; even an occasional feast at Nirvana, a luscious Indian restaurant nestled into the penthouse of a posh East Side high-rise, windows all around, the city spreading like liquid silver in every direction.

Eva's first major purchase was a secondhand Volkswagen bug—

lemon yellow, convertible—which she fussed over like a mother hen. Next came a brand-spanking-new ten-speed bicycle, electric blue, with all the bells and whistles. On the day Eva brought it home, before she had so much as taken a test drive, I begged her to let me sample it.

"No way," she insisted wisely. But I pressed and pushed until she caved. "Just once around the block," she warned.

"I promise," I replied, and meant it . . . until the smooth, zippy handling of the bike seduced me into going a little farther. I rode over to St. Lucy's to impress my friends. On the way back home, I picked up a tad too much speed heading across Waring Avenue, and lost control of the bike as I approached the intersection at Boston Post Road. Realizing in a flash that I could either head into oncoming traffic or crash into the massive pillar of the El, I chose the latter, blasting full on into the unyielding colossus, smashing myself up pretty good . . . and totaling the bike. Panicked and bleeding, I dragged the mass of mangled metal and rubber into the nearest gas station, begging for help.

"Nothing we can do for you," said an unhelpful mechanic. "Try a bike shop."

Eva was waiting for me out front as, dragging the destroyed vehicle in tow, I approached the house. She screamed when she saw what I'd done, and ran toward me in tears. After confirming that I hadn't been too badly hurt, she started howling like a coyote, clutching the gnarled remains to her chest and cursing me to hell. New Jersey Grandma came toddling out of the house.

"Whats-a-matta you yella, hah?"

My sister was inconsolable. It wasn't the first time I had rendered her thus. There had been the Windy incident, of course—and the infamous accident with the ceramic sculpture Eva had been working on in art class for almost the entirety of her senior year of high school. It had won several awards and had been displayed in the school lobby. When she finally brought it home and installed it on a bookshelf in the living room, I found myself irresistibly drawn to the object. Mounted upon a small, black block of wood, the brown-hued bust bore a striking resemblance to my father's old friend, Jack Singer (thick lips, wide eyes, bald pate, ring of curly hair around the back and sides of the head). I gazed into it fixedly, entranced and amazed. I picked it up to take a closer look. It was heavier than I thought. *Boom!* It fell to the floor and shattered into rubble.

"Arrgghh!" I heard Eva scream from two flights up.

I was able to have the bicycle rebuilt eventually, but remained forever powerless to salvage Eva's demolished masterpiece—which I feel guilty about to this very day.

My big sister's new life as a working girl was one of many big changes happening right then. The halcyon Paramus days had ended with sudden ignominy when Aunt Terry and Uncle Danny filed for divorce amid messy circumstances—a scandalous heartbreak for the entire extended family. The details were kept from us kids, but we gathered that another woman was involved . . . maybe more than one. New Jersey Grandma, blaming the victim, started referring to Terry as *la strega* (the witch) when she put Danny out of the house.

"What eeza theese—'kaput'?" I remember her asking my mother. "La strega say the marry-ash ess 'kaput.' "

And it was. Aunt Diana tried for a while to carry on the tradition of Sunday dinner, but it had become awkward, my cousins arriving sans parents, sullen and confused, the crack-up of their family an elephant in the room. I could feel them drifting away from my sisters and me slowly, with dreamlike languor, as if we occupied opposite ends of an ice floe that had broken in half, dividing us, each frozen mass yielding independently to the inevitable forces of nature.

On the heels of her twenty-first birthday, in 1973, Rosette moved out of the house and into an apartment in Yonkers, despite my father's violent objections. They had been doing serious battle over Paulie, Rosette's heroin-addicted boyfriend, whom she'd been dating off and on (mostly on) for years. Paulie was an abstract concept to me. I never met him and glimpsed him only once or twice. He was never discussed. He was not supposed to exist. But he did. Very much. Exist. My father disowned Rosette when she left, and our contact with her became limited.

Even the physical arrangement inside the house was shifting: When my father and I completed our renovation of the raw half of the attic, Eva moved into an irregular patch of it, cordoning off the area and draping the slanted walls and ceilings with Indian-print fabrics, covering the floor with a plush white faux fur rug (which she brushed regularly on her hands and knees and forbade me from treading upon except when shoeless and specifically invited to do so), swathing the entrance to her lair in layers of sheer fabric—a nifty harem effect. Maria moved into the other half, opting for a spare contemporary look that would become her signature. Across the hall, Rosette's bedroom remained empty and untouched, many of her belongings still in place, a still-life shrine to our missing sister, an omen of her eventual return.

I was upgraded to the second-floor bedroom earlier shared by Eva and Maria—a veritable studio apartment compared with my former digs, with four big windows (they'd soon be closed up or replaced with little ones) and space enough to create separate and distinct areas: lounge, study, boudoir. I hung brightly colored fishnets from the ceilings and, in a nod to Eva's design scheme, draped Indian-print bedspreads on the walls, daydreaming obsessively about doing up the room all in black and white with bold splashes of red—a look I'd seen in a movie or a magazine. I started saving up money for a bedroom ensemble like the ones so many of my friends had—matching bed, dresser, mirror, desk—but never managed to acquire one.

The only steadfastly unchanging element in our world was a constant drumbeat of hard labor. The titanic task my father had tapped for us seemed to grow exponentially with every fresh strike of the crowbar. My labors were not only misery-making but thankless. My father seemed to disapprove of every move I made. I don't know why it never occurred to me to rebel; instead, I became hell-bent on earning praise. For a while it was my habit to make performance-rating charts for him to fill out and return to me. Drawn by hand in carpenter pencil, they were arranged like grade school report cards, with a column down the left listing various tasks I'd completed (cleaning basement, threading pipe, burying debris, et cetera) and a row of boxes next to each task to be checked according to how well it had been executed (excellent, very good, good, satisfactory, poor, unsatisfactory). I never actually gave these charts to my father but often filled them out myself. I tried to be honest about my performance in each case, and designed a grading system so I could arrive at an overall score for a given week. Some part of me was aware, always, of how poignant these charts were, and how pathetic, yet I was compelled to go on creating them. The times I can remember my father praising my efforts, or even acknowledging them, are few.

Like the day he rented a Dumpster to facilitate the removal of demolition debris, which had begun to overwhelm our property. I worked alone for twelve hours or more, filling the massive steel container with wheelbarrowful after wheelbarrowful of pulverized plaster, mangled lathing, discarded doors and windows, trims and moldings, radiators and flooring, and so on. It was a stifling Saturday in August, the kind of New York City summer day when the body is simultaneously fried from above by the naked sun and baked from below by ovenlike heat pulsing out of buildings and beating up from the pavement; the kind of heat that softens metal, melts blacktop. I worked tirelessly despite the burn, thrilled to be ridding the property of a haunting mess that depressed me daily, embarrassed me when friends came over, crushed any potential for normalcy—a neat little yard with a table beneath an umbrella, say, a few flowers blooming nearby.

The potential for that existed. When we first moved into the house, Eva had bought loads of gardening books and catalogs, and started planning the creation of lush woodland. She was going to hang a hammock between two trees in the side yard and install beside it a little pond (available by mail order). She was going to plant water lilies in the pond, stock it with goldfish, carpet the whole area in a soft blanket of pine needles. In the opposite side yard, long and skinny, she was going to plant a bed of flowering ground cover in a rainbow of colors. The scrappy backyard she'd transform by planting squares of sod in a checkerboard pattern, which the catalog said would soon grow toward each other to form a dense, velvety carpet of green. Along the back fence there would be a flower garden—pansies and impatiens, buttercups and morning glories—and off to the side an organic vegetable garden. She got started in small ways, ordering the sod and a few other items, clearing away dense weed patches, hauling rocks out of the ground.

But then we came home one day to find that my father had done a little gardening of his own: all the trees around the property—most of them tall and slender, except for the ancient backyard oak (which would later have to be felled for safety reasons)—had been cut down. But not completely. For reasons unknown, my father had sheared the trees at about the five-foot mark, leaving stripped, leafless poles where verdant shade givers once swayed. Eva screamed when she saw the massacre, and cried for a week. The sod she'd ordered ended up rotting in its cardboard boxes. Her garden was never planted. I was crushed to see my sister crushed this way. Her dream for us was sweet. The end of it made things feel hopeless. I was sorry for her, sorry for us, sorry for all of it.

So it was with glee that I loaded up the Dumpster that summer day, freeing the property of its abusive load, making it possible for grass to grow there again, or even just weeds. When the huge container was filled to overflowing, the yards were finally clear. A wasted, burnt-up thing, but happy, I slumped into the house to wash up for dinner. (Still no air-conditioning, of course, and no fans to speak of.) I think it was on my way to the bathroom, or maybe later, nearer bedtime, that my father spoke admiringly about me to my mother loud enough for me to hear.

"He put in some day today, your son. What a job. *Nice work.*"

I remember swelling with pride, smiling uncontrollably, feeling a surge of energy. At the same time, I felt embarrassed to be fussing so over having been tossed a bone. Good doggy.

My father seems to have been bent on preparing and training me not for life in general, or for the world, but simply for life under his rule, in his house. What kind of man did he think would grow from such a boy? Would I learn to be confident and secure, aggressive in proper measure, prepared to assert myself in the world—all on my own? My disdainful peers—those sloped, leering boys draped against chain-link fences or crouched on stoops and benches, expressing revulsion at the sight of me, repudiating with ease the value of my very existence ("what a waste," they'd say)—had sealed the deal. I wound up being secretly scared of my own shadow well into manhood, insecure and self-conscious to an unbearable degree. I too much surrendered my power, in big and small ways, to lovers and salesclerks, employers and friends, passersby—everyone; too frequently sought approval and affirmation from every human transaction; too reflexively apologized to everyone for everything, as if trying to erase any trace of myself as I went; too willingly asked for permission where none was due, from people who had no authority to grant it in the first place. I learned too well to hide, learned to lie too freely, found too much comfort in isolation. I wasted too many years not knowing that I was young and beautiful and the world was my oyster.

Our already overwhelming workload was compounded by my father's initiation of several additional grandiose projects and undertakings—one such behemoth being the planning of an international pilgrimage and celebration to mark the thirtieth anniversary, in 1974, of the liberation from Nazi occupation of the town of Maastricht, Holland, by the 30th Infantry. Dad had maintained regular contact with his army buddies through the Old Hickory Association and, as the anniversary approached, summarily appointed himself president of the self-formed Maastricht Reunion Committee. His plan was to lead a couple of hundred men and their wives on a chartered trip to the Netherlands, where they would retrace the steps of their battles and be reunited with those they'd liberated thirty years earlier.

Recruiting my mother, sisters, and me as staff, my father coordinated the whole affair out of the master bedroom, posting hundreds of letters, making thousands of phone calls, organizing scores of meetings. My poor mother typed letters, labels, mailing lists, and other correspondence on the old Royal well into the night. The rest of us were put to work folding and collating letters, stuffing envelopes, licking stamps. The phone had to be clear at all times for any international calls that might be coming through. We became, for a long stretch of time, a bustling, family-run travel and event-planning agency, even as the systematic demolition of the house continued at full throttle around our very ears.

My father convinced KLM Airlines, the Dutch carrier, to sponsor several trips to Holland and Belgium so he could make the proper arrangements. We were like prisoners on furlough when he was away, filling the house with music, eating at odd hours, coming and going at will. He'd return home boasting about being on a first-name basis with the mayor of Antwerp, a *Bürgermeister,* and several diplomats. We just shrugged—but he ended up pulling off a success that well exceeded our imagination. The infantry was given a heroes' welcome. Street celebrations sprang up all around the event, attended by thousands of people. Tearful, wrenching scenes abounded of local people recognizing the men they called their "liberators." My father cried countless times, an unusual emotional expression for him, and was duly celebrated everywhere we went. He had managed to scrape enough money together to bring our family along: my mother, his mother, Eva, Maria, and me. We were thrilled to be traveling abroad, and amazed by what my father's machinations had wrought. I remember ending up alone with him in a department store at one point, squirming with my usual discomfort.

"What a trip this is," I said, just to break the silence. "I feel sorry for all the people who didn't come." Clutching some socks and underwear for purchase, my father gazed off into the distance, his eyes watering.

"They didn't believe," he said, "but they don't matter, the ones

MY FATHER (FAR RIGHT) WITH
ASSORTED DUTCH DIGNITARIES
AND SUPPORTERS OF THE MAASTRICHT REUNION

who didn't come. The ones who came—they matter. They know. They know . . ." This was an utterly private moment. It did not include me.

"Enna whatsa theeza place-a we inna now?" New Jersey Grandma kept asking at every stop, "becooz I wanna tella Concett'."

A week later, back at home, on the phone: "That's-a right. My sonna take-a me to Brucella, Ollanda, Germana—all ova-da."

She was in constant competition with Concetta, her Old Country friend, whose son was a doctor. "Enna he take-a me for-a fly onna da privada jetta," Grandma continued, exaggerating. The jet wasn't private—but the flight *was* chartered, the cabin a flying party, familiar passengers climbing through the aisles, chatting and drinking, ignoring the annoyed stewardesses' constant entreaties to "return to your seats and fasten your seat belts."

My father commandeered the PA system and stopped speaking into it almost never for the duration of the eight-hour-plus flight, reading aloud letters from various Dutch dignitaries, discussing the upcoming itinerary, reviewing policies and procedures. When he played the Dutch national anthem and tried to get the crowd to sing along phonetically, several fellow travelers shut him down.

"Shut up, Cappi. That's enough now," I remember one drunken man yelling across the plane, his pants open for comfort, his hairy belly hanging out, a Dutch stewardess looking on disapprovingly.

My recollections of that ten-day excursion are a random assortment of animated postcards: checking into the little hotel in the center of Maastricht, with its hand-operated elevator in a gilded cage and long, spindly room keys from another century; wandering the quaint cobblestone streets of that town, becoming hopelessly lost and discovering Maria to be a natural bloodhound, able to guide us instinctively back to where we'd started with eerie precision ("I think we make a left here and turn right at the next corner and then go across that park down there and through the outdoor market"); a daylong bus trip to Paris, where we were dropped off in Pigalle, the red-light district, and given a few hours to kill before having to hit the road again—our travel mates opting to dine at McDonald's, my mother breaking us free to dine at a little *tabac*—breaking away myself after lunch, sneaking into a few of the porn shops lining the avenue, swiping some hard-core chapbooks and leafing through them feverishly in the bus john on the ride back to Maastricht; a side trip to Amsterdam—a cloudy day canal ride; a street festival in Brussels in which thousands of bundles of superstinky Limburger cheese were distributed as souvenirs, repellent to all but Grandma ("Aldo like-a theeza cheeza," she insists, collecting a shopping bag full of the stuff and carrying it home on the plane, marching boldly through customs denying its existence, stinking up the entire plane cabin on the way home); visiting a Dutch couple and going out to a pub with their teenage son—tearing through town in a tiny sports car at a hundred miles an hour, thinking Eva and I would not make it back alive; Grandma urging me to steal decorative objects from every restaurant we entered, pointing up at various displays and whispering, "Carlo, get-a for me this-a potta and that big-a spoon-a"; arriving back home in the Bronx feeling immediately like the trip had happened in the distant past, the souvenirs in my hand—miniature wooden clogs on a key chain, a mirrored elephant figurine, a Delft medallion—objects from another dimension.

A year later, in the fall of 1975, Eva, about to turn twenty, leaves home to attend college at SUNY New Paltz. One day she loads up her yellow convertible Volkswagen bug, hugs and kisses us all, and is gone. The house is strangely silent without her. All I can hear for a while is her missing voice. Maria and I are suddenly a twosome—she on the brink of puberty, I in its throes.

The sister whom I had always considered a kind of twin had been gone just a few weeks when Missy skipped breakfast one day and moped around listlessly, her eyes dull, her nose warm and dry. We called Eva, and she recommended a few home remedies—softening Missy's food, feeding her water with a dropper, creating a "sickbed" for her. We vowed to take the dog to the vet if she didn't improve in a day or two. By the next morning, she was dead. She'd tottered into my parents' room overnight, sat on the floor at my mother's side of the bed, and whimpered for a while, waking my mother and asking for attention—highly unusual. When Mom found her lifeless and stiff as wood a few hours later, the house erupted into a storm of grief and bewilderment: What could possibly have killed Missy so suddenly? Had we failed to notice that she'd been sick for a longer time? Was it something we'd fed her? Could we have saved her with swifter action? Eva came down from school to hammer together one last coffin. We buried Missy in the side yard, which my grief-stricken sister had once imagined enchanting with hammock and pond, our hearts racked with guilt: surely we could have prevented this somehow; surely we were responsible. Linc searched for his little buddy for days afterward, rattled and confused by her sudden disappearance.

Only Niffi soldiered on, having grown into a proper grimalkin by then, mangy and nasty and mean. Why couldn't the invisible illness have stricken *her*? She lounged about stiffly, hissing whenever anyone approached, leaving disgusting stains everywhere she went from the wet rash plaguing her entire underside. Nothing cured that condition, not even the wide plastic collar we attached to her neck for weeks at a time to keep her from licking the mess (and which reminded me of the costume worn by Bette Davis in *The Virgin Queen*). When she'd ruined enough furniture and bedding, Niffi was confined to areas where heavy towels, changed regularly, had been set down over every surface. Still, she managed to slither out and roam free, soiling the house with a trail of colorful effluvia.

13.

Disco changed my life.

When first I heard the extended-play version of Donna Summer's "Love to Love You, Baby," in 1975, I was stunned into silence, stilled midstride. I'd heard a few earlier expressions of this brand-new music on *Soul Train* and WBLS-FM—jams like "Wicky Wacky" by the Fatback Band, the Hues Corporation's clunky "Rock the Boat," George McCrae's "Rock Your Baby," "The Love I Lost" by Harold Melvin and the Blue Notes, "Never Can Say Goodbye" by Gloria Gaynor—but Summer's seminal recording was operating at a whole other level. Expansive, transportive, epic, it sounded like nothing else. I boarded the bus to Alexander's in a trance, bought the album (the young singer's U.S. debut), and played it over and over on my trusty Lloyd's quadraphonic sound system with built-in eight-track cassette player and space-age flip clock, recording the title song (which clocked in at just under seventeen minutes, the longest continuous track I'd ever heard) on my father's portable cassette tape player, getting into big trouble for leaving the house with Dad's only high-tech toy so the music could be in my ear all day long. Even as the batteries on the old Flintstones-era device wore down and Summer's voice became a low-pitched warble, I found the sound rapturous. It wasn't just the spare, cunning vocals: the luxuriously extended musical changes and lush, driving orchestrations moved me and moved my body. (Pete Bellote was the album's brilliant British producer. His partner, the now-legendary Giorgio Moroder, collaborated with him on nearly all subsequent Summer recordings, building masterfully upon the sumptuous template Bellote had laid down with "Love to Love You, Baby.") Rumor had it that Donna's intense moaning and wailing were the sounds of live masturbation.

"She had eighteen orgasms while she was making this record— no, *for real!*" went a typical claim. The number climbed as the rumor gained traction.

"She had twenty-six orgasms while she was making this record!"

"She had thirty-two orgasms!"

"Sixty-eight orgasms, yo!"

I became a devoted aficionado, hungrily lapping up the grooves of a parade of fierce divas, trailblazing bands, and cutting-edge producers as they stormed, one after another, into the spotlight. Miss Summer was the High Priestess (her 1976 follow-up album, *A Love Trilogy,* took the sound to new heights, a trend that continued with *Four Seasons of Love,* released later that same year, its cover photo inspiring a fresh rumor that Donna was secretly a man—"Just look at her *hands!*"—and peaked with *Once Upon a Time* in 1977), but fabulousness abounded: there was Thelma Houston, Gloria Gaynor, Barry White and the Love Unlimited Orchestra, the Salsoul Orchestra, the Trammps, Dan Hartman, Van McCoy, Chic, Cerrone, Silver Convention, Grace Jones, Carol Douglas, Shirley and Company, the Three Degrees, MFSB, the First Choice (whose "Philly sound" recordings on the Philly Groove label, produced by MFSB's Norman Harris, form a critical link between pre- and post-disco dance music), the Oasis, Salsoul, Casablanca, TK Records labels, and so many others.

The music provided a transcendent sound track for high school— supplemented, of course, by the continued output of folksier faves like Melanie, Carole King, Carly Simon, and Cat Stevens, along with exciting new sounds from Elton John . . . and a brooding upstart named Billy Joel. (Bette Midler, another rip-roaring newcomer, blew my mind three times in a row with her first three albums: *The Divine Miss M, Bette Midler,* and *Songs for the New Depression.* I staked out a stretch of Barrow Street in the Village when I read that she lived there, hoping to catch a glimpse of this strange, staggeringly original chanteuse, and sent her a fan letter to which she replied with a hand-typed note, replete with typos and ink-drawn corrections. Eva loved to mimic Bette's bathos-laden cover of Karen Carpenter's "Superstar": *"Ya called me baby / Baby, baby, baby, oh bay-bay . . ."*) My St. Lucy's friends, now attending area Catholic high schools, were almost as hot for disco as I was. The finished basement of Peter Mazzoni's house on Bronxwood Avenue, a few doors down from the church, was our headquarters for sharing new music and practicing the hustle. I had some experience with salsa, and a few of our crew knew swing; between us, we were able to perfect a dance vocabulary of tricky turns, dips, strides. I soon became a proto–Tony Manero, living the life long before he gave it a name. (When *Saturday Night Fever* came out, a couple of years later, my friends and I scoffed: Travolta's game was corny. He wasn't doing it right. His partner couldn't dance *at all.* We were the real thing, and we knew it.)

Still hesitant to venture fully into the larger world of Manhattan, we'd go to nearby discotheques like the Second Floor in Yonkers or Peachtrees in New Rochelle to showcase our skills. Hustling required great energy and abandon . . . along with equally great *control.* I loved the stillness and swivel in the hips as the feet worked fancifully; the elegant, high-speed port de bras; the drama of the dance itself, swelling with the swell of the music; loved the look on my partner's face, my hand on her hip, our wordless communication, my authority in leading. I earned a reputation for making any girl, no matter how inexperienced, look good on the dance floor.

"Just relax and follow me," I'd say. "Don't try to do anything special. Just move with the beat."

I felt sexy saying that, sexy on the dance floor, sexy leading these sexy girls—but it wasn't about sex. I was just trying to find the ideal hustle partner. She came to me in the form of a schoolmate named Margaret, whom I happened to run into at a club one night and who turned out to be an expert, showing me a few new tricks and executing her moves with hard polish. She was ebullient and wild on the dance floor, but always in total control. We seemed to meld completely into the dance, eyes locked on each other's, bodies in smooth motion, people respectfully clearing space all around us so we could really break it down. I understood in our best moments that dancing was the closest I'd ever come to flying. I came to need it on a regular basis. Margaret and I started practicing in empty schoolrooms between classes or during lunch. We couldn't get enough. It felt good to be physically intimate with a girl like this without the pressure of sex.

Columbus High turned out to be a vast improvement over my previous public school experience, perhaps because it had an actual name, not just a numerical assignation. Two St. Lucy's friends became fellow students, along with a few good pals from 135. We were quickly joined by a couple of new faces—and suddenly school was *fun.* I became heavily involved in extracurricular activities, joining the debate club, the school newspaper, the chorus (whose leader, Mr. Horn, after a bit of vocal coaching, suggested I just lip-synch), the poetry club, the merit club . . . If they offered it (and it was not sports-related), I joined it. At one point, late in my high school career, I was simultaneously performing in the school play; serving as both editor in chief of *The Admiral,* our school newspaper, and class vice president; performing community service at a local nursing home; and being featured in a lobby display as Poet of the Month. (I'd won for a trippy ditty, lost to time, called "Into My Mind.")

Gym class, which I continued to dread and despise, was now optional. Thanks to an ambitious lesbian fitness instructor, students could choose instead to attend unisex lessons in fencing or modern dance. Delighted for a chance to escape the oppressive environment of traditional phys ed—with its humiliating rituals of volleyball, basketball, dodgeball (all balls were problematic)—I gleefully elected fencing, finding instant romance in the accoutrements: white jacket, knickers, slippers and gloves, black-and-white mesh mask, silver épée; romance in the basic stances and lunges; in shouting *"En garde!"* and *"Touché!"*

Miss Jaffee, another hip, young teacher making welcome changes, insisted that we call her Marlene—a novelty and a thrill, very adult—and offered an English class called WOW: World of Women, in which she exposed us to radical feminism and other incendiary ideas. She arranged the chairs in a circle and invited us to consider each class "a rap session." The WOW reading list included *Our Bodies, Ourselves* and *Sisterhood Is Powerful,* the latter containing Valerie Solanas's "S.C.U.M. (Society for Cutting Up Men) Manifesto," which caused great upset in the classroom. Solanas argued for the complete eradication of the male species, except for a few specimens to be spared for breeding purposes until a more efficient means of procreation could be found. My classmates, girls and boys both, were universally outraged. I was in the small camp not taking the writer seriously—a foolish mistake, of course, since Solanas had already gotten started on her ambitious agenda by shooting Andy Warhol (which Marlene conveniently failed to mention)—and guffawed at Solanas's observation that the average man "will swim through a river of snot, wade nostril-deep through a mile of vomit, if he thinks there'll be a friendly pussy awaiting him." Marlene moderated the heated classroom debate with authority and bemusement. She loved pushing our buttons. And we loved having them pushed. (At home, I hid my WOW books like pornography. My father *could not know* about any of this.)

Marlene also offered classes in drama and film studies, exposing us to playwrights like Tennessee Williams and Lillian Hellman; early film directors like Fritz Lang and Sergei Eisenstein; dramaturgical concepts like subtext and story structure; technical concepts like cinematography and the persistence of vision (a natural trick of the human eye that makes motion pictures possible). She took us to see student productions at Pace and Lehman Colleges (Hellman's *The Children's Hour* and Arthur Miller's *All My Sons* were highlights), and enrolled us in a city outreach program sponsoring special weekday matiness of popular Broadway plays especially for public high school students.

"I loved it!" I'd gush erumpently after each performance—we saw *Pippin, The Wiz,* and *Your Arms Too Short to Box with God*—wowed by what I considered wondrous virtuosity.

"You love everything," Marlene complained, egging me on to think more critically. She took us to a series of afternoon symposia with Broadway luminaries (sponsored by the same city program), and I remember staring, starstruck, at George C. Scott and Trish Van Devere sitting casually on stools on the bare stage of a Broadway house, fielding questions from the student audience. My father had taken us to see George C. Scott play George S. Patton in the movie *Patton*. I'd been awed by the actor's ferocious tour de force—and also by the abstract understanding that my father had served under this fabled warrior. Patton, Scott, and my father were linked inextricably in my mind in some muddled way. Scott, in person, actually looked a little like my dad, which added to the confusion, and his name was eerily similar to the general's. That day is a blur.

A more vivid recollection is the Tennessee Williams symposium: Pandemonium threatened to ensue as restless high school students awaited a very late playwright. When finally he arrived and was introduced, Williams stumbled out onto the stage of the Winter Garden Theatre, smashed, wearing an overcoat with a bottle of booze sticking out of the pocket. The first words he uttered were almost exactly these:

"You know, this used to be an old vaudeville house. Back in those days, there would have been a ramp running out from the stage, cutting right down the center aisle. I wish that ramp were still here. I'd get on it and keep walking until I was out the front door."

When a precocious student asked why he never wrote comedies, Williams quipped, "You apparently haven't read my plays."

Afterward, a tabloid reporter working the Broadway beat, a character out of Damon Runyon, solicited comments from exiting students.

"Whadja think?" he asked me. I looked at Marlene.

"Tell him the truth," she suggested. I reported that I was disappointed; Williams was a "hero of mine," I said, and it was "disturbing" to see him drunk and belligerent onstage. I was mortified to find my words in print the next morning.

Marlene reestablished the Drama Club, long defunct, and started mounting full productions every spring. *My Sister Eileen* was the first of these, produced in my sophomore year. I had not yet joined the Drama Club but attended several performances of the play, impressed by the level of professionalism on display. A raven-haired beauty named Joanna Bonaro, a junior and the club's star actress, played the title role with great style and panache. I became friendly with her and her shy twin sister, Virginia (who preferred to work behind the scenes, as a stage manager), and they introduced me to sexy, swarthy Victor Almonte, their good friend and another rising Drama Club star. Victor was a Mediterranean Montgomery Clift—slim and slinky with olive skin, jet-black hair, and soft brown eyes twinkling behind gold-tinted aviator lenses. I knew he was gay, and I was sure that he knew I was too.

We became great pals, discovering in short order that we shared a taste for pot, a love of disco, and an attraction to the stage. The following season, in the spring of 1976, Victor played Tony Kirby opposite Joanna's Alice Sycamore (the male and female ingenue roles) in Marlene's production of Kaufman and Hart's *You Can't Take It with You.* Girls squealed and swooned upon his entrance, literally stopping the show to fuss over the quiet stud, slightly effeminate, in his powder blue three-piece suit and slick black hair. Poor Virginia collapsed into a lachrymose heap when she marred the last moments of Victor's final performance by closing the curtain too early. The earnest young thespian had taken a long, actorly pause before saying his line; Ginny heard the silence, thought she'd missed her cue, and released the curtain.

The resulting confusion in the audience didn't stop dozens of girls from rushing down the aisle and throwing themselves at the foot of the stage during Victor's curtain call. He was pursued hotly in the hallways for weeks afterward but took it all in his stride. I don't think he even dated.

I'd very much wanted to play the role of Paul Sycamore (Alice's father) in that production but was instead cast in the bit part of Mr. Henderson, the tax collector. Mr. Henderson's entrance is a feint for Tony's, a sight gag: the eccentric household is swirling with preparations for the arrival of Alice's fancy suitor; the doorbell rings; the family arranges itself for the young man's entrance; Alice, smiling nervously, swings open the front door—to reveal nerdy, nervous Mr. Henderson in a cheap suit, crushed fedora, and goofy spectacles, clutching an old-fashioned briefcase. I enjoyed the big laugh, but was secretly embarrassed to be cast in the doofus role, a walk-on, while Victor, debonair, strutted the boards as the dream lover.

At Marlene's prodding, I eventually penned a short play of my own, my first, a seething melodrama called *Victims of Circumstance*, about a pair of neglected suburban housewives who become lesbians. Joanna and Victor played husband and wife in the classroom production—a triumph of casting. In the penultimate scene, she begins to break the news to him.

"What are you trying to say to me?" he demands, shuddering. "That you're a—"

"Say it, Bill. Go on—just say it!"

"—*a lesbian?*"

"Yes! Yes, I'm a lesbian!" she screams, sobbing convulsively.

The actors went for broke, chewing up the scenery like hungry beavers. *Victims of Circumstance* got a standing ovation. A girl named Millie told me it was better than watching TV.

Through Victor I became an active member of the Student Council, presided over by a math teacher named Stan Stein, another young hipster—Jewish 'fro, Geraldo Rivera–style mustache, elephant bells, and platform shoes—who happened to be a good friend of Marlene's, and under whose tutelage the student government office was transformed into a groovy seventies lounge: chocolate brown walls with harvest gold trim, Peter Max posters, rice cakes and natural peanut butter to snack on. The office became home base, a room of our own, a place to be utterly free. Our young teachers were friends and mentors. They didn't judge us. They treated us like adults. Marlene lived with her longtime boyfriend on the Upper West Side on Manhattan; Stan lived alone on the Upper East. They invited us into the city frequently, turning us on to funky little restaurants and cafés in their respective neighborhoods.

Stan's meticulous, antiques-filled apartment featured an audiophile-quality stereo system with high-tech speakers and woofers. He loved disco as much as we did. I have a vivid memory of his arranging Victor and me on his chocolate brown sofa (he favored the color), right between the two main speakers, and blasting a demo pressing of "I Need a Man" by Grace Jones. We all agreed that it was splendiferous.

I knew instinctively that Stan was gay, and I knew he knew that Victor and I were too. But it was not discussed. I plotted in my mind over and over again to make a move on Victor, to just lean in real close when the moment was right. I tried to manufacture serendipity by booking as much private time with him as possible. He seemed to be doing the same—as when he invited me alone to his grandparents' apartment while they were away. We had the run of the place. We kicked off our shoes and lounged on the carpet, watching TV, smoking hits, acting silly. Over and over again, our bodies and lips were near enough to touch—but did not.

I remember thinking that I had blown my one best chance with Victor as I donned my shoes again and prepared to leave the quiet apartment after that long, lazy afternoon. He was a senior now, and would be on his way to New York University in the fall. He'd be living in a dormitory in the Village, meeting new people, exposing himself to the whole wide world, gone from me. I attended his—and Jo's and Ginny's—graduation ceremony that June with a heavy heart; my last year of high school was going to be lonely. Stan and Marlene watched the unfolding drama with knowing eyes, quietly shepherding us the best they could, never pushing or prodding, letting us be. For the first time, really—just letting us *be*.

At home, my mother prepared the elements of dinner before leaving for work in the morning. I'd race into the house at the end of the school day—late, on account of all my extracurriculars—quickly complete one or two of the hideous tasks on my to-do list, wash up, change into clean clothes, and get dinner started as per her written instructions. (Maria's jobs were to set the table and help wash dishes.) Eventually I became an excellent cook, but not before destroying several barnyards' worth of sausage, cutlets, chops, and roasts. After dinner, it was time for homework and other duties, but sometimes I'd manage to slip out for a quick visit with my St. Lucy's friends, or to other friends' houses in the neighborhood. I had learned how to disappear for minutes, sometimes hours, at a time, having consciously and unconsciously practiced the art unto mastery.

Bicentennial fever was sweeping the nation, building to a frenzy as Independence Day approached. Peter Mazzoni and I, like other teens in the neighborhood (and around the country), painted fire hydrants and curbstones in patriotic patterns of red, white, and blue. Murals and flags abounded. Everyone was stocking up on fireworks. Big block parties were planned. My father had decided to mark the occasion in his own special way—with an international event even more ambitious in scope than the Maastricht reunion: Torch 200 was his complex scheme to arrange for the Athletiekverening, or AV34—a society of Dutch athletes that began running liberation marathons in 1949—to carry a lit torch from Europe to America, and to then run across the country with the living flame in an athletic bicentennial tribute. He designed logos and letterhead, wrote countless letters (which he insisted upon reading aloud to us over and over again), worked the phones to the point of farce. Again, he traveled to Europe to make arrangements, recruited his family as staff . . . and pulled off a remarkable success.

When it was all over, the mayor of Antwerp presented my father with an engraved plaque bearing the Torch 200 logo, dubbing him "Cappi, The Running Ambassador." The self-styled citizen diplomat had single-handedly mapped out an itinerary that started in Holland, blazed a path across the ocean, and wended its way cross-country, coast to coast; he'd coordinated marathon routes, made travel arrangements, and arranged food and lodging for the team of runners and their entourage all along the way; he'd advertised and promoted the event in every town and hamlet they passed through, had even purchased and carried the spare torch fuses. All unpaid, of course; these were labors of love. My father's rewards were success and the adulation of strangers. He complained bitterly that his family didn't understand or appreciate his monumental achievements. And it was true. We did not. We were unenthusiastic about Torch 200 and the extra work it meant, bored by Dad's letters, nonplussed when foreign dignitaries phoned the house. We perked up only when my father announced that he'd be going away for a few days. I suppose there was casual cruelty in our apathy. It was not our intention.

Somewhere in the swirl of all this, or perhaps earlier, a VW van festooned with Flower Power decals and rainbow stripes—a genuine hippiemobile—pulled up in front of our house one morning. The doors popped open and Rosette tumbled out onto the sidewalk in a cloud of patchouli and pot smoke, her hair frizzed out to there, wearing a fringed suede vest and hip-huggers, hauling a backpack and a couple of carpetbags. She and her girlfriend had hitchhiked their way back to the Bronx from California, where they'd been living for a year or so, Rosette having moved there to escape her addled lover. He'd ended up following her across the country, and now she was back. That was all I knew. Only a few more details emerged in the weeks following her surprise return: she and her girlfriend had lived in San Francisco for a while, then moved to a little place near the beach in San Diego; she'd tended bar at a Hells Angels hangout; abalone stew was delicious.

Rosette settled back into her attic bedroom as if no time had passed at all, freshening it anew, festooning it with seashells, concert posters, and other tokens of her real life. She gave me a huge, brilliant conch shell, a pinecone the size of a football . . . and a brown suede fringed vest that I treasured but never wore. It just wasn't my style. Seventies fashion was in high flight, and I was on it like ink on paper: designer jeans (a new concept) by Jordache, Sassoon, and Gloria Vanderbilt, with matching denim vests; clingy Huk-A-Poo shirts in vivid prints; mile-high platform shoes in mod colors; and, my personal pièce de résistance, a wide-collared denim maxi coat with bright plaid flannel lining and matching trim. (My hair, of course, was blown dry and shellacked into a smooth helmet using Consort hair spray for men.) I shoplifted whatever items I couldn't afford to buy, a fairly easy feat in those days—especially at Alexander's. Craig Scott, a mod boutique under the El, was an important source for the very hippest fashions. I dared not steal from there; instead I saved my money and chose discerningly.

I don't think my father and Rosette exchanged two words during that time, not even an initial greeting. The perennial drone of our black-and-white TV, propped in a corner of the dinette, helped mask simmering tensions at the dinner table. *Bowling for Dollars* was usually on. We watched even the reruns.

"Oh, this guy. He ends up winning a lotta money," we'd remember about a given player. Or: "This one can't bowl at all." When a one-armed contestant showed up to compete, the toupee-wearing host was thrown for a loop. He got quiet for a moment.

"So. How'd it happen?" he asked.

"Machine accident," the grim reply.

Awkward pause.

"Okay! Let's bowl for dollars!"

Despite my father's refusal to acknowledge Rosette's existence (and she his), I think he was relieved to have his daughter home, back at his table. He had long maintained that the only acceptable circumstances under which a grown child may "leave home" were to marry, attend college (with certain caveats), or escape the clear and present danger of criminal and/or drug-addicted parents. He wasn't kidding.

My oldest sister and I became bosom bodies, hanging out in earnest for the first time—she mixing with Victor and Joanna and other high school friends, as well as with my St. Lucy's friends, whom she'd known since childhood; I mixing with her best friends Joni, Christine, and Charlene, a trio of complementary party girls who were also smart and focused on the larger world. Together, we formed a buzzing social network. True rock 'n' rollers at heart, Rosette and her crew were not especially fond of disco—but they loved to dance. I taught them how to hustle in the attic bedroom, our arms colliding with the slanted walls and ceilings, our feet slipping on the tiles.

My father yelled occasionally for us to quiet down, but he rarely ventured up there.

14.

On a Saturday night around nine, the attic bedroom is aflounce in satin, sequins, and feather boas as Rosette and her girlfriends and I—joined, perhaps, by a couple of my friends—primp for a midnight screening of *The Rocky Horror Picture Show.* Stills and publicity shots from the new cult sensation out of London are taped to the walls for reference: Tim Curry, Richard O'Brien, Patricia Quinn, and Nell Campbell leering at us through heavy layers of glamour Goth. Charlene and my sister, both handy with a sewing machine, have built sweeping black satin capes with blood-red linings and high, stiff collars; custom-altered tops and skirts and bustiers; spray-painted dangerously high platform shoes in Day-Glo colors. Christine, a professional beautician, has teased out their hair and is tying it into irregular knots. She is responsible for my new hairstyle, a perm, the "white Afro" look I've wanted for so long.

"You gottu permanett'," New Jersey Grandma declares authoritatively the minute she sees it—the only family member, oddly, to acknowledge my transformation.

"No I didn't," I lie, not wanting to admit to time spent in a beauty parlor.

"Dotsa permanetta, you."

"No. I just didn't comb it."

"Nunna you tella me," she presses, "theeza permanett'."

(Grandma knows her salon treatments.)

We drive down to the Eighth Street Playhouse in Greenwich Village in Charlene's sixties Volvo sedan, navy blue. The line outside the theater, snaking halfway down Eighth Street to the corner of Sixth Avenue, is a party, costumed revelers passing joints, sipping flasks, singing songs from the sound track. When the house opens, a parade of fans dressed as characters from the movie tromps back and forth in front of the screen, warming up the crowd and winning fans of their own. During the movie, the audience shouts phrases in unison with the action, throws things (rice, water, frankfurters) at the screen on cue, jumps into the aisles to dance the Time Warp.

Later, party seekers linger on the sidewalk before disbanding reluctantly. The girls and I walk west to the Waverly or Washington Square Diner for eggs and coffee, or east to Kiev, for cheese blintzes and pierogi with sour cream. They freshen their makeup in the bathroom or right at the table. (I will usually have opted for a simple cape worn over street clothes, too self-conscious to exploit this legitimate opportunity to apply makeup or expose some flesh.) We pile back into the car, swing by Astor Place Square, pull over, and, in a tradition started by Charlene, jump out to give "the cube" a twirl before heading home. (She was the first of our crew to point out that the sculptor Tony Rosenthal's *Alamo,* a massive black metal form balanced on one of eight corners, would spin handily on its axis when given a push.)

Arriving home late from anywhere was risky. And I arrived home late from everywhere.

"You're cutting into the next day!" my father would say about staying out past midnight. "Only people who are looking for trouble are out at that hour."

I'd creep into the house as soundlessly as possible, whispering through the door for Linc to stay quiet, praying I wouldn't find my father sitting up at the kitchen table, watching TV, drinking coffee, engaging his restless leg syndrome at full tilt. "What time is it?" he'd ask flatly on such occasions. (Only on my luckiest nights was he already in bed when I got home.) I pretended to listen to the long lecture that usually followed, feigning contrition, attempting to defend myself with elaborate lies:

"But Charlene's car broke down and we didn't have a spare tire so we called Triple A but they took a really long time to get there and I tried to call you but there was no pay phone anywhere and by the time we finally got near a pay phone we were almost home so I thought—"

"Peter's sister Donna's boyfriend got a promotion at work and he took us all out for burgers and milk shakes and I didn't have my own ride home so I had to wait with everybody until it was all over and when I tried to call you the guy in the restaurant said the pay phone was busted and I couldn't use the restaurant phone unless it was an emergency and I said it really was an emergency but he didn't believe me so—"

"Marina's grandmother on her father's side had a heart attack and her mother was really upset so she asked me to stay until the aunt and uncle came over but they were late because they got in a car accident and the uncle was badly hurt and—"

Most often, though, I kept the story simple: it was John's birthday or Joni's birthday or Peter's mother's birthday or Father Oliverio's birthday.

"Awful lotta birthdays in your crowd," my father would mutter, frequently letting me slide in spite of himself.

Rosette did not have to jump though any such hoops, just one of many perks of being on nonspeaking terms with my father—and also a function of age: she was twenty-five years old now, a working girl, trying her hand at a number of different jobs and potential professions, taking sudden backpacking trips to Europe (via Laker Airways before it went bust), generally pushing at the boundaries of convention and the limits of my father's tolerance. He clenched his jaw but kept his distance. I envied the freedom Rosette enjoyed, tucked safely above the fray in her sunny garret. I smell perfume when I think of her room in those days. I see rolls of gift wrap and curling ribbon, vintage dresses in sequins and lace. (For all Rosette's gumption, she was pretty girlie at heart.) At Christmastime, her groovy pad was the place to be for wrapping presents, modeling holiday fashions, and keeping an eye on the back driveway from her little twin windows at the top of the house.

"They're here!" we'd yell as we spotted cars pulling in, guests arriving.

Our place had become the new official headquarters for family gatherings, even as we continued to rip it apart. Though the ritual of Sunday dinner with the extended clan was pretty much a thing of the past, we still practiced the tradition among ourselves, sometimes joined by Aunt Diana, Uncle Aldo, and New Jersey Grandma. Grandma continued to be a one-woman bread and pasta factory when she stayed over, filling our kitchen with globes of dough rising beneath damp dish towels and boards full of drying pasta—sauce bubbling on the stove. During downtime, she'd crochet afghans in zigzagged rows of vivid color, her eyes glued to the TV screen, miles of woven blanket piling up at her feet, miraculously spun from a single needle.

"You louse-a!" she'd yell at a fictional cad on *General Hospital* or *Days of Our Lives*. "Nunna you talk-a to the wife-a like-a that!"

In the late afternoon, after watching one show after another for hours:

"Carlo. Essa theeza the same-a stow-ree?"

"What, Gram? You mean like from this morning? No. You've watched about ten different stories."

"No! Theeza the same-a stow-ree."

"No, Gram. It's not."

"Yes-a-yes," she'd protest, returning to her work. "Eeza the same-a stow-ree, theeze." She never believed our answers to her queries.

"Carlo. Whatta time eet eeza now?"

"Almost four o'clock."

"Fow o'clock-a! Nooo. Whatta time?"

"Grandma, it's *almost four o'clock*."

"Nooo. Eeza a no fow oo'clock-a."

We'd roll our eyes and chuckle. "Hey! Nunna you leff onna the Gremma!" she'd yell.

Gremma. That's how she spelled it on birthday cards, her loopy, shaky scrawl painstakingly etching the words: "Opi Boida, Lob Gremma." (Her gift on such occasions, and every Christmas, was a glance at your passbook from the savings account she held for each of her eight grandchildren, the funds to be dispersed upon her death. The highest lifetime total ended up being around four hundred bucks.)

Grandma had recently sold her two-family brick house in Fort Lee and moved into the finished basement apartment of Diana and

Aldo's house in the same town. I missed her immaculate little home, its scrubbed flagstone walkways lined with corpulent blooms of stunning variety. Grandma produced the most beautiful tomatoes, zucchini, basil, parsley, radishes, cucumbers, and other greens and vegetables from a small plot out back. My all-time favorite of the dishes she created from her backyard harvest was fried *gagutz* (zucchini) flowers. The sturdy yellow blooms—lily-shaped, their petals running with delicate veins of pale green—were rinsed, dried, dipped in egg, dredged in flour, fried in vegetable oil, drained on brown paper, sprinkled with salt (or sometimes powdered sugar), and served hot. They were sweet, bitter, crunchy, tender, pungent, and mild all at once. They tasted like the colors green and yellow, folded inside the flavor of golden brown.

Sometimes Grandma picked the flowers in the early morning, while they stood open to feed on sunlight and dew. (They were otherwise closed tight, podlike.) She'd stuff the open blooms with chunks of fresh mozzarella, fasten them closed with toothpicks or thread, and prepare as usual. Maybe she'd add a few pebbles of cooked sausage, or bits of fried bacon. The melty, creamy, juicy center made an already exquisite confection almost unbearably delectable. Grandma would have prepared truckloads of them had they been available, but the *gagutz* blossom is a sometime thing. It takes time for the plant to make them, and it makes them in moderation. We seemed to know, even as kids, that this food was special. Not just the *fiori fritti*—all of it. We neither took Grandma's kitchen wizardry for granted nor hid the pleasure it gave us.

"*Mangia, mangia,*" she'd encourage from her post at the stove, obviously pleased. "*Mangia più.*"

The white-lacquered front door of her house led into a spotless foyer, set off with wrought-iron railing. Beyond it was the living room, a formal affair, never used for actual living. There were linen drapes, a brocade couch, a couple of printed wing chairs, a lovely old carpet, a mahogany coffee table, a bookshelf with a few knickknacks and figurines—including a large crystal ball encasing a vivid red rose that seemed for all the world to be vibrantly alive, raindrops glistening on one or two of its petals. The brilliant orb held a magical allure. I lifted it carefully and turned it around and around in my hands over and over again, wanting to break the crystal apart so I could touch the living rose . . . the flower for which my grandmother was named. *Rosa.*

We usually entered from the back, stepping right into a shiny, sunny kitchen, the room I loved best: starched yellow curtains, gleaming white stove and pale countertops; shiny chrome-and-enamel dinette set in lemon yellow; small, vibrant plants in glazed pots lining a tiled windowsill; herbs in tight bundles tied with bakery string, hanging on brass hooks to dry. There was an old perpetual calendar on the wall near the phone, one of the few possessions Grandma had carried with her from Bari—painted wooden figures of a pair of children, boy and girl, walking cheerfully through the rain, a blue-and-red umbrella above their heads. Beneath their feet was a series of three slots, into which were slipped long ribbons denoting day, month, and date. *Lunedi, martedi, mercoledi . . . Gennaio, febbraio, marzo . . .* (The calendar was not kept current. It counted time in another way.)

When, in the old days, Grandma hosted sleepovers in this house for all eight of her grandkids—my four cousins, three sisters, and me—she'd have us bathe in batches of four to save money on the water bill: boys in one shift, girls in another. I think she changed the water between batches, or at least freshened it, but Grandma was nothing if not frugal, having come through extreme poverty and hardship to wind up a landed lady with two houses, some good jewelry, and a modest but tidy savings. We could pretty much get away with anything at her slumber parties. It was Christine and Eva's idea to drink quarts of water before bedtime so as to be awakened in the night by the need to pee. We'd meet up groggily and tiptoe around the darkened house, tending to whatever poor critters we'd caught, engaging in whatever silliness we could muster at that hour, sneaking into Grandma's room as she snored to spy in horror at the full set of false teeth floating in a glass on her bedside table—old-fashioned choppers that looked quite capable of starting up a conversation all on their own. Daniel liked to pluck them out of the glass and chase the girls around the house with them, threatening to "bite."

This is the house where Grandma regularly entertained Mrs. Sinatra, Frank's mother, a neighbor and friend from her first place in Fort Lee. Mrs. S was not especially handy in the kitchen, and she prevailed upon Grandma to prepare Frank's favorite dishes—*cavatelli, ravioli, focaccia,* Sunday gravy—whenever he was planning to visit. (We kids hatched a rumor about how Mrs. Sinatra told her son that she had cooked the meals herself, and also about how Grandma hid behind the drapes to steal a glimpse of Ol' Blue Eyes chowing down on her grub.) Her friend returned the favor by showering Grandma with gifts of increasing value, culminating in crisp one-hundred-dollar bills tucked into elegant boxes of silk stockings, designer scarves, or fine leather gloves. (The women began to lose touch when Frank moved his mother to a bigger house far away—in Queens.) It was thrilling to know that the Chairman of the Board himself, big cheese of the Rat Pack, former teen idol over whom my mother had swooned as a wartime bobby-soxer—whose smoky vocal stylings filled our house on a regular basis—was smacking his lips over the same succulent dishes I was, prepared by the same hand.

A favorite memory of that house is sitting alone with Grandma on the front porch during heavy summer rains, as was her habit, cozy and dry beneath the wooden eaves as the air went damp and chill around us. Hard raindrops pelting the beams; the smell of green rising up in a mist; Grandma shifting in her chair, sighing contentedly; a sudden sunburst piercing heavy clouds—these simple childhood pleasures were now things of the past. Grandma's new digs were cramped and impersonal. And I hardly ever saw my cousins anymore.

"Carlo, whatsa dot *bubble-a bubble-a*?"

"It's the fish tank, Grandma."

"Da veesh-a dank? No."

"Yes, Gram. It's the filter. In the fish tank. It makes that sound." (I'd revivified my aquarium since the unfortunate boiling incident . . . this time investing in a heating element with an automatic cutoff feature.)

"No da veesh-a dank-a theese. Carlo! Tella Gremma! Whatsa dot *bubble-a bubble-a*?"

She shared my bedroom when she stayed over (since it still contained two beds, a vestige of its former life as Eva and Maria's room), performing her nighttime ablutions with heavy sighs—removing her corset, donning her nightgown, washing her face, netting her hair, soaking her dentures. She'd fold the coverlet back neatly, slip her slippers off, and climb into bed. She'd pray for the longest time, streams of words chanted in a beseeching singsong. This praying would devolve eventually into grunts and moans; the grunts and moans, into quiet sobs; the quiet sobs, into snoring. Every night. Sometimes I could hear the name Theresa on the mournful river of whispered words. All the sadness of life seemed to cover Grandma like snow whenever she lay her head down.

"Arrgghh! Argh! Argh! *Arrrggghhh!*" Her bloodcurdling screams in the middle of the night are terrifying. I have not seen the movie *In Cold Blood,* or even read the book, but I know the basic story and am certain as I bolt out of a sound sleep that I will face a pair of psychotic gunmen standing in a sea of carnage.

"What is it, Grandma?" I shout.

My father rushes in, the rest of the family piling up in the doorway behind him, lights being flicked on everywhere.

"What happened, Ma?" Dad urges.

She is sitting up in bed, red-faced, panicked.

"Esta gatt'!" she blubbers. "It-a walk onna my bod-ee!"

Niffi had climbed atop Grandma's sleeping form in the night, as cats will do.

"It's okay, Mom, calm down. We'll put her out and close the door. Okay?"

"Please-a! *Chiuda la port'!* My god-a! *O dio mio . . . o . . . o . . .*"

What a drama queen she could be when it came to our pets.

"Estu can'! He's-a too big-a!" she always said about Linc. "Take-a him to a *farm-a!*" The concept of pet ownership was foreign to Grandma. She believed in raising animals solely for the purpose of eating them.

My mother generally yielded the kitchen to her opinionated mother-in-law ("it's easier that way"), but her own culinary skills were legendary. At Christmas, a massive affair, Mom opened the meal (following a proper buffet of hot and cold antipasti and other appetizers) with her exquisite 'scarol soup with little meatballs. Some people refer to this hearty chicken broth floating with tender escarole and succulent cherry-size meatballs as "Italian wedding soup," but we always just called it 'scarol soup with little meatballs, as in "Mom, you making the 'scarol soup with little meatballs for Christmas?"

"Why? You want it?"

"Well, *yeah.*"

"Okay then, I'll make it."

(She would have made it anyway, of course, but we both enjoyed the ritual.)

For the pasta course, Mom served homemade *manicotti,* her secret being that she used crepes instead of pasta dough, yielding cakes so light and fluffy that they barely remained aplate. Then, of course, the great platter of gravy meat, and all the other requisite courses: several roasts, a few kinds of potatoes, vegetables, stuffed mushrooms, salad—each prepared by my mother to absolute perfection. The Christmas dessert table was an embarrassment of riches: Mom made towers of *strufoli* (fried balls of sweet dough drenched in honey and sprinkled lightly with crushed toasted almonds), two kinds of cheesecake (Italian, made with ricotta, and American, made with cream cheese and sour cream), and several types of cookies (including melt-in-your-mouth butter balls rolled in powdered sugar, and golden sesame *biscotti*); Grandma always made at least a half dozen varieties of traditional Barese Christmas pastries, including *gatata* (delicate deep-fried rosettes dipped in honey), *castagnelle* (small, crunchy crescents of chocolate and nutmeg, ideal for dunking), *torrone* (the hard-sugar variety—amber-colored, nut-studded, smooth as glass), several types of *biscotti,* and others, some forgotten, whose guttural-sounding names belied their true nature. Aunt Diana might have made an English trifle ("*very* continental, you know"), and there were bowls of warm chestnuts, chilled clementines, dried dates and figs, plates of chocolate, marzipan, rock candy, bacchanalian clusters of grapes in red, black, purple, and green.

I took great pride in the table and the overall presentation of this epic meal, eagerly volunteering every year to iron yards and yards of linen tablecloths (my father had purchased some fine specimens at an employees' sale at Saks), polish sterling silver serving pieces and utensils (which my parents had received as gifts for their twenty-fifth wedding anniversary), shine the few pieces of crystal we had, hunt down vases and candlesticks and other accent pieces. My goal was to render a table setting worthy of *House Beautiful,* an oasis of opulence and glamour. I created clever patterns with the mismatched plates, glasses, flatware, and chairs so as to make the variations look purposeful. Luckily, the plush, creamy linens, with their silk embossing and woven monograms (the initials *KJC,* I think, presumably belonging to a Saks customer who'd abandoned a large custom order) cascaded over the sides of the table and fell all the way to the floor—handily masking the fact that our revelries were taking place atop two double sheets of plywood nailed to a few rough-hewn horses. We simply didn't have a table big enough to accommodate this formal sit-down affair for twenty or more. For the first time ever, my mother's family had started joining the annual festivities—New York Grandma; Aunt Virginia and Uncle Frank; cousin Marie and her husband, Ronnie; cousin Frankie and his wife, Joan; their two kids; Joan's mother.

My father eventually acquired a massive, four-piece Depression-era dining room suite: extendable table with ten chairs, eight-foot-long sideboard with slightly smaller matching cabinet, glass-front hutch the size of an upended Cadillac. The dark, hulking pieces consumed every inch of space in the dining room, greedily soaking up what little sunlight managed to squeeze through the now-tiny windows. He attempted to brighten up the funereal ensemble (which we all hated on sight) by reupholstering the chair backs and seat cushions in bright orange Naugahyde. They now made a funny sound when you sat on them, something like a quiet fart. (No longer would I have to slip a whoopee cushion under New Jersey Grandma's ample butt to get a big laugh at dinner; the chairs themselves were the gag.)

By Christmas 1977, Uncle Frank and New York Grandma were gone from the table. He had died of a heart attack on a shoulder of the Cross-Bronx Expressway while changing a flat tire. She had slipped away quietly in her sleep, after living the last nine of her ninety-one years in a state of vegetation, a kind of hell, mind alert inside a withered body. Her deliverance through death was merciful, but I still mourned the woman she had once been. My mother, I knew, felt the same, as she sobbed quietly in her only black dress.

The corpse in its tufted casket at Marchiselli Funeral Home was a garish doppelgänger of my homespun grandma, mocking and strange: hair poofed, makeup heavy, adorned in pink chiffon.

"But look at her hands," offered a woman, a friend of Aunt Virginia's, I think, as we stood before the coffin. "Such a story they tell. When you think of all they've been through. You know? I always like to look at the hands."

Grandma's were folded neatly across her rib cage, heavy-veined and patted with makeup, draped with a string of rosary beads, elegant and purposeful even in their osteal condition. Their story spanned a century:

Upon her arrival in New York City in 1900, Grandma moved into a Hell's Kitchen apartment with some relatives who'd settled there a few years earlier, doing piecework and other at-home labor, factory work, housecleaning—whatever was available—eventually reconnecting with a young man from her hometown, a jaunty fellow named Luigi, when he moved to New York a few years later. She married him in a simple civil ceremony, and the newlyweds moved into a tenement apartment of their own on Fifty-second Street between Tenth and

Eleventh avenues. Grandma had three children—Joe, Frank, and Virginia—all delivered at home, while Grandpa Louis (my middle name) worked as a hired barber until he'd saved enough money to open a business of his own, the Shamrock Barber Shop, on West Eighty-sixth Street and Amsterdam Avenue. (The Irish reference remains unexplained.) He disappeared one day, abandoning home and store to hide out in Chicago until the ruffians from whom he'd borrowed money stopped looking for him—or, perhaps, until he'd raised enough cash to settle his debt. (Grandpa Louie had a bit of a gambling habit . . . and a *gumada* or two on the side.) Grandma, suddenly alone, struggled to keep the family together until her husband resurfaced. My mother was born on the heels of his return, a late love child whose oldest sibling was already nineteen years old. In a familiar trajectory, the immigrant couple eventually saved enough money to move up to the Bronx, and bought a pair of brick houses on Paulding Avenue and 219th Street, living in one and using the other for rental income. Grandpa opened a new business on Fordham Road, Louis' Barber Shop, and the family weathered the Depression more successfully than most.

Their neighbors in the Bronx were the Mineo family, and when my mother was old enough, she started babysitting their youngest child—a pretty, pouty, quiet boy named Sal. Grandma had become great friends with Mrs. Mineo, the driven stage mother determined to make her oldest son, Michael, a star. When Mike went on an audition for the original Broadway production of *The King and I,* Sal tagged along for the ride. He was spotted on the sidelines by a casting director and hired the same day (his first big break).

At around the same time, 1950 or so, my grandfather died suddenly of a heart attack, and my mother met and married my father. Grandma sold her houses and moved into a rental on 237th Street and

GRANDPA LOUIS (FAR LEFT) AND ASSOCIATES, IN
FRONT OF ONE OF SEVERAL BRONX BARBERSHOPS HE
OPERATED OVER THE YEARS—THIS ONE ON
LACONIA AVENUE

White Plains Road (where she remained for most of the rest of her life). She knew that her new in-laws frowned upon her because she was Sicilian. *"I Africani,"* New Jersey Grandma would say, not meaning it as a compliment. New York Grandma never addressed this directly, but instead asked me questions like "Which-a you Gremma eez-a mo' funna? Me? Or de othra one?" Or: "You like-a stay mo' wit-a you othra Gremma? Or wit-a me? Which-a one?"

"You, Grandma," I always answered. She knew it was true.

I resented the fact that my father's family regarded New York Grandma as somehow inferior and, at her wake, felt a kind of angry pride as I watched them file up to her coffin respectfully, hands folded, heads bowed, kneeling before her lifeless body in prayer, turning reverently to offer solemn condolences, finally giving my mother's mother her due.

Her hands: a child's—deflecting the blows of a tyrannical father, pumping water into a bucket on a rocky hillside, stroking the face of her dead mother, taken from her in girlhood; a teenager's—gripping the rail of a ship sailing from the Old World to the New, presenting papers to officials in a strange land, carrying bundled belongings into the teeming ghetto; a young woman's—accepting the ring of her be- trothed, birthing her own babies, laboring tirelessly with needle and thread, reaching for the arms of an absent man; a mature lady's— buffing her proud new home to a shine, digging gardens, cooking and baking and sewing, bringing cures to sick neighbors without being asked; an old woman's—bouncing her grandchildren above her head, weaving hats out of strips cut from brown paper bags, hanging laun- dry, feeding mouthfuls of buttery *pastina;* an invalid's—brittle and motionless, stiffly clutching the side of a blanket, raising a trembling spoon to her lips, reaching for her grandson's hand and pulling it close; a corpse's—restful at long last, white and blue.

"That one," Eva asserts definitively.

We're standing in the outer yard of Boston Post Road Garden Sup- ply, surveying stacks of Christmas trees for sale. Eva has asked a worker where they keep "the biggest ones" and is pointing to a speci- men at the bottom of the pile. I struggle to retrieve her choice without causing an avalanche. When finally I've wrestled it free, I stand it up, bounce it on the ground a few times to loosen its branches, and ro- tate it slowly—like Carol Marol displaying a Broyhill living room en- semble or a sterling silver tea service by Michael C. Fina on *Let's Make a Deal.*

"Nope. Too small," Eva says dismissively, already moving on down the line. "How 'bout *that* one? Show me that."

This has been an annual tradition since childhood. It continues into her college years, when she comes home for winter break. Eva is the family Christmas maven, always has been. She insists upon the tallest, thickest, fullest, freshest tree, devoting hours—sometimes *days*—to finding it, making increasingly desperate-sounding contingency plans:

"If we have to, we'll drive upstate, go into the woods, and cut our own. *We'll just cut our own!*"

When finally a candidate is deemed worthy, we store it in the backyard to keep it fresh until the day before Christmas Eve, when we attempt to drag it into the house, usually finding that it's way too tall and wide to fit in the living room—or even through the front door. Eva always ends up chopping it down from the bottom, fretting about "losing the shape," twisting the discarded branches into wreathes to hang on the front and back doors. (Sometimes she'd be forced to hack at the top as well, resulting in a bushlike shape that really unnerved her.) Even once they'd been cut down to size, our trees were usually incapable of standing on their own, and had to be anchored to the ceiling and walls with complex wire-and-hook trussing. My father had a fit every year when he saw how we'd hacked into his freshly painted Sheetrock. ("Too bad!" Eva would whisper to me hotly. "How else does he expect me to get the thing to stand up?")

My ambitious sister filled the house with the sound of classic Christmas carols, almost panicking when any other type of music was played; wound fresh evergreen garlands around the old oak banister (which she herself had stripped, stained, and polished years earlier), tying the twin posts at the bottom of the staircase with big red ribbons; taped our many Christmas cards to the walls in the shapes of wreaths and candy canes (again getting into trouble with Dad for marring the paint); sprayed fake snow in the corners of all the windows; scattered decorations throughout every room of the house, replacing regular towels and dishrags and bath mats with Christmas-themed ones; fastened sprigs of mistletoe over every doorway; draped the exterior of the house and all available railings with blinking colored lights; led midnight expeditions deep into Bronx Park to raid the holly bushes, filling every available vessel in the house with great bundles of spiky-leaved branches crowded with juicy clusters of (poisonous) berries.

She read *The Night Before Christmas* and *A Christmas Carol* aloud to anyone who would listen (Maria, usually) and scanned the *TV Guide* for showings of the many movie adaptations of the Dickens tale—especially the 1951 version starring Alastair Sim as Ebenezer Scrooge—watching them over and over again, year after year (including the animated version starring Mr. Magoo). *Miracle on 34th Street, It's a Wonderful Life, Holiday Inn, The Homecoming, A Charlie Brown Christmas, Frosty the Snowman, Rudolph the Red-Nosed Reindeer*—Eva made certain they flickered endlessly across every TV screen in the house. She was dripping with Christmas at Christmastime, drenched in it, ho-hoing a tad too merrily from the helm of a ship of spruce and fir, riding the waves of a candy-striped sea with fierce determination.

It's Christmas Eve. The Yule log burns on Channel 11—a poor man's fireplace. We begin the serious work of trimming, a complex and delicate operation since everyone (especially Eva) is highly opinionated. Tensions run high, but the tree always ends up looking gorgeous.

"Ma, come see!" we call proudly to our exhausted mother, still toiling at the stove.

In addition to working full-time, cleaning, grocery shopping,

Christmas shopping, wrapping presents, and preparing the next day's massive feast, Mom would have just finished making the traditional Christmas Eve meal of seven fishes prepared seven ways: shrimp cocktail, scungilli salad, fried flounder, baked cod, sautéed scallops, clams casino, mussels marinara—for example. (My father loved this meal and usually contributed to its preparation, excelling at batter-and-fry jobs.)

"Oh, it's nice," she'd wheeze in the direction of the tree, collapsing onto the couch for a minute before getting back to work. "You gonna have room to fit any presents under there?"

Later, I run off to midnight Mass with my St. Lucy's friends, perhaps stopping at one or two of their houses for a quick visit ("You gotta come see my tree!"), and stay up for hours, wrapping presents and writing special holiday messages for each member of the family. I try to sleep for a while, but Christmas morning comes quick. It always holds a special magic, despite whatever else is going on. And there is usually *a lot* else going on. Christmas is not my father's favorite season.

15.

Cappi's first response to any request was "no." Only through mental and verbal gymnastics did I manage to secure as much time out of the house as I did. It was my policy to ask permission to attend upcoming events while he was napping.

"Hunh? Yeah," he'd mumble, still asleep.

Later, when he balked at my plans: "But you gave me permission! Don't you remember? I asked you and you said yes!" I learned to talk a blue streak, constantly inventing emergency situations, very special occasions, and one-time-only opportunities, endowing each invitation with great urgency.

"But *everybody* is gonna be there!"

"Everybody? Am *I* gonna be there? Is *your mother*? Your *grandmother*? No? Then *everybody* is *not* going to be there."

Or: "But I have to go! It's gonna be *gigantic*!"

"*Gigantic*? Look up the word in the dictionary. What you're describing is a physical impossibility."

Or: "But John is sick and the team *needs* another player!"

"Do they really *need* another player? Or do they just *want* to hang out and kibitz around?" (He often peppered his speech with simple Yiddish words and expressions. We all did: "You're *meshuga*" or "it's a *mitzvah*" or the ever-useful "*Oy vey iz mir.*")

A habit of his that I especially resented was to keep working right up until dinnertime. "You can clean up after we eat, Bub." That could easily take another hour or more, depending on what we'd been up to. My father was very particular about how certain tasks should be accomplished, even instructing me on the proper way to sweep a floor (*brush-brush, tap-tap; brush-brush, tap-tap*). Some of his advice was useful, like sprinkling water onto crushed plaster before sweeping in order to control the dust, or "letting the tool do the job"—swinging a hammer easily, for example, lightly gripped, the motion focused in the wrist, instead of banging away like a madman; or handling and guiding a screwdriver gently, allowing its own weight and balance to perform its function without muscle.

But more often than not, the particulars he insisted upon seemed random, and served only to slow me down. When finally I'd finished, Dad would inspect my work and release me. (Or not. Usually there was "just one more thing" for me to do. And "a last thing" after that.) Afterward, I'd jump into the shower, scrub myself clean, get dressed, and attempt to head out for the evening. It was typically past eight o'clock by then, sometimes closer to nine.

"Not worth going anywhere now," my father would say. "You'll only have to turn around and head home in a little while." (Eleven o'clock was my standard curfew, though I honored it almost never.)

I rebelled hard against this, one of the few issues over which I was willing to butt heads with my father.

"But that's not fair!" I'd say, ready for a fight.

"Who said life was fair?" he liked to counter. I'd usually end up pleading.

"Come on, Dad. I've been working all day. I need to unwind a little. I'll be home on time. I swear. Come on. Pleeeease."

Unless he was in a particularly foul mood, he'd let me go. My mother helped by corroborating my stories and otherwise providing cover and encouragement where she could. She knew that I needed an ample social life. In all fairness, so did my father . . . or he never would have let me have one. (My older sisters insist that, as a boy, I was given much more freedom than they were; we all agree that Maria, as the baby, got away with murder.)

"What are you wearing? Eye makeup?" Dad grunted disgustedly, looking up from his coffee cup as I approached the kitchen table, dressed for Saturday night.

"Eye makeup? *What?* No! Of course not!"

And it was true. I was not wearing eye makeup. But I did enjoy a long toilette and devoted considerable time to buffing, scenting, and smearing my face and body with herbal-scented moisturizer (Raintree, I think, which, combined with the already powerful fragrances of Clairol Herbal Essence shampoo and Jōvan Musk for men body spray, made me stink like a fecund forest). I had seen my sisters and their girlfriends take special care to lubricate the delicate tissue beneath their eyes, a soothing-looking regimen. I copied their technique using Vaseline. All this primping and pampering, antidotes to grit and grime, worried and irked my father to no end. I knew he was already concerned about my sexuality. I could feel it in a thousand ways. I remember him eyeballing me anxiously one day as I paused at the kitchen table to listen to Ann Lazerta gossip with my mother about how Rock Hudson was said to be having an affair with Jim Nabors.

(*Gomer Pyle?* I remember thinking. Surely hunky Rock could do better.)

"Can you imagine it, Mary? I just can't imagine it."

"Grrrr," growled my father, quite literally, as he opened the basement door and called me away. "Bub! Come downstairs and give me a hand."

Downstairs: "Don't believe everything you hear. You believe all that?"

"Well," I began meekly, horrified by where this was going. "Who knows? Maybe it's true. I guess it doesn't matter."

I remember his response exactly: "Doesn't matter? Doesn't. Matter? Oh, it matters, fella, it matters. Know this: There is no such thing as a happy homosexual. They're perverts. They're child molesters. They're miserable people. They're sick. Sick, sick people. Oh, it matters. It matters very much."

I knew he was addressing me directly, laying naked my secret before us both. I stayed real quiet, desperate for escape.

"What, Ma?" I yelled upstairs in response to an imaginary page. "I'll be right there. Mom's calling me. Gotta go."

Dad had already intercepted some gay porn I'd ordered through *Gay Times,* a newsprint fag rag I'd picked up in Times Square. I had started cutting school occasionally to wander downtown alone, sneaking into porn theaters, picking up copies of *Screw, Gay Times,* and *Michael's Thing,* sidling into smut shops and feverishly searching for the "fetish" section, where the "all-male" porn was kept. By my eighteenth birthday, in January 1977, the lack of even a hint of sex or romance in my life was driving me mad. Straight teens all around me were dating and smooching and fucking and falling in and out of love. They were trading preengagement rings and ID bracelets, pawing and cupping and squeezing each other, lustily exploring their nascent libidos right out in the sunshine. There was simply no equivalent for an undercover gay boy. I continued to date obligatory girlfriends, but had yet to experience anything close to what I longed for. My explorations "down the city" became increasingly bold, my curiosity peaking exponentially, culminating in the audacious move of sending away for the Mr. G catalog—which promised "XXXplicit photos" of "beefy studs" with "huge endowments." I prayed for the illicit material to arrive on a weekday, when I could grab it before my parents got home. It did not.

I will never forget the Saturday afternoon, around lunchtime, that my father went out to the mailbox and lingered a little too long. I peered through the window anxiously; his back was facing me; he was opening items and inspecting them. I had a terrible sinking feeling. After a while, he came into the house. He looked stricken, white as ice, and approached me with strange quiet.

"You didn't order something from a company called Mister G, did you?"

"Mister—what? No, I don't think so, nope. No," I lied, gulping so hard that I nearly swallowed my own tongue, my scalp and face aflame.

"You sure?" he pressed.

"Yeah, why? What is it?"

I knew he didn't believe me. Thinking fast:

"The only thing I ordered recently was the Charles Atlas catalog. I'll show you."

I raced upstairs, grabbed my old black-and-white brochure, studded with pictures of musclemen in skimpy posing suits, and raced back down again, shoving it eagerly into my father's hands. "See? This is what I ordered. Maybe they gave my name and address to some other company or something? Is this Mister G, or whatever, something about bodybuilding?"

I considered this improvised ploy a stroke of brilliance on my part, a highly logical explanation that ought to absolve me of any further suspicion. But my father seemed unconvinced. He grew somber, saying nothing further as he wandered away from me, floated up to his bedroom, and shut the door.

After a while, I could hear that he was on the phone. I pressed my ear to the door but could not make out his words, so I went up to Rosette's room and, ever so gingerly, picked up the extension. My father was talking to a priest—the rector, in fact, of historic Trinity Church on Broadway at Wall Street, whom he'd befriended through Torch 200 and whose sumptuous private quarters I'd joined him in visiting once or twice. (My father had a penchant for cozying up to powerful people.)

"Have you found other such materials in the boy's possession?" the kindly old Episcopalian was asking.

I was quaking in my boots too hard to have retained much else, but I think Dad's unofficial spiritual adviser wrapped up the conversation by suggesting that the mailing might very well have been erroneous, and that my father would be wise to play it cool and just keep a close eye on me going forward. Dad was bleating my name up the attic staircase even before I set the receiver down.

"Yeah," I answered, in a sweat, bounding down to him.

"Were you just listening in on that call?"

"Huh? No. Why? Were you on the phone?" I'd been worshipfully studying Gracie Allen on reruns of *The Burns and Allen Show* for years; I knew how to play dumb. But again I could read my father's disbelief. He slinked away in a sad funk. I don't think we ever got back to work that day.

I continued my explorations undaunted. The call of nature was more powerful even than fear of my father. While he and my mother were at work, I searched their room for the Mr. G mailing: full-color photos of muscled-up male models shot from low angles, their "huge endowments" crowding the foreground of each frame. (Truth in advertising.) Pity, I thought, that I couldn't put the material to proper use, given the buzz-kill nature of its troubled history. I don't remember getting up the nerve to go to my first gay bar, but somehow I found myself one night at Uncle Charlie's North, in the East Twenties, an establishment listed in *Gay Times* under the heading "Watering Holes." I had never heard this expression before and it worried me. "Watering hole?" Was this some kind of gay code? Was I supposed to recognize its meaning? I scoped out the joint for a good half hour before I could bring myself to enter, walking around the block multiple times, stealing furtive glances through the darkened windows. It seemed an innocent enough place, a neighborhood pub with a few bodies inside, but still I found the whole affair impossibly intimidating.

At the bar, my limbs shaking, chills whipping up and down my spine, head spinning, eyes burning, I ordered a Seven and Seven, spastically taking the drink from the bartender and sipping nervously. Some horrid old queen, drunk, was holding court nearby:

"Oh not me, honey. I don't mind at all. Give me a *hairy ass* any day of the week. I'll be on it like white on rice, honey. A nice *hairy ass!*" The words cut right through me. My father was right: these people were perverts. A young bartender gestured to me as he pushed a fresh drink my way.

"Courtesy of him," he said, pointing to his hirsute, beer-bellied co-worker at the other end of the bar. My not-so-secret admirer (a "bear" in gay parlance, I'd later learn) winked at me as I glanced his way.

"*Hairy ass,* honey," continued the queen, "I LOVE IT!"

I was just about to bolt out of there when, out of nowhere, a sweet-sounding brogue filled softly my ear.

"I don't know why people come here and act so nervous sometimes, you know? It's just a bar, after all. You know? Just some guys hanging out."

I turned in the direction of the voice and found myself nose to nose with a nicely pickled blue-eyed Irishman, thirtyish.

"I'm not nervous," I countered. "Just—maybe—well, maybe a little."

He tacked gently with me, which was wise, introducing himself as "Patrick, like the saint," speaking in soft, reassuring tones, quietly but deeply holding my gaze. Eventually he was saying something about going back to his place. And I was saying yes. I excused myself and backed into the bathroom, experiencing one of the only full-blown panic attacks I've ever had in my life.

"But this is what you've been wanting," I told myself. "Don't chicken out now."

My diminutive new friend, inebriated, drove us out to his dank basement apartment in a two-family house somewhere in Queens, and we immediately got busy. I liked making out at the door, slipping our clothes off on the way to the bedroom, feeling for the first time a man's bare flesh against my own. But as we fell into bed and things got serious, I stopped liking it. The tastes and smells were salty and musky and vaguely gross; the sensations, totally foreign and not particularly enjoyable. I carried on dutifully, uninspired, without climaxing. When it was over, Patrick made me a sandwich, American cheese on white bread, and showed me a picture of his mother, in long dress and apron, standing at the gate of a little farmhouse in rural Ireland. She reminded me of Auntie Em in *The Wizard of Oz,* espe-

cially in the scene where she appears to a captive Dorothy as a fleeting
image in the Wicked Witch's giant crystal ball:

"Dorothy—Dorothy, where are you?" "It's me, it's Auntie Em."
"We're trying to find you! Where are you?"

"I'm here in Oz, Auntie Em! I'm locked up in the Witch's castle . . . and I'm trying to get home to you, Auntie Em! Oh, Auntie Em,
don't go away! I'm frightened! Come back! Come back!" (In one of the
film's most genuinely chilling moments, Auntie Em's gentle visage in
the glass gives way to the horrifying mask of the Witch, mocking and
sadistic: *"Auntie Em, Auntie Em, come back!"* "I'll give you Auntie Em,
my pretty! Ah-ha-ha-ha!")

I was poor, lost Dorothy Gale, imprisoned and trembling in a
strange and treacherous land, wanting more than anything to just go
home again. Patrick, sweetly enough—at once the Witch and the
Wizard—drove me there, all the way to the Bronx. He was sober now.
He asked for my number, and I gave it to him. He called the house a
few times after that (luckily Maria happened to answer each time),
and I just kept making excuses until he stopped trying. I never saw
him again, never wanted to. I was through with sex. It was a relief to
discover that I didn't like it, didn't want it, didn't need it. Problem
solved. (Until my next erection.)

The more time I spent out of the house, the more freedom I craved. By
now, I was violently sick of our toxic labors. I hated and dreaded them
like nothing else, my heart sinking as Thursday gave way to Friday,
and Friday night became Saturday morning. *"Up and at 'em, Bub!"* I
nursed fresh fantasies of patricide and suicide. And then, a brainstorm: I would get a job! Because *work* was something my father re-
spected. It would be guaranteed time out of the house. Duh! Poring

over the pages of the *Bronx Press Review,* I found an opening for part-time work at McDonald's on Fordham Road and scheduled an interview immediately.

Freshly scrubbed and showered, lavishly moisturized and fragranced, dressed in my best designer jean ensemble and brand-new blue suede Earth shoes by Anne Kalso (they and Converse All Star sneakers being the only acceptable alternatives to proper platforms), I worked hard on my interview to impress the store manager, a certain Mr. Curtis Sliwa . . . who would soon go on to found the Guardian Angels, the cultlike New York City–based paramilitary organization, and then become a right-wing radio talk show host. But at that time he was the night manager at the Fordham Road McDonald's, and a very ambitious one, at that. He'd gone to McDonald's Hamburger Institute and earned a degree in Hamburgerology, which he'd framed and mounted proudly over his little desk next to the deep fryer. He described the job:

"You'll come in at six-thirty, work the floor, you know, sweep, mop, clean the bathrooms, bus the tables, empty the trash, hose down the sidewalks, wash the windows, wash the chairs, mop up vomit, that kind of thing. Then, when we close at midnight, you'll scrub down the dining room, clean and shine the counters, the grill, and all the other fixtures, mop the floors, scrub the floor mats, go down to the basement and push vast piles of five-hundred-pound sacks of garbage that have been festering since breakfast up over your head and out through a trapdoor leading to the street above, praying that a band of thugs doesn't descend upon you, push you back into the hole, and take the store hostage." Which, I later came to discover, was exactly what had happened just a few weeks prior to my being hired. The store was robbed after hours, with the intruders gaining entrance in the manner I've described. They locked the staff in the walk-in freezer and shot the manager in the back of the head, killing him instantly. That was why there were some job openings, luckily enough for Curtis and me. I prayed this would not happen again as I hungrily accepted the job, agreeing to start that very weekend.

Curtis proved himself to be as eccentric as he was driven, stripping his shirt off after closing and walking around bare-chested, a set of nunchucks flung across his bony shoulders, our protection against the bad men with guns. He put us to work cleaning parts of the store that weren't even in the manual. I'm sure Ray Kroc himself couldn't identify some of the obscure machine parts Curtis instructed us to shine and polish. It was sweaty, nasty, backbreaking work at minimum wage (two dollars and thirty cents an hour)—and I loved it. *Loved it!*

"Uh, Dad, it's five o'clock. I gotta get ready for *work*."

Freedom, baby! I was willing to risk my life for it. And risk it I did, both inside the store (the clientele packed heat) and out in the street after my shift. Curtis would typically work us until after two o'clock in the morning, and I'd wait alone on the eerily still commercial avenue for a bus that hardly ever came, often forced to walk home, a good five miles or so. There were all the usual dangers of the street at that hour, but there was also, for a while, a new and terrifying threat: the killer who called himself Son of Sam, who received commands to kill from his dog and whose sickening diatribes and letters to Jimmy Breslin were published in the *Daily News*. Two of his earliest victims—when he was still known as "the .44 Caliber Killer"—were friends of mine, Valentina Suriani and Alex Esau, shot dead right in front of Val's apartment building while making out in Alex's burgundy Mercury Montego during the early morning hours of April 17, 1977.

Valentina, a few years older than I was, had been best friends since grade school with Donna Mazzoni, Peter's older sister. We spent a lot of time around each other in the Mazzoni house, where Mr. and Mrs. M referred to us as their "other kids." Val and I, though not on intimate terms, always joked that this made us siblings.

"Hey, sis," I'd say.

"Yo, bro," she'd answer.

She'd been a counselor at St. Lucy's Day Camp while I was still a camper, and it was she who'd taught us many of the songs we bellowed on bus trips, helped organize camp talent shows and giant end-of-summer parties, and was always first on the floor at CYO dances. Val was giggly and full of fun, the very spirit of vivacity—but streetwise too, with a hard streak. One Saturday night just a few weeks before her murder, my play sister really saved my butt.

I had smoked a joint passed to me by a school friend, which, unbeknownst to either of us, was laced with angel dust. No sooner had I slipped the crushed-out roach into my cigarette pack for safekeeping than I had begun hallucinating. This was nothing like the usual mild buzz I got from pot. I didn't know what was happening to me. Suddenly the dark street exploded into a Technicolor dreamscape, the night sky pulsing and throbbing in luminous hues of pink and purple. The Sun-Maid raisin lady—a ruddy-faced peasant carrying a straw basket filled with grapes, the product's mascot—appeared before me as a huge figure looming from the clouds. I thought she was warning me about an unseen cliff ahead. I thought she wanted me to step into her basket for safe passage. Then I thought she was going to hurt me. My friends became alarmed.

"Let's get him a cup of coffee," Peter suggested.

We went to a diner and I stood outside, afraid to enter. I was just a few blocks from home but remember thinking that, if my friends never came back for me, I'd be lost forever. I had no idea how to get to anywhere from here. The world through my eyes had now morphed into a Peter Max poster. I reached above my head to touch floating rainbows and shooting stars. A huge, funky character out of Robert Crumb's "Keep on Truckin' " cartoon went stepping by overhead, nearly crushing my skull with the sole of his giant shoe. The coffee fed me by my faithful friend served only to heighten and speed the swarm of psychedelic images. Peter brought me home to his house, installed me in the basement, and summoned Donna and Val.

"Is he drunk?" Donna asked.

"Your friend is tripping," Valentina said at a glance.

I heard and understood her words clearly. It helped to know what was happening. Val settled me into a comfortable corner, dimmed the lights, put on some soft music, and sent Peter to fetch me a glass of water and some juice. I don't think she said even a word to me as she busied herself, nurselike. The rest of the night is a blackout, but I know it ended safely. That was the last time I saw Valentina alive.

"You can hear the rats scratching inside the walls," I remember Alex saying about the Hell's Kitchen apartment he'd grown up in. He and Val were soon to be engaged, and would probably have ended up married. (Alex, though quiet and shy, was considered "trouble" by Val's parents and other adults in our world, but he was no trouble at all.)

Val's wake at Farenga Brothers Funeral Home was the most mournful event of my young life. Hundreds of grieving friends and relatives crowded the hall, spilling out into the street, shocked and tear-soaked, anxiously looking over their shoulders for a gunman still at large. I remember Val's mother collapsing at the coffin in a hail of shrieks and being carried downstairs to the lounge by a group of women in black dresses, black lace veils pinned to their heads. I followed them with heaving chest and wet palms, feeling the agony of this woman, wanting to stay near her, embrace her, be a child to her. But we'd never even met. I watched as the women lowered her onto a vinyl-upholstered love seat, Mrs. Suriani screaming and sobbing, flailing her limbs with savage abandon. One of the women was squeezing her hand, leaning into her face, and urging her to "be good now, honey, come on. Be a good girl. Be a good girl for me, honey, please—"

The serial killer was stalking the very streets I navigated on my way home from McDonald's, usually striking at just those midnight hours. I'd think of him and quicken my pace. As long as there was some light, I felt safe. But the dark stretches were terrifying, especially the long hike past the Bronx Zoo and through the creepy tunnels leading to the great juncture where Fordham Road becomes Pelham Parkway and White Plains Road converges with Boston Post Road. Sometimes I'd get a ride home from a co-worker, but only in exchange for agreeing to hang out for a few hours. The weekend closing shift was a wild and freaky collection of seventies party people.

Kitty (who'd been a well-paid mortuary beautician at the Walter B. Cooke Funeral Home but quit because she found it too depressing), Yvonne (maybe five feet tall in heels, bleached blond, three hundred pounds of sheer fun-loving Nuyorican womanhood going through an ugly, protracted divorce), and a butch dyke named Gina (who carried a variety of weapons and needed no excuse to use them) knew about all these little after-hours speakeasies and basement dance parties tucked into hidden corners of the neighborhood and neighborhoods south of us. These were places that literally had little windows cut into their doors through which a secret password had to be uttered in order to gain entry. Inside there was usually just some tinny music, a few ratty folding chairs, and maybe an ugly lamp with a bare bulb on a makeshift bar serving shots of whiskey or gin in little paper cups, like in a dentist's office. But these dens were nocturnal and forbidden, peopled by shady characters in flashy clothes, throbbing with mystery. If this was ghetto fabulous, it was all me.

The sexiest of these outings was the time our besotted crew—reeking of cheap booze, cooked meat, stale grease, garbage, cleaning fluid, and body odor—wended its way down a long, dark alleyway, through a series of doors and hallways, and down another alleyway that opened, finally, onto a thundering basement dance hall, Latin style, with multicolored cellophane palm trees banking a glittering dance floor. Yvonne grabbed my hand and pulled me into the crush of bodies.

"Dance me, papi! Dance me hard!" We salsaed ourselves into a frenzy.

My father, of course, had no idea about any of this. I'd explain the extra-late nights in some work-related way and he'd grudgingly accept. I even managed to slip away from the house one Saturday afternoon and evening in order to attend the wedding of my co-worker Ralph, the fierce snapping queen of our crew, from whom I first heard the pronoun "she" used in reference to a male.

"Oh yes, my boyfriend Vinny? She and me is gonna be married. Oh yes, child. You're all invited. And Curtis, she's gonna do the service!"

And so it was, child, because Miss Ralph's mouth never wrote a check her ass couldn't cash. Curt seemed to have a special fondness for Ralph, which I found endearing. He was protective of him, and tolerated no fag-bashing comments at the counter.

"Take a look," I remember him quipping affectionately as, after closing, attending his chores, Ralph paraded around the dining room swinging his rag and bucket for all they were worth. "It's the Dairy Queen."

On their wedding day, the blushing bridegrooms were chauffeured up to the entrance of their South Bronx project building in an immaculate white stretch limo. A driver in formal dress opened the car doors for them, and they emerged into the sunlight wearing matching white-on-white tuxedos with white satin lapels and cuffs, and white patent leather shoes with white silk spats. Preceded by a formal bridal procession, led by a blushing flower girl and the mothers of the grooms wearing heavy velvet gowns and corpulent wrist corsages, Ralph and Vinny marched regally into the building, down the fluorescent-lit hallway, and into the thickly festooned community room, where they exchanged vows and rings and were married before—well, before Curtis Sliwa. Then we partied and ate food from aluminum trays, and drank rum and RC cola from paper cups. Curtis danced the Robot all night long, way too intensely, his eyes wide and distant, dripping sweat and poking out moves in a freakish trance.

If it's scandalous to out the founder of an urban paramilitary organization and right-wing radio talk show host as the trance-dancing mock presiding minister at a gay marriage ceremony more than thirty years ago in the South Bronx, then I've dropped a bomb. But for me, Curtis Sliwa was a Freedom Rider.

16.

"Wanna do the hills?" moon-faced Marina Ogliotti asks devilishly from behind the wheel of her '76 Ford Mustang, electric blue, with black hardtop and white leather interior.

"Hell yeah!" we respond.

It's a ritual. Now she drives to the top of a long avenue (I forget which, maybe Mace or Waring), way up past St. Lucy's, and then, pedal to the metal, tears at top speed down twelve blocks or more, the car dipping and bouncing over several steep "hills" along the way. We scream as if aboard the Dragon Coaster at Rye Playland, Marina providing a live operatic sound track at the top of her lungs. (She loves to sing.)

An old buddy of mine from day camp and the CYO, and a child-hood friend of Donna's and Valentina's, Marina had by then become one of my very favorite people in the world. She, Peter, and I formed a frequent threesome. Zaftig, with inky black bone-straight hair, wide, dark eyes, and sweet, funny features (reminiscent of a young, meatier Kaye Ballard), Marina was a natural mimic and comedienne, regularly sending our crowd into dangerous convulsions of laughter. We'd beg her to stop, fearing for our lives, but she was relentless. Marina killed, trading in high camp long before any of us even knew what that meant.

Her best friend from St. Catherine's Academy for Girls, Joanne Puglia (a compact, oversexed little vixen with a part-time job at a bread shop on a sleepy stretch of Morris Park Avenue, where she was known to hang the Closed sign on the door from time to time, to make it in the basement with a deliveryman) was constantly trying to mount and mate me in the backseat of that car.

"I'm so fucking horny I could fucking fuck that fucking fire hydrant" was a typical declaration. "In fact—you know what?—pull over." She'd hop out and straddle the nearest Johnny pump, bounce up and down a little, then hop back into the car and start yanking at my pants, shoving her tongue down my throat.

"Drive out to Orchard Beach parking lot," she'd pant at the driver's seat, "and don't look back here."

"No, Marina, don't do it," I'd squeal, peeling Joanne's fingers off my zipper. "Joanne, cut it out. You're like my sister. I can't do that with you."

I'd usually clamber up to the relative safety of the passenger seat, leaving Joanne to writhe and moan alone.

"Hey, hey, don't stain my leather back there," Marina would bark. "Fuckin' nympho." She claimed most of the Catholic high school girls were like this.

"Oh, yeah," she'd say. "You didn't know? They're a bunch a' *who-ahs.*"

Marina displayed the makings of a young Anna Magnani in her performance as the maid in the CYO production of *A Day in the Life of Archie Andrews* (in which I was cast as Reggie Mantle, and recruited

Linc for a cameo as the Andrewses' family dog). The audience roared as my divinely silly friend prattled on in an outrageous accent she'd invented for the character, slipping trippingly from Irish to Swedish to Cockney to Russian to Italian and back again. She even managed, from out of nowhere, to work in her pirate impression, her favorite bit from some old movie: "So ya say ya wanna take a walk, ay? Well to-morra mornin' at sunrise, you'll *walk the plank!*"

Stopping the show more than once with her over-the-top physical antics, Marina raised the bar she herself had set a season or two earlier, at the annual CYO talent pageant, with her audacious rendition of "I've Got a Lovely Bunch of Coconuts"—performed in a home-made Carmen Miranda costume while juggling a pair of hairy brown coconuts and belting out the lyrics in a ridiculously broad Cockney accent:

> *Oh, Oy've got a lover-ly bunch o'cokey-nuts*
> *Ere they are all standin' in a raaow . . .*

Her parents, mid-century immigrants from Abruzzi, were labor-ers: her father, a groundskeeper at a Westchester County office park; her mother, an office maintenance worker on the midnight shift. The living room of their attached brick house on Paulding Avenue was cordoned off by a velvet rope, beyond which loomed dreamily a green-and-gold-flocked velvet couch encased in plastic slipcovers; a smoked-glass, kidney-shaped two-tiered coffee table; a glass and brass curio cabinet displaying delicate porcelain figurines; and several large pieces of Romanesque statuary, including a painted lady holding a huge bunch of grapes that lit up when you plugged them in—all set neatly upon a spotless carpet of bright fuchsia. Marina's bed-room was a vision in pink and white, with a ruffled canopy crowning her queen-size bed. Mr. and Mrs. Ogliotti showered their American-born daughter with more luxury than they could afford. She was their princess, ambassador, spokeswoman, translator, business manager—their eyes and ears in a world they found endlessly baffling. She had an older brother living in San Francisco with whom the family appeared to have little contact, so she was for all intents and purposes a pampered only child, accustomed to getting what she wanted.

"Gimme that," she said, when I showed her my copy of *Hot Line: The Letters I Get . . . And Write!* by Burt Reynolds, a paperback I'd found in the book rack at Royal Stationery on White Plains Road, featuring steamy fan mail allegedly received by dreamy Burt and his equally steamy alleged responses—along with several pages of seminude photos. Marina snatched the book from my hands and buried it in her underwear drawer. I never saw it again.

She was sullen and depressed for weeks and months after the double murder. We all were. The killer was out there, killing still. Some neighborhood boys formed a posse and vowed to "hunt the fuckin' psycho down and string 'im up from a lamppost by his fuckin' balls." It was just an empty pose. Whenever we managed to forget for a while and found ourselves laughing at some silly thing or other, one of us would express guilt and shame for enjoying ourselves while our pals lay cold and rotting in their graves. We dragged ourselves to the CYO spring dance, moping around on the sidelines, not at all our usual selves. Finally, we gathered in a cluster to do a simple pony, our old standby, the standard dance of our pre-disco youth. (Irene Murphy shook her huge rack while performing the little hop step. "Cut that out!" her stoner boyfriend, unseen, bellowed from a dark corner.) I was just starting to feel the music when a handsome thug approached me menacingly, his boys in tow. It was Fernando, my old junior high school nemesis, not a regular here. I couldn't tell if he recognized me or thought I was fresh meat.

"We don't like the way you dance," he said.

"So what?" I responded, sounding in my own ears like a girl.

"You dance like a fag," he continued.

"Too bad," I shot back lamely.

He stamped on my foot, punched me hard in the stomach, and stalked out of the gymnasium. Humiliated, I left the party. My sympathetic friends and I headed over to White Castle to smother our sorrows in tiny steamed cheeseburgers, shoestring fries, and vanilla milk shakes.

Stephen Patrick, the musical genius of our crew—a fair, fey wisp of a boy with a hushed speaking voice and fine hands—had recently been hired as the church organist, and he had his own key. We snuck into St. Lucy's on a regular late-night basis, getting high and gathering around the organ to hear Stephen perform "Love Lies Bleeding" (including the long, extended intro) and other selections from Elton John's *Goodbye Yellow Brick Road.* The windy strains of the old Hammond, pumped out hard by a driven young player, echoed off the plaster walls and marble surfaces of the empty church. We usually ended up wandering alone in different directions, each taken by the experience in our own way, achieving something like spiritual fulfillment in that room for the first time.

I experienced a brief calling to join the priesthood. A "life in God" seemed both a ready solution to the problem of my sexuality and a chance to inhabit a permanently enhanced, heightened state of consciousness—akin, perhaps, to being high all the time. The heavenly summons came during a CYO retreat at a dude ranch in upstate New York, where trained counselors and young priests led us through a weekend of spiritual exercises, meditation, and prayer. At one point, well greased for it, we were invited to lounge on the carpeted floor of a large studio and listen to a recording of "Everything I Own" by Bread:

> *I'd give up my life, my heart, my home*
> *I would give everything I own*
> *Just to have you once again*
> *Just to touch you once again . . .*

We were encouraged to cry, to "just let it out"—about nothing in particular, about everything, anything, our sins perhaps, our fear of God, our unworthiness—and to then stream up to a podium where several young priests sat ready to hear our confessions. This solemn sacrament was usually performed in the absolute privacy of a darkened booth; the theatrical public arrangement in the room was intended, I guess, to create a kind of fever of penitence. It worked: my friends and I became undone by the exercise, sobbing deeply, rising to our feet, and stumbling up to the podium one by one.

I remember sitting before an earnest cleric—his head bowed and his hands folded—unable to do anything but weep. I wanted to tell him that I was overwrought with anxiety; that I found the world around me terrifying and wild, and couldn't see my place in it; that my own body and mind had become foreign territory, daily doing battle with me; that I was prepared and willing to turn to God and devote myself to Him with all my heart, to throw myself at His mercy and put myself completely into His hands—if it would mean deliverance. I wanted to say all this and more. But all that came out was "boo-hoo." Finally the priest spoke in a cold voice.

"What are you crying about?"

I dried up instantly. "I'm not sure," I said.

The moment was gone, evaporated. I confessed a few sins, said my penance, and returned to the group. By the time we were on the bus back to the Bronx, my celestial caller had hung up the line.

The trip home was a mess. Those foolish priests had led us deep into the forest of ourselves and abandoned us there. Most of my friends, tear-streaked, looked wounded and lost. Especially Billy. He'd been a fellow altar boy, the kid originally responsible for introducing me to all the others and my most treasured friend when we were younger. Billy had a profound and completely distracting long-term crush on a handsome boy named Adriano. He'd confessed his forbidden love to a priest during the "Everything I Own" exercise, rocking back and forth afterward, sobbing the words "I don't want to be this, I don't want to be this, I don't want to be this." The poor kid never recovered, his slender little frame quivering in the arms of one female friend after another the whole way home. Days later, he denied it ever happened.

"What? No. I was just upset because JoJo is sick and we might have to put her to sleep." Somehow we were supposed to believe—and pretended we did—that the phrase "I don't want to be this" had something to do with an ailing Chihuahua.

West Side Story was Marlene's ambitious choice for the school play during the spring semester of my senior year of high school. I didn't mind being cast in the small role of Snowboy, one of the Jets. As senior vice president, editor in chief of the school newspaper, and active member of the Yearbook Committee, my plate was already filled to capacity. Plus, the Jets got plenty of stage time. The kids in the lead roles of Maria, Anita, and Tony (Laura Rodriguez, Wilma Rivera, and David Santiago) were genuinely talented singers, and natural actors. Laura's brother, a professional Vegas-style choreographer (whose unsubtle stage name was Rick Sextos), had been signed on to stage the musical numbers, a task he approached with no holds barred, setting us to leaping, twirling, kicking, humping, grinding, and sliding our way across the auditorium stage on our knees, bellies, and butts. It was thrilling. Mr. Dzig, the music teacher, rehearsed the orchestra and taught us the difficult vocal material.

I will never forget our performance of "Tonight," the climactic Act One finale (heralding the fateful event that will quickly spiral into tragedy for all). The song is sung contrapuntally by the entire cast, building thunderously until all voices join in unison for the final surging note. In Marlene's staging, cast members entered from various points around the two-tiered set, slowly making their way to a riser at the foot of the stage. She'd filled the Jets roles with Italian, Irish, and Jewish kids; the Sharks, with Puerto Rican and black kids. The parallels between the characters and ourselves were intentional, of course, and Marlene exploited them by convening rap sessions for the cast so we could discuss and explore the issues. But most of the kids who'd ended up in the Drama Club were more evolved types, "not prejudiced," so we pretty much agreed on the basics. All we really wanted was to get back into rehearsal: we had a theatrical coup to stage.

The Sharks and Jets flowed into the big number from the back of the auditorium, singing down the side aisles, paced to arrive at the riser just before the final few notes of the song. The rush of adrena-

line I felt as we took our places among a sea of openmouthed school-
mates singing huge this glorious song—Mr. Dzig waving wildly in the
pit, whipping his student orchestra with remarkable success through
the burning forest of Leonard Bernstein's cacophonous score, his
Eraserhead-like hairdo bouncing to and fro in a frizzy column, wire-
rimmed spectacles vibrating at the bridge of his nose, sheet music
tumbling off a wobbly stand; the audience, rapt and suspended,
clearly stunned, gazing upon the spectacle with emotion before exploding into an earthquake-like ovation; the shimmering twinkle of
silence occupying that shiver of space between the song's hard finish
and the thunderous outburst—all this, on top of the profound beauty I
had discovered in the material itself and in the very acts of rehearsal
and performance, bound me forever to the romantic ideal of a life in
the theater.

Victor came to check out our final dress rehearsal, bringing
Joanna and Virginia along, and he and I hung out alone in the student
government office beforehand, munching on dry rice cakes and rem-
iniscing about "old times." Victor described events unfolding in some
other reality, a world away from the Bronx. His style of dress and
grooming had grown slicker, more cosmopolitan ("he looks like he's
from down the city"), and he wore a square leather pouch, like a sad-
dlebag, with a long, slender strap slung diagonally across his torso.
When he asked how everything was going with me, I said without in-
tending to that I'd been going through some big changes.

"I think I'm bisexual," I stated plainly, much to my own surprise.

"I know, me too."

Gulp. Had Victor just come out to me?

"Did you say you too?"

"Yeah." And then, quickly, "Hey, where is everybody? Shouldn't
we be getting downstairs?" The details of the rest of that day escape

me. But I remember a bright sun shining in my brain: Victor and I had come out to each other. (We both knew that "bisexual" was code.) Anything was possible now.

I had started answering personal ads from the back pages of *Gay Times,* at first responding only to those with telephone numbers, nervously clutching fistfuls of dimes in the smelly phone booth at the Esso station under the El, or, preferably, one of two clean little compartments at the back of the Golden Dragon Restaurant (which the grumpy owner let me use only when the dining room was empty). The first guy I called asked me how big my dick was. I didn't know. He told me to go home, measure it, and call him back. An hour or so later I reported, with some exaggeration, that my dick was three inches long.

"Was it hard when you measured it?"

Well no, it wasn't. It was all curled up into itself like a turtle, freaked out by the cold wooden ruler, cringing from the sharp edge of the built-in metal strip—intended for line drawing but suitable as a dick-slicing device.

"Go back, get it hard, and measure it again."

I tried, without success. When I called back the third time, I said I'd counted seven inches.

"Let's meet," he panted. "Give me your number and I'll call you back."

"Okay," I said. "My number is—" and hung up.

I knew better than to have this freak call my father's house. Regretting my haste a few weeks later, I called again, explaining that we'd been cut off because I'd run out of change, and that I'd then become homeless for a while. But I was back on my feet now and ready to meet. When did he want to get together? Following a brief silence, suddenly not horny at all, the stranger on the other end went through the motions of excusing himself before disconnecting.

The "better" personal ads, the less desperate-sounding ones, the ones with accompanying photos, all required written responses. In a fit of hormonal urgency, I posted a letter to a guy named Vinny, pictured in his ad as a handlebar mustache–wearing Italian in his late twenties, naked from the waist up, with a tight, hairy torso, low-slung jeans, and well-worn black Fryes (I had the same boots in tan, a hopeful omen). I included a picture of myself—my graduation photo, in fact, in which I wear a navy blue blazer over a subway-themed Huk-A-Poo shirt, gold cross on a gold chain, blown-dry hair, and a tight, thin smile aboard thick lips—and guarded our mailbox for days until Vinny's response arrived . . . actually a greeting card from a guy named Don explaining that Vinny had to go away for a while, but that he, Don, would be happy to meet me instead. He didn't provide a physical description, but he gave me his phone number. I called from the safety of the Golden Dragon, and we arranged to meet.

Don lived in Chelsea, when it was still a grim industrial district dotted by rough projects, in a fabulous duplex apartment he'd built himself. He'd bought the small building a few years earlier with a friend, a former lover, he said, who occupied the upper two floors. (Early Chelsea queens.) He was black, thirty-something, slightly overweight, not particularly handsome but appealing in his way; soft and warm to the touch. He told me that some photographs he'd taken of skinny teenage boys writhing on bedsheets or submerged in bubble baths, their erect penises poking through foam, had been published in *Gay Times* and pointed out several framed prints mounted on clean white walls. I had seen some of these pictures before and was duly impressed.

"Took 'em right up there," he said, gesturing overhead. "Want me to take a few of you?"

My answer was an emphatic no. Don backed off right away. Soon,

HIGH SCHOOL GRADUATION, 1977

he leaned in to kiss me. His freshly scrubbed skin was the texture of velvet, his breath was clean and minty, he was moving nice and slow. I began to relax. We took off some clothes and rolled around. After a while, he led me to the spiral staircase, and hopping onto his bed, we collided our bodies together some more. Suddenly I was ejaculating. "Not yet, not yet!" poor Don yelled, but I could no more control the timing of the physical explosion than I could direct the course of stars and planets. This was definitely an improvement over my experience with Patrick . . . not nearly Nirvana, but getting warm. Maybe sex was an option, after all.

Don had planted a huge hickey on my neck, my first.

"What are you dating, a vampire?" my mother asked. "Better cover that up before your father sees it." I wanted to tell her everything, wanted to tell somebody something, wanted to stop lying and step out of the shadows but knew, of course, that I must not. At least there was Victor. I wanted him. I decided to make another date with Don and invite my old friend along. Perhaps a ménage à trois would break the ice. I phoned Don from the Dragon and asked his advice.

"You can try it," he said, "but you have to be ready for rejection."

He counseled caution but agreed to play along, suggesting that a foursome might be less awkward. Though Vinny was "still out of town" (I understood by then that Don's ad had been a bait and switch, but it didn't really matter), he had another friend he could invite. I ran the whole idea by Victor, my heart in my throat, and to my surprise he was game.

Don's friend was roughly Don's age, also black, tall and nicely built, quite handsome. He sat smiling in a club chair, wearing an oxford shirt and dress slacks, Don and I stiffly occupying a leather couch opposite him. Victor was spending an awful lot of time in the bathroom. We'd met up at the Twin Donut on the corner of Twenty-third

Street and Seventh Avenue, and he seemed cheerful enough as we headed over to Don's nearby address, laughing and gabbing and approaching the whole thing with a healthy sense of fun. Boys at play. But he grew listless once we'd gotten inside, complaining of a persistent stomach ailment. Finally, he asked if he could lie down for a while. Don escorted him to a spare bedroom, and then sat very close to me on the couch. Soon, his friend was sitting beside us, his hand on my thigh. Nixing this development immediately, Don ushered me into his bedroom . . . where he knew not to maul or paw me, knew not to hurry, knew that this was new to me and that I was frightened; knew, even, that he was not the teacher I would have chosen, which seemed to humble him. He was *respectful*. I liked that. Our second encounter lasted only a few minutes longer than the first, but my twin experiences with Don were newsy and enlightening.

I showered, dressed, and tiptoed into the guest room to rouse Victor from a sound sleep. As we headed out, Don's friend rose from his club chair and set down the magazine he'd been reading the whole time to accept Victor's apology.

"Stan gave me something for my stomach," Victor said, "and it really knocked me out."

"He should know better than that," I remember scolding.

And then, to Don and the stranger: "He's our teacher. Er, um—*friend*."

Outside on the street, Victor snapped to immediately and erupted into raucous laughter. It had all been a gag. He wasn't attracted to Don's friend and couldn't think of how else to get out of it. He was tired and needed a nap anyway.

"You *are* a good actor," I marveled. And he was. I'd swallowed the bait whole. We laughed over grilled cheese sandwiches at a seedy local diner. (Victor has become a vegetarian.) Later, he pulled out his leather-bound weekly planner, nearly the size of a phone book, and looked to see when he'd have time to meet again. He wasn't sure. We agreed that we'd talk over the next week or two to set something up. We never did. I saw Victor only once or twice after that. A decade or so later, he would die of AIDS.

I had taken my SAT high on pot, scoring just below 900. (There'd been no formal preparations, and no one told me I could take it again.) Now I was searching for colleges by mileage—in order to qualify, a school had to be far enough away that I'd need to board but near enough that I could get into the city with ease. My father, fortunately, stayed out of the application process, occasionally dropping just two hints: Columbia University and West Point. The first was out of the question for several reasons—proximity to home, for starters; the second was just plain strange. Bone-chilling, really. West Point? Exactly which part of the boy living in his house did my father believe would thrive and bloom at a *military academy*? On the morning he announced that we were taking a drive "just to see the place," I made every excuse I could think of. He would have none of it. Hiding behind huge, cheap sunglasses and an oversize windbreaker, I sat silently in the car as my father drove us up to the compound. Dr. Meltzer was on the radio with his popular program, *What's Your Problem?*

"Helen in Baychester," old Meltzer might have been croaking. "What's your problem?"

"Oh, Dr. Meltzer, thank you for taking my call," a woman named Helen might have gushed. "I'm a lifelong listener and I just love you, I really do. You should run for president, you really should. You'd have my vote, you really would. Really you would. I'm calling today about my sister. She has a large goiter on her abdomen that has to be removed, or at least drained, but her health insurance ran out because she recently lost her job and now the doctors say they can't treat her. Anyway, Dr. Meltzer, the point is, the goiter recently ruptured. And now my sister—"

"Listen, sweetheart, I hate to cut you off but I have to go to a commercial break. Tell you what I'm gonna do. Stay on the line, I want you to stay on the line, sweetheart, it's very important. My producer is going to come on the line and get your personal information and we're gonna send your sister an original Dr. Bernard Meltzer T-shirt. A hundred percent cotton, very comfortable. How's that? And I'll even include one for you—stay on the line, dear. We'll be right back."

The old radio huckster, not a medical doctor, freely dispensed expert advice on all and any topics: health, career, finances, parenting, even romance. ("Remember, darling, love means never having to say you're sorry. Hmm. Where have I heard that before? This is Dr. Bernard Meltzer. Stay tuned.")

"How does he know so much about so many things?" I asked my father, just to say something.

"Common sense. And he knows how to talk to people."

"Really? Well maybe he could talk to *you* about not subjecting *me* to the torment of this fucking trip to *West Fucking Point*!" I screamed silently, inventing car phones right on the spot.

The uniformed officer in whose stately office, dimly lit, I soon found myself was saying something like "Your father tells me you're considering a career in the military." I don't think I responded, busy as I was realizing that this was a scheduled appointment, not just a spontaneous visit, stealthily casing the exit, planning my escape should I be compelled to stay. But the benign officer just gave us a generic soft sell, handed me a few pamphlets, and showed us a bit of the campus: low brick buildings on trim green lawns, erect cadets milling about in various styles of uniform. My favorite was the torso-hugging blue-gray gabardine zippered waistcoat with mock turtle collar and a wide dark border around the entire perimeter. I picked one up at a surplus store a few months later. Got a lot of compliments on that jacket. Looked great with a pair of wide-legged jeans.

Ohhhh baby! My heart is full of love and desire for you
So come on down and do what you got to do . . .

The swelling chorus of Thelma Houston's "Don't Leave Me This Way" is pulsing out of giant speakers ringing the dance floor of a steamy discotheque in Quebec City. I am hustling with Margaret, her blazing eyes and openmouthed smile spinning around my ears as I lead her in our most complex spins and twirls (the triple fake, the behind-the-neck switcheroo, the walking turn). We're on our Senior Trip, organized by Stan—three nights and four days in Canada. I have taken a hit of THC, but am feeling nothing yet. We leave the club, planning to check out another. (Stan and Marlene have given us a curfew but have allowed us to explore the city unattended.) I swallow another white pill. Maybe the first was "beat." As we approach our destination, I am starting to feel a little numb. I think I might pass out.

"Hey, guys—gimme a minute."

I pause to gather myself, leaning against a building. I place my hand on the brick wall . . . and my hand feels like one giant block of cement scraping another. It sends a bizarre shiver through my *gums*.

"I think I have to go back to the hotel."

By the time we get to our room (we are bunking in same-sex groups of three or four), I can neither walk unassisted nor speak a single word. My friends lead me to the bed and summon Stan and Marlene.

"What did he take?" I hear Marlene asking.

"They're taking THC," Stan says knowingly.

"How much?" Marlene presses.

"I think he only took one," says a friend.

"No. I took a second one. And I'm actually totally alert. I can hear you quite clearly. I just can't open my eyes or close my mouth or lift my head or stir my limbs at all. Please just keep talking and stay with me. It's not entirely unpleasant. But it's not what I was hoping for either. How about you? How's your night going? You feeling anything?" I asked inside my head.

Marlene to the others, looking down at my corpselike form:

"He's fine. He's breathing normally. He'll sleep it off. No more pills. Let him rest. Give me a key. I'll check on him again."

"Noooo!" I scream from inside a prison of total paralysis. "I don't want to be alone. Somebody stay! *Don't leave me this way!"* With that, I flash back to my thrilling flight across the dance floor with Margaret. We are burning the boards with our moves. But I am also alone in a darkened hotel room, far from home, hoping I will not die. The two realities are equally vivid.

The next morning, Stan and Marlene descend upon me and the other student government officials—my good friends Mike and Alan, and a kid named Ira (whom we never particularly connected with but who'd won the presidency square and fair on a platform of "Students First")—for a stern talking-to. We'd already tried the patience of our mentors by smoking pot in the bus bathroom on the way from the airport to our hotel.

"You're supposed to be setting an example for the others!" Stan hisses.

"We thought we could trust you," Marlene laments, her genuine disappointment cutting to the quick. "We were wrong."

We vowed to change our ways, and did. No more pills. Just pot and liquor. But I never could drink much. That night, I downed three or four glasses of Amaretto, and threw up on the cobblestones outside a quiet little bar. The last time I remembered being that sick from drink was New Year's Eve a few years earlier, when I'd downed an entire bottle of sickly-sweet sparkling wine, Giacobazzi Lambrusco, on my way to a pre-party at Billy's house. His mother, draped in a flowing Pucci print lounging gown, noticed my particular shade of green and put her arm around my shoulder, an Eve menthol 120 bouncing on her lip.

"Whatsa matta, honey? You don't look so good. Wanna glass a' water?"

"Yes," I said, turning to her. "Water might be—*blwrraghhh!*"

A river of vomit flowed up from my stomach, out of my mouth, and onto the neck and chest of my hostess. The traditional New Year's Eve dinner my mother had prepared—roast pork, lima beans, and escarole (the beans and greens representing coins and dollars, auguring wealth in the new year; the pork representing . . . well, pork), a dozen or more half-digested Christmas cookies, the quart of Giacobazzi Lambrusco—it all rushed out in a hot, rancid stream onto the elegant garment Billy's mother had purchased just days earlier at Enza's, *the* high-end boutique on Allerton Avenue.

Her face fell. She removed the cigarette from her mouth.

"That's all right, honey," she said flatly. "Wanna clean yourself up and go lay down? I'm gonna change my dress . . ."

Stan and Marlene were still pissed at us when we got home from Canada.

"You're going to find that you won't have so many privileges now," Stan warned, but it wasn't true. Things went back to normal after a day or two. No choice. We still had the Senior Party to pull off, the yearbook to distribute, the graduation ceremony to produce. Stan's plans were zealous all around. "Goodbye, Columbus" was his theme for our fete at the Marina del Rey in Throgs Neck, a sought-after catering palace on the waters of the Long Island Sound. No prom tradition existed at Columbus, so there was no budget. Stan dug into his own pocket, selling mugs and banners printed with a logo he'd designed to help raise money. Most of my classmates ordered THC or mescaline for the affair. I did not. At the party, I found the inebriation of my friends unattractive and wandered off alone several times, smoking cigarettes, roaming the manicured grounds, gazing westward into the twinkling Manhattan skyline.

I'd be leaving home in a couple of months, having recently been accepted to SUNY Purchase despite my idiotic SAT score. Good grades, a mother lode of extracurricular and community service activities, a handmade chapbook of poems and stories, and an impassioned admissions essay had all qualified me handily for this progressive institution. (Lucky thing, since I don't recall being invited to attend anywhere else.) Founded by Governor Nelson Rockefeller in 1967 as the jewel in the crown of the state university system, Purchase housed both a traditional liberal arts college and an arts conservatory offering rigorous training in dance, theater, music, visual arts, and film. It had easily passed the mileage test, and had charmed me completely when I visited. The campus was mellow and highly symmetrical, its uniformly brown brick buildings and walkways at once oppressive and soothing. Several of the flat geometric structures—including a massive performing arts center with four state-of-the-art theaters, an art museum, and a sprawling glass and steel building devoted entirely to the study of dance—were still being completed. A humongous Henry Moore statue sat in the center of a great brown brick plaza. Another oversize artwork was parked nearby, the temporary installation of a grocery store shopping cart the size of a small building. Beyond the plaza was a great rectangle of green; beyond the green, a valley of hills, with an old stone mansion tucked deep into the center of the scene, its mighty bulk dwarfed by nature's sweep. A sprinkling of earnest-looking young professors and artsy students ambled about, some in tights and leggings, others lugging art supplies or musical instruments. I understood intuitively that it would be safe to be myself here, and can remember smiling Cheshire-like as I settled comfortably into a hollow of the Henry Moore to gaze lazily across at the sylvan woods.

"There is *God* in mescaline," Georgina, a girl I know only peripherally, is propounding from deep inside her trip, tugging at my arm and pulling me back into the party. "And I didn't even do a whole one! . . . Come with me, I wanna dance, dance with me."

I move stiffly about the room in my beige polyester three-piece suit, solid mauve Huk-A-Poo shirt, and coordinated two-tone platforms, never really warming up to the party. The buildup has been too intense. How could anything live up to the hype? Plus, my mind has chosen this particular night to grasp the understanding that I am standing upon the precipice of a massive change.

Many parents, including my own, balked at the fact that our high school graduation was held at the Brooklyn Academy of Music—we were Bronxites, what did we need with Brooklyn?—but the grand hall was the only affordable option Stan deemed suitable. He led the proceedings from behind a walnut podium like a professional emcee, having decked out the stage in tasteful floral sprays and arrangements. He'd put me in charge of recruiting the keynote speaker, suggesting that I try Tony Randall and Anne Bancroft, the former because he was witty and articulate, the latter because she was a Columbus alumna, having graduated decades earlier, when she was still known as Anna Italiano. Randall couldn't make it, and Bancroft never responded. (A rumor surfaced that Miss Bancroft, another favorite—we watched her over and over again in *The Miracle Worker* and *The Prisoner of Second Avenue*—held a grudge because she'd not been given the lead in a school play, but I doubted its veracity.) The best I could do was Alison Steele, a sultry-voiced FM radio deejay known as "the Nightbird," who turned out to be a hoot. As class vice president and winner of several awards—Community Service, Honor Roll, Creative Writing—I was seated prominently onstage, an honor and a thrill. I never wanted to remove my gown, and kept it flapping against my body until well into the evening.

One Saturday night a few weeks later, my friends Alan and Holly and I gussied up hard and drove downtown in Alan's father's silver Cutlass Supreme with burgundy interior (a floating living room, we called it), determined to get into Studio 54. Alan, a high school friend, not part of my St. Lucy's crew, had replaced Victor as my closest pal and deepest crush. (His girlfriend, Holly, must have seen my struggle but never let on.) As we cruised slowly past the world's premiere nightclub, on the northwestern edge of the Theater District, not far from the Hell's Kitchen tenement in which my mother was born, we sensed a problem: muscle-bound bouncers stood behind ropes and stanchions, handpicking patrons from the crush of bodies pressing in on them, gruffly clearing a path for VIPs arriving in long stretch limos.

"Uhhh. Any other ideas?".

I'd heard talk of clubs like Les Jardins and G. G. Barnum's, but the best option seemed to be a place Holly knew about called New York New York, chief rival to Studio 54. We headed over there.

The management must have mistaken us for the children of some designer or celebrity, because we were whisked past a series of velvet cords, ensconced at an excellent table astride the dance floor, and served drinks on the house. Confused but asking no questions, we gazed around at the all-white interior—copious clouds of mist diffusing multicolor laser light effects, a gloriously crisp sound system pumping my favorite jams, designer-clad club goers moving smoothly across a glassy dance floor—and sipped our Seven and Sevens quietly, too intimidated to dance.

17.

Wednesday night, July 13, 1977:

My mother, father, Maria, and I are gathered around the kitchen table in candlelight, listening to the news of the Big Blackout on a transistor radio. The entire city is dark as pitch. The killer, in our very midst, is watching, waiting, stalking, striking. Rosette and her girl-friends are staying upstate until his reign of terror ends. She and Charlene are accustomed to hanging out in Charl's car, gabbing and smoking, double-parked in front of our house, exactly the kind of scenario Son of Sam preys upon.

By the time he is caught quite by accident a few weeks later, David Berkowitz, a pudgy, schlubby postal worker around Rosette's age, has killed six people and seriously wounded seven more. My friends and I want justice, want it our way, want him disemboweled in the public square. Reporters and camera crews gather outside Valentina's build-ing seeking comments from neighbors and family.

"How do you feel now that the killer has been caught?"

"What would you like to see done to the killer?"

"Will the killer's capture bring you *closure*?"

When we hear that a few enterprising reporters are poking around St. Lucy's, my crew and I race over to *our corner* to give them a piece of our minds—only to catch the tail end of a white news van disappearing at the end of the block.

"And don't ever come back!" we yell pointlessly into a trail of dust.

I was working full-time that summer as a shipping and receiving clerk at the Saks warehouse, a job my father had wrangled for me. We'd wake at around five, hop into the car before six, and arrive at the waterfront facility by six-thirty—with plenty of time to stop in the employee cafeteria for coffee and doughnuts before clocking in at seven. As the car turned off the West Side Highway and onto local streets, we'd drive past a tasty array of hookers, drag queens, and grizzled Marlboro men in full leather gear, stumbling out of darkened doorways and cruising the bloodstained streets (the area was a bustling wholesale meat market by day). My father growled long and low, like a bulldog, as I squirmed with obvious interest at these first glimpses into a forbidden underground world I hadn't even known existed.

"*O! Lo figlio di Filli!*" hailed the lumpenproletariat freight elevator operator, a Calabrese immigrant shaped like a *zepolle* (who reminded me of Marina's father).

"*Che se dice?*"

My father had introduced me all around the plant, given me the lay of the land, shown me off to his co-workers. ("Your dad's an asshole," said one guy, pretending to be kidding.) Philly, as everyone called him, even trudged me up to the administrative offices and introduced me to management.

"He's won a couple of writing awards," he boasted to Bruce in Copywriting.

"Oh, yes?" said the hopeless queer, looking up at me. "Interested in learning to write copy?"

"Maybe," I answered dully, wanting to get away from him.

As he led us hither and yon, I could see—for the first time really—that my father was proud of me. He was proud of himself too, having just made foreman, and demonstrated his new authority by casually issuing orders and instructions as we navigated to his tiny basement office. I overheard him in the locker room once:

"That motherfucker's a real cocksucker."

I'd never known my father to use such language. At home, he objected hotly even to words like *damn, crap,* or *shut up.*

What a hypocrite, I thought to myself, not for the first time. But some part of me understood that he was just trying to be one of the guys. My father was every bit the social misfit I was.

I worked on the fourth floor, away from him, breaking down huge shipments of clothing and accessories from worldwide suppliers and redistributing the merchandise to Saks stores nationwide. I am confessing nothing when I observe that several fine garments—silk blouses by Ungaro, wool skirts by Givenchy, jersey tube dresses by Diane Von Furstenberg—went missing that summer, and that several pieces fitting these self-same descriptions ended up upon the backs of my sisters and their friends. My only confessions are that I was young, reckless . . . and very, very lucky.

Manny and I—he was a fellow worker around my age, maybe a year or two older—took walks along West Street during overlong lunch breaks, wending eastward until finding ourselves on the streets of the Village. We'd stop in to head shops to buy pipes and bongs—sometimes trying them out on the way back to work, happy to operate our forklifts high on pot.

"*Where you been?* Ya way late comin' back, youse two!" our boss, Vinny, would yell.

"Carl hadda do somethin'. I hadda help." (I'd encouraged Manny to blame any and all fuckups on me, since I knew I'd be leaving in a few weeks.)

"You should know better than to throw your lot in with him," Vinny whispered once, as I walked away. "That guy's on another planet."

And I was.

I disappeared from the floor for great swaths of time, climbing into the maze of giant boxes hugging the perimeter and finding a comfy niche to settle into for a nice long nap; or else I'd bring a pad and pen to scribble random thoughts and senseless strings of words. It was from here that I wrote my first Dear John letter, to Don. I hadn't seen him since the Victor debacle, but he'd been sending notes to the house—dangerous in the extreme, especially now that I was gone all day. In a fancifully cursive missive, I thanked him for everything and explained that I was planning an engagement to my childhood sweetheart, *Theresa*. "What can I say?" I remember writing. "She makes me feel happy." I told him that I'd soon be leaving for college and promised to forward my new address. We had no further contact.

"Ho! Carl-o!" Vinny is yelling.

I tumble out of my hiding place and head in the direction of his voice, trying to look busy as I tuck some papers into the pocket of my ink-stained gray smock.

"Yeah, Vinny? I was just checking on that shipment back there. Was I supposed to break that one down?"

"Phone for you," he spits testily.

This is highly unusual. I never get calls at work. It's Donna Mazzoni. She's tracked me down through my mother. Peter is in an Intensive Care Unit of Einstein Medical Center. They think he's had a stroke, possibly stemming from a seemingly minor head injury he suffered earlier that summer. He's in a coma now. If he survives, there is a good chance he'll be brain damaged, or completely paralyzed. I tell Vinny that I have an emergency and need to leave immediately, then go downstairs and report the same to my father. Over the serious objections of both men, I push off into the subway.

At the hospital: Peter is shrunken and cadaverous, tubes and hoses snaking through ports cut right into his limpid flesh, clunky machines clicking and beeping and buzzing and humming all around him. The medicinal, urine-tinged stink of the room, sharply metallic, is suffocating. I step into the hallway. Donna runs up behind me playfully. She loops her arm in mine. *"Weeee're off to see the Wizard, the Wonderful Wizard of Oz,"* she begins singing incongruously, skipping with forced gaiety down the long, fluorescent-lit corridor, past empty gurneys and overlit cubicles filled with the near dead—the yellow brick road from Hell. I play along gawkily, nauseated, feeling like the sweaty back end of a dancing donkey in some lurid vaudeville.

Peter: with whom it had always been safe to be fully myself; whose privates I'd touched in public pools, and who'd touched mine, but purely for exploratory purposes, free from sexual attraction—and therefore wildly liberating; who'd told me in the heat of a childhood fight that my mother's London broil, prepared especially for him back when we were still living in the apartment, "tasted like it came from Russia," the harshest insult he could muster; who, years later, was not afraid to hustle with me in his finished basement so he could learn the moves firsthand; whose household was calm and nurturing, an

Italian-American *Leave It to Beaver,* his kindly father (a cop) and gentle mother (a schoolteacher) creating an atmosphere of warmth and
solidity; whose maternal grandparents had been born in New York
and spoke perfect English, a novelty, and whose paternal grandfather
had helped tile the Holland Tunnel; who wasn't a Bette Midler fan but
hunted down a full-color photograph of my favorite diva, framed it,
and presented it to me on my birthday, inscribed "With love from
your pal"; whose special kinship was a two-way cure-all for teenage
angst, and with whom the unspoken understanding I'd always shared
provided true solace across the years.

I went off to college still uncertain of my friend's fate. (He ended
up recovering fully, becoming a doctor, and pioneering early treatment of HIV/AIDS—before succumbing to the disease himself in
1990. Today, the Mazzoni Center, formerly Philadelphia Community
Health Alternatives, bears the name of my boyhood friend, one of its
first medical directors.) Our utterly vivid Marina, third cog in our
youthful wheel, died the year before Peter, of leukemia. The old-
timers would say that she "snatched" him because she was lonely.
They said the dead could do that.

.   .   .

Mom, Dad, Rosette, Maria, and Grandma all drive me up to Purchase
on the appointed September day, my belongings stuffed into the
trunk and piled onto the roof of my father's sputtering clunker. They
escort me onto the strange bricky campus and help settle me into my
room—a cell with two beds and two dressers, cemented to the floor.

"You bring an extra blanket?" my mother asks. "Ooh—don't forget the groceries. You gonna get a little refrigerator?"

"He's fine, he's fine," grumbles my father, jingling coins in his
pocket. "There's one more box," he says to me, leading me out toward

the car, mumbling disapproval as we pass a few rooms with their doors open—post-hippie love children laughing and touching each other, Crosby, Stills, Nash & Young playing in the background. (*"Teach your parents well / their children's hell / will slowly go by . . ."*)

At the car, the trunk is empty.

"Guess you got it already," my father fibs. "So . . . you ready?"

This is awkward. We don't do this. He knows it too.

"Huh? What? Sure. I guess."

He looks away, squinting into the sunlight. I am staring at the dorm building. The brown bricks are glowing red. He reaches into his pocket.

"You okay for money?"

"Sure." I'm not. He thrusts a well-worn twenty-dollar bill at me. "Oh, Thanks."

My mother appears on the walkway above us.

"Phil? You coming back up?"

Later, we linger at the car for a while longer, my mother and sister crying.

"Butta why you cry?" Grandma keeps asking.

She knows that I'll be less than twenty miles away, and that I am planning to come home on weekends and holidays. But my mother and sisters understand: nothing will ever be the same. They drive away, and I am alone. I turn to face the campus.

From here on out, my time will be my own.

Epilogue

On a Friday night in March 1998, I attended the opening ceremony of a weekend-long quasi-theatrical event hosted by the Foundry Theatre, "A Conference on Hope," in which a few hundred people gathered around Earth-themed banquet tables in a funky downtown ballroom, enjoyed a light supper, listened to various presentations, and offered our own thoughts about the future of humanity and the politics of . . . *hope.* Some friends and I went out for drinks afterward to continue the lofty discourse, breaking up just after midnight with plans to gather the next morning for a daylong session of workshops and performances. I'd had a sideline conversation with someone about the eighties disco diva Joyce Sims and promised to deliver a tape of her twin club hits, "Come into My Life" and "All and All." At home in my Park Slope apartment, I slipped on some headphones and went to work at my amateur deejay station, making a mix of these and other recordings. I was mildly buzzed, not tired at all, my mind bright with utopian ideas about the coming millennium, my heart filled with . . . *hope.* Flipping through my vinyl collection for a few bonus tracks, I heard the phone ring, unusual for that hour of the night. Fred, my then-companion of nearly twenty years, picked up.

"Oh hi, Mary," I heard him say.

My mother. Not good.

"Oh my God . . . I'm sorry. We'll come right over . . . He's right here." Fred handed me the phone. "Your father's dead."

My mother was near-hysterical. "He's on the floor, Carl. He's blue. The cops are here. I tried to save him. Eva's on her way. I don't know what to do. He's dead, Carl. Carl, he's dead—"

"We're getting in the car right now, Mom. I'll call Maria and Rosette. I want you to do a me a favor: make a pot of tea for yourself and the cops. We'll be there by the time you're done drinking it. Will you do that for me? Will you make a pot of tea?"

"No, that's all right, Carl," she said. "It's late, you're tired."

Even at this moment of gravest extremity, my mother's reflex was self-effacement and retreat. "I don't want to bother you." Fred was already downstairs, pulling the car around. I dialed Maria, who'd just recently moved into a sweet little flat on St. Marks Place, only blocks away.

"You mean he's dead?" she asked after I'd repeated it several times. I told her yes. She went silent then.

"Throw some clothes on," I said. "We'll be in front of your house in a few minutes."

Fred stopped at Junior's on Atlantic Avenue for three cups of coffee to go and drove us up to the Bronx. It was strange: there was an air of adventure about the trip, almost a sense of *fun* in meeting up in the middle of the night like this, sipping coffee against the cold, zipping along a blissfully quiet Bruckner Expressway, the city shimmering, half-dozing. The fact that my father's dead body awaited us remained an abstraction. I felt nothing, really, beyond the simple pleasure of the drive; felt blank.

Maria, Fred, and I entered the house to find my mother hunched over the kitchen table, head in hand, no tea brewed or brewing, a pair of young police officers sitting at the Draculian dining room table, their radios periodically rasping out static-filled transmissions. City law requires that an official of the coroner's office sign off on any and all deaths occurring inside the home to rule out foul play. The cops, as they politely explained, were required to remain "at the place of death" until such official arrived, which might take several hours.

"So he's still upstairs?" I asked my mother, after hugging her for a long time.

"Yes," she said. "On the bedroom floor." The story came pouring out:

My parents had been to a German restaurant in Peekskill with two other couples, old friends. My father had eaten pounds of Wiener schnitzel, bratwurst, knockwurst, weisswurst, and other cured meats and sausages, his favorite. He'd downed mounds of sauerkraut and pickled vegetables, two or three steins of dark beer, some red wine, four or five cups of coffee, perhaps a few nibbles of strudel and assorted *Hausgebackenes* (though he was never too big on sweets). He'd driven home, an hour-long ride, dropping one of the other couples off in Yonkers, and then he and my mother had settled into bed to watch a little TV before falling asleep. He'd died in a flash, midsentence. We all expressed gratitude that it had not happened while he was still behind the wheel; people in the initial shock of grief often find themselves rooting around for such hidden blessings.

My father had mellowed somewhat in his later years, slowed by a persistent cardiac condition and several heart attacks. He'd re-

sponded well to triple bypass surgery in 1994, recovering fully and feeling better than he had in years, quickly abusing his renewed health by returning to a steady diet of red meat and coffee. (He'd quit smoking after his first bout of angina.)

Pop, as his granddaughters—Sophia, born in 1988, Rosette's

child; and Mia, born three years later, Eva's—liked to call him, was a
dream grandpa, doting in the extreme, indulgent of the girls' slightest whims, abundantly loving, deeply nurturing. They adored him; he
was luminous in their presence, giddy. He phoned them daily, even
when they were preverbal and could but gurgle into the receiver, and
insisted upon a heavy schedule of babysitting. He and my mother figured mightily in the early lives of their grandchildren.

"He had just changed the channel—you know how he changes
channels, ooh, it drives me crazy, I always say, 'Phil, just pick one,'
you know?—and a movie came on, *The First Deadly Sin*—you've seen it,
with Frank Sinatra and Faye Dunaway, it's not so good—and I said,
'Oh, I don't want to watch this. Isn't this one where she dies in the
end?' and he turned to answer me and all of sudden he went blue—
and this froth—his mouth—he started frothing—and I knew, I knew
right away. And I dialed 911 and they told me to get him on the floor,
they were yelling at me, it was terrible—oh my God it was horrible—
and I rolled him off the bed—that's what they told me to do—right onto
the floor—and he just fell, he just fell there, and they told me to get
down and pump his chest, and I got down and I was pumping his chest
and pumping his chest . . . but I knew he was dead, I knew he was
dead . . ."

We sat quietly around the table, our five heads leaning into a
circle—Eva having arrived just minutes after Maria, Fred, and I. Now
Rosette came storming in through the back door. She marched toward
the kitchen but stopped short of entering.

"Where is he?" she asked from the doorway.

"Upstairs," Mom responded, Rosette flying away even as the word
was still falling. None of us had yet dared approach the body.

"Should I make a pot of coffee?" offered Fred. I enjoyed seeing
him at ease in this house. He had not been allowed to enter for the

better part of two decades, venturing in only when my father was away. My father had never come to accept the fact of my sexuality. Fred and I had met and fallen in love during the summer of 1979 when we were both working as counter boys at Curds n' Whey, "a yogurtarian café" outside Grand Central Station. My father had grudgingly tolerated my "new best friend's" frequent visits to our house that season and the following fall, grumbling and moaning but looking the other way, trying hard to deny what he knew to be true. That Fred was a black man didn't help.

"You have sisters in this house!" he hissed at me once, when I'd announced that Fred would be sleeping over, sharing my room for the night. "You really think this is safe?" I think he knew that it was.

On the night in January 1980 that I moved my remaining belongings out of the house and into Charlene's waiting car to be driven out to Brooklyn, where I would begin a new life with Fred, my father careened from room to room, sounding bizarre distress calls, desperately offering me "one final chance to stop what you're doing before you are damned forever in the eyes of God!"

"Keep moving. Don't think. Just act," whispered Rosette at the awful height of it, as I finished loading up Charl's car against the horrifying sound track of Dad's guttural ululations—the wailings of a mighty bear being stabbed in the skull with a hunting knife.

He disowned me and I was cut off from the family for several years afterward, having to sneak around in order to maintain contact with my mother and sisters. I'd explicitly "come out" to all but my parents just months prior to the move. (It was not until years later that I was able to speak candidly to my mother about the nature of my relationship with Fred. She responded with relative ease; it was not news.)

By Christmastime 1983, I'd begun to sense that Dad wanted a way out of the corner he had painted himself into: He and Rosette were still not on speaking terms, and he'd "temporarily disowned" Eva when she opted to remain in her college apartment one summer. Rosette and I approached him and asked what had to happen to end the impasse.

"Number One: Admit you've done wrong. Number Two: Apologize. Number Three: Never mention 'that name' [Fred] in this house again."

My big sister and I agreed to all three conditions. We hugged and shook hands.

"Well," I sighed, relieved and hopeful, "I think this deserves a toast."

"Mary, get the anisette and some glasses. Come inside."

I tested the fragile bonhomie a few days later by stubbornly trying to bring Fred to Christmas Eve dinner. My father, sitting with his granddaughters at the kitchen table, stringing popcorn and cranberries in a warm pool of light from the mock Tiffany shade hanging just overhead, started making those strange animal noises the minute he heard my lover's voice at the door. ("I thought it was feeding time at the zoo," as Alice Kramden once quipped.) Fred and I turned right around, wandering the blustery streets until I thought to call Charlene, whose parents, our beloved Nick and Goldie, Italian and Jewish respectively, proudly eccentric and gloriously theatrical, invited us to their table for the traditional meal. I have never forgotten that simple act of kindness. Something precious, unspoken, transpired among us that night, a kind of alchemy.

"Look at Fred, what a good eater. Did you try the stuffed calamari?" asked Goldie, passing a platter his way. "They came nice."

Fred and I refilled our plates as Charlene stepped away to slap a record on the turntable: *Christmas in New York.* We were spackle and knife to each other that night, in the finished basement of the Mangialardi house on Buck Street, filling in each other's blank spots, masking blemishes, smoothing over rough patches with a few deft strokes.

"Came nice?" Nick scoffed. "They're like *butter!*"

Relations with my father improved when I gave up trying to get him to accept the fact of Fred and started obeying his directive to pretend my spouse didn't exist. He never came any closer to accepting the truth, but he was pleased with me in other ways, impressed that I was attending Columbia University as a graduate student, and generally supportive of my aspirations as a playwright.

"Are you doing anything I wouldn't be proud of?" he once asked. I answered—honestly, but from a universe apart—that I was not.

"Okay then," he said.

Now he was lying dead above our heads as Fred moved freely about the kitchen, brewing coffee at the stove, asking if anyone needed to "eat a little something." My mother had always liked Fred, instantly sensing his essential goodness. He felt the same about her.

"She's kind and gentle," he said after their first meeting, "and she knows all about us. I can see it in her eyes." My sisters quickly came to embrace him as a long-lost brother, and some of my favorite memories of married life are of them surrounding him at the kitchen table of our Brooklyn apartment, driving him into fits of uncontrollable laughter with their stories and antics, tears rolling down his cheeks as—gasping and pleading for mercy—he reaches into a back pocket for that ever-handy wad of Kleenex.

Only my father held out, never softening an ounce or yielding one inch of ground, his objections silenced now as Fred puts a plate of anisette toast on the table and fills a cluster of deep green mugs with steaming java.

"Mary—Cremora for you. And nobody takes sugar, right?" He doesn't really need to ask.

Rosette came back down to the kitchen after a while.

"It would be nice if one of you would go up there," she said.

My feet as I trudge up the stairs are lead-filled cinder blocks. My mind flashes upon Bert Lahr as the Cowardly Lion in *The Wizard of Oz* in the scene where he agrees to help rescue Dorothy from the witch's castle: "I may not come out alive, but I'm going in there. There's only one thing I want you fellas to do. . . . Talk me out of it!"

I pause at the bedroom door, slightly ajar, screwing my courage to the sticking place as I'd done so many times before in this very spot, when preparing to request permission to attend some upcoming event or responding to a solemn summons delivered by messenger ("He wants you"). I enter slowly. Candlelight from several sources, the room's sole illumination, casts shape-shifting shadows, huge and ghostly, against the bare beige walls.

My father is lying on the floor next to his side of the bed, limbs assembled neatly, eyes and mouth closed, white sheet draped over his body, face exposed, votive candles surrounding the still form, framed photograph placed nearby—the dead man being kissed on either cheek by his cherished granddaughters, a huge, silly grin on his face. Rosette had not found him this way. His body, my mother told us, had contorted in death: mouth and eyes open, arms and legs akimbo. It had taken courage and strength of stomach to transform the horrifying scene into one of peaceful repose: Rosette's hands busy upon the corpse of her father, tugging gently at the rapidly stiffening limbs, wrapping her palms around his mouth to press it closed, lowering his eyelids with her finger, combing his hair—a tender communion between father and daughter after a lifetime of blood-soaked battle.

"Oh, Dad," I sigh down at the dead man.

I referred to him that way but rarely, maybe two dozen times in my entire life. When summoning him from a distance I'd usually just yell, "Hello? Hello—can you hear me? Hello?"

"Phil—Carl's calling you," my mother would interpret.

"Hello" was my version of "Dad."

"Oh, Dad." I hear myself sighing again.

My father was no monster: he was a man possessed by a force that had already been given a name generations before he was born; a man of clashing parts, at war with himself and the world around him, his mind not entirely his own. There is much I have not said about him here, facets I've left unexplored, acts of gentle fathering I have failed to chronicle:

"The answer's in the book," he'd say whenever we complained about a difficult homework assignment. "Flip through again, check the index and the table of contents—it's in there. All you have to do is find it." Or, when we were very young, poking a hole in either end of an egg, its contents to be slurped directly into the mouth, a treat we found delicious: "Who wants an energy boost?" Or at the dinner table, when we thumbed our noses at asparagus or peas or Brussels sprouts: "It all turns to sugar if you chew it long enough. Try just one." And it was true: the longer you chewed it, the sweeter it became. "Toldja so," he'd say with a smile. "Let's go to the movies," he'd announce suddenly, striding into the nearest theater heedless of schedule, staying for the next show to watch the parts we'd missed, stopping off for hot dogs or Carvel—or both—on the way home. There were spontaneous trips to his uncle Angelo's shoe-repair shop on Arthur Avenue, where the smell of yellow glue and black polish made my head float; and to his aunt Suzy's house—with its twenty-two-year-old cat, talking parrot, and wall full of cuckoo clocks that would screech and jangle every hour on the hour. There was Perna Florist on 238th Street, it's soft-spoken proprietor, an old friend of Dad's, always sending us home with fresh flowers for Mom; and Al's Pizza on Zarega Avenue. "Who's the better cooker?" Al would ask. "Me or your daddy?"

"You're both the same," I'd answer, the grown men laughing at my reflexive diplomacy.

And more. There is more.

Whatever else may be said about him, my father never exempted himself from his own ungodly demands. His labors were mightier than any of ours (except my mother's). He was a fierce provider, loyal and self-sacrificing; buried deep beneath the tumult of madness had always been a sense of dogged devotion. I guess that's what held us all together and made our family ultimately work—in its crazy Tilt-A-Whirl way. I guess that's what makes it work still.

In February, around his seventy-sixth birthday, less than a month before he died, my father had engineered some time alone with me. The whole family—Rosette and Eva, their husbands and kids, Maria, Mom, Dad, and I—was going out to a restaurant to celebrate the January and February birthdays (mine, Mom's, and Dad's, in time order).

"Let's take all the cars," he said. "Carl, I want you to come with me."

I resisted: "But we can fit in two cars, can't we?"

He ignored me: "Let's go."

I climbed into the front seat reluctantly; it was still my policy to avoid being alone with my father whenever possible.

We headed north on the Bronx River Parkway, the rest of the family in a caravan behind us. Silence. I hated this. Then my father spoke haltingly, his eyes on the road:

"You know . . . your sister says—Rosette says—she says I've said some things and done some things—she thinks I've treated you badly . . . and I guess . . . I guess you could say that I have. I guess you could."

A pause. This is difficult. For both of us.

"But—you're my son. And you know the bottom line. You do know the bottom line, don't you?" My scalp went all hot and prickly. I wanted to jump out of the moving car. At the same time, I wanted to brand these words into my brain: my father had never spoken to me like this. I needed to hear it.

"I know, Dad," I said in a voice not quite my own. "I do know. And you know it's the same for me. Right?"

"Well, okay then," he said, adjourning the meeting. "Now where the hell is this restaurant?" Just a few weeks later, he was dead.

"Oh, Dad." I sigh again, sitting on the edge of the bed, looking down at his corpse. It's becoming purple now and hard to the touch. Rigor mortis is setting in. It's nearly four in the morning. He's been dead for several hours. I feel the house vibrating all around him, radiating out from the center of his body—so small really, such a small man inside all this house. I think of the thousands of hours he has spent laboring wretchedly under its roof over the course of nearly thirty years, and I wonder why. There is no answer.

During my first year of college, I'd returned home every weekend to continue toiling at my father's side, but by sophomore year I had learned to stay away: "I've got a *giant* paper due on Monday!" Dad carried on alone, maintaining the Saturday work tradition right up until the time of his death—even after his heart had weakened and the heavy chores represented a direct threat to his life. Much of the work we'd completed decades earlier was in disrepair; and much of his newer work was in various stages of incompletion. My father's master opus was still in progress.

Just a few weeks after we buried him, and at my mother's behest—as spring sprang all around us, the tulip bulbs my father had recently planted in the hilly, rocky front yard sprouting juicily—I sold the monstrous dining room suite to an antiques dealer (a thousand bucks cash, not bad), my sisters and mother and I wandering around the empty room after the last piece had been loaded out, marveling at the sudden lightness, considering new design possibilities. Next I hired a contractor who brought in a team of workers and accomplished in a few weeks what Bub and Cappi couldn't have done in a decade. The sound of their hammering and drilling and sawing and tiling and roofing and plumbing and sanding and painting was the sweetest music, a soothing symphony of the exertions of *other men*. I busied myself with prep work and cleanup, humming happily as I buffed the rooms to a shine, one by one, after the army of builders had stormed through, the ragged interior of the house transformed, ultimately, into a sparkling gem. Each of those men—and especially their leader, the one-in-a-million Ray Lewis, a father himself, a grandfather, a soulful family man who seemed to understand the deeper implications of the job he was doing and really put his heart into it—earned a special kind of blessing that season.

Deep in the midst of it all, while doing a solo walk-around after a long workday, jotting notes and making lists, I suffered what I guess was an anxiety attack, suddenly overcome by doubt and fear: maybe this was costing my mother too much money (though Ray's price was ridiculously reasonable); maybe I was going too far, or maybe not far enough; maybe my father was turning in his freshly dug grave at the unsubtle changes I was overseeing; maybe we had acted too soon, or too late; maybe we should have held on to the dining room set after all; maybe we should be selling the house as is, or maybe we should sell it never—and on and on. These thoughts scorched themselves into the pillow as I tried to sleep in my old bed, alone in the house. (My mother was staying at Eva's while the work was being done.) I drifted off just before daybreak, and had a dream that seemed as real to me as life itself:

I am sitting at the kitchen table, the renovation complete, obsessing about having done the wrong thing. My father approaches quietly, smiling and benevolent. He looks younger, softer, lighter. He sits down opposite me and puts his hands on the table, palms down. He looks squarely into my face, eyes shining.

"Thank you, Carl," he says. "You did good. The house looks beautiful. *You finished the job.*"

I awoke with a start, the pressure gone from my chest, a reply forming on my lips, dawn breaking through the streaky windows— they would all be washed today.

The official from the coroner's office had arrived "at the place of death" just after eight o'clock in the morning. My father had been dead for over seven hours by then. His skin had gone dark, almost black in spots, his body preparing to decompose. Following the inspection, a couple of men in dark suits arrived from Farenga Brothers Funeral Home, zipped the corpse into a black plastic body bag, and carried it down the stairs—my mother, sisters, and I clustered at the bottom, Fred at a distance, in the kitchen. I touched the body as it passed.

"Love you, Dad," I whispered. And it was true: even during the worst of it—and in spite of everything—I always did love him.

My mother cried briefly at the back door, recovered quickly, and then went into the kitchen to wash a few dishes. We'd need to head over to the funeral home later that morning to make arrangements. She climbed upstairs to shower and change, slowly, with dread. I could hear her moving about in the master bedroom, putting things in order, stripping the bed, cracking a window open.

Her maiden name is Cuffari. I'd always been unable to discern a meaning. Sometimes a name is just a name. But then she mentioned, only a few years ago, that her sister Virginia had always said that a letter, probably an *i*, was missing from the original spelling of the name. Playing around with placement, I quickly came up with Cuffiari. After confirming that this was most likely the original spelling, I researched its meaning: bonnet maker.

Crikey! Twisted head married a hatter!

It's just like my mother to have been standing there all along in quiet possession of the answer, patiently waiting to be called upon: Twisted head? Build a custom bonnet.

Next question, please.

Acknowledgments

This book wouldn't exist had not Kristine Dahl, my agent at ICM, suggested I write it, coached me through a year of developmental work, and stayed at my shoulder every step of the way. She is a dream partner and a mighty muse. (Her former assistant, the writer Montana Wojczuk, made some valuable contributions.)

It is my great good fortune that when Kris sent the finished proposal to Gerald Howard at Broadway Books, he took a shine to it right away. Gerry has been a heroic editor. I can't imagine being in more soulful, able hands. His wife, Susanne, has also been a nurturing presence, and my overall experience at Broadway has been ideal. (Hearty thanks to Katie Halleron, Gerry's assistant.)

Annabelle Gurwitch led me to Kris; Dave Simonds (and Hip Replacement, the artists' collective) led me to Annabelle; David Briggs led me to Dave . . . my gratitude to all. (Old pal Briggsy gets special kudos for being a longtime source of cheer and wisdom—and a stunningly insightful reader of early drafts.)

Much of this material was developed in live performance, made

possible by adventurous impresarios such as Chris Fields at the Echo
Theater Company; Paul Stein at Comedy Central Stage; Michael and
Victoria Imperioli at Studio Dante; Steve Olsen at the West Bank Café;
Susan Albert Loewenberg—and the late, lovely Susan Raab Simonson,
who, along with her husband, Eric, was so kind and helpful when we
worked together, despite being extremely pregnant—at LA Theatre
Works. The inspired documentary filmmaker David Gaynes shot and
edited several live performances, providing an important early training tool.

Many other friends, scores of them (lucky me), are owed a ton of
thanks for a raft of reasons. Here, but a few:

Suzanne Shepherd, for long urging me to mine this material, and
for providing critical early direction, and decades of loyal friendship;
Laura Shaine Cunningham, for her absolute faith in me from the
start, and for her practical guidance; Alexandra Gersten-Vassilaros,
treasured friend and sometime collaborator, for her sage counsel and
abundant generosity of spirit; Alex's husband, John—and the boys,
Tonio, Luka, and Stefano—for embracing me as family, and graciously
offering up their magical country place as a writer's retreat; Roma
Maffia, my old pal, for talking me off the ledge during a couple of serious creative blocks, showering me with praise when I needed it, and
opening her dreamy Los Angeles home to me for weeks at a time.

Heartfelt thanks to Fred Carl, my former spouse, forever my soul
mate; Barbara Hencheck, cherished friend and adviser; James
Cascaito, longtime buddy—and chairperson of the Foreign Languages
Department at FIT—who, along with his colleague Isabella Bertoletti
helped me nail down the Italian words and phrases that appear in
these pages; the brilliant Terence Winter, whose enthusiasm for my
work has been vastly heartening; the luminous Edie Falco, first to
read the finished manuscript (after my agent and editor), her effusive

appreciation putting a permanent strut in my stride; Hilton Als, another early reader (and old college chum), who said the most wonderful things at just the right moment; Sam Rudy, Jeff Marchetti, and the venerable Joey Reynolds, for their help in promoting the live shows; Anne Pollack, whose friendship is a healing elixir; Donna DeMatteo, Norman Kline—and my fellow scribes at the HB Playwrights Unit—the best listeners of early drafts a fellow could hope for.

Thanks, too, to Onomé Ekeh for designing a perfect website; Susan Vitucci, for her butt-saving technical assistance; the Actors' Fund and the Episcopal Actors' Guild, for helping me out of a couple of tough spots in the years immediately preceding the sale of the book; and to Alan Dienstag, Marion Koltun-Dienstag—and their kids, Ruby and Emmett—Elizabeth Berridge, Kevin Corrigan, Annabella Sciorra, Ray Abruzzo, David Margulies, Hattie Gossett, Kiera Coffee, Toba Singer, John McCormack, Susan Kouguell, Tatiana Kouguell, Lauren Malkasian, Chris Donahue, Claire Malkasian Donahue, Holly Webber, Rebecca and Ben Egozi, Darrell George, the late Renton Kirk Learmont, and others, whose names should probably be here—they know why.

Curses on the foul, obnoxious bar that opened right across the street from my apartment building several months before I finished the manuscript, dashing any hope of being able to work at my desk past six o'clock or so, seven nights a week; blessings on Todd Senzon, trusted friend and adviser, who quietly slipped me a key to his nearby, Zen-like office, and invited me to work there instead.

To my boyhood friends—Peter, Marina, John, Patrick, Valerie, Patricia, Alan, Holly, Mike, Joanna, Virginia, Anthony, Frank, Nina, Charlene, Christine, Joni, Terry, Goldie, Nick, Robert, Adele, Bernie, Mr. and Mrs. M., Donna, Valentina, Alex, Jeffrey, Eric, and the rest . . . you're with me always.

To the late Carlos Arévalo Gómez, my brother in spirit, who helped me become (for better or worse) the man I am today—thank you.

Above all, I owe a profound debt of gratitude to *my family*. They have been amazingly patient and supportive throughout this process, trusting me to tell fragments of their stories as I tell my own. My mother, especially, has worked hard to remember dates and details, softly setting aside her apprehensions about what might get revealed here. She is my rock—together with my sisters, Rosette, Eva, and Maria; their husbands, Larry, Johnny, and Joe; my nieces and nephew, Sophia, Mia, and Monte. I don't know where I'd be without them, or how I'd live to tell the tale.

To the entire extended clan on both sides of the veil—especially Anne, keeper of the flame, who provided vital historical information and some wonderful photographs—I send love and salutations. You are alive in me.

Finally, thank *you*, gentle reader.

Now put the book away and go out into the sunshine!

Carl Capotorto

© Eric McNatt

CARL CAPOTORTO was born and raised in the Pelham Parkway section of the Bronx, New York. He received an M.F.A. in playwriting from Columbia University School of the Arts in 1984 and has been a playwright, screenwriter, and actor for more than twenty-five years. He played Little Paulie Germani on *The Sopranos*, and is currently co-developing a new original series for HBO. *Twisted Head* is based on his solo show of the same name, which he has performed in New York and Los Angeles. He lives in Manhattan.